MY BRUTAL AWAKENING

PART 1

Karen Patricia

Copyright © 2024 (Karen Patricia)
All rights reserved worldwide.

No part of the book may be copied or changed in any format, sold, or used in a way other than what is outlined in this book, under any circumstances, without the prior written permission of the publisher.

Inspiring Publishers
P.O. Box 159, Calwell, ACT Australia 2905
Email: publishaspg@gmail.com
http://www.inspiringpublishers.com

 A catalogue record for this book is available from the National Library of Australia

National Library of Australia The Prepublication Data Service

Author: Karen Patricia
Title: My Brutal Awakening
Genre: Non-fiction, Paranormal / Ghosts

Paperback ISBN: 978-1-923250-54-3
ePub2 ISBN: 978-1-923250-55-0

"SO MANY PEOPLE HAVE SEEN SO MANY THINGS, WE CAN'T ALL BE GOING MAD." —ADRIAN PAYTON

This book has been 50 years in the making. It took me 47 years to finally wake up after my near-death experience and undergo what I can only describe as a brutal spiritual awakening. I was told that writing my story would help me heal from the cataclysmic trauma that my family and I had experienced over many years. We moved to a brand-new house in a brand-new estate for a brand-new life, but what we got was anything but that. Being house number 13, it was all too easy for family, friends, and even ourselves to dismiss the incessant occurrences that plagued us from the day we arrived as mere bad luck. But that was far from the truth.

There were dark, malevolent forces with us that we were completely unaware of. My story is DIABOLICAL. There are things here in our midst that will do everything they can to torment us and cause absolute devastation in our lives. They can strike with lightning speed, before we even know what has hit us. They are so hostile, and we as humans are so vulnerable to the parasitic nature of these monsters that both hunt and haunt us. They remind me of trapdoor spiders, lying in wait for their unsuspecting victim, ready to seize and devour. They are like energy feeders, attracted by negative emotions. That's why you must think positive, happy thoughts and raise your vibration to literally cut off their food supply. They can rip families apart, wreck lives, and cause the most incomprehensible runs of bad luck. They are the most frightening and forbidding enemy we will ever know, latching on with no intention of ever letting go.

Their evil will drive us into stress, fright, terror, overwhelm, panic, fear, anger, and many other emotions at every chance they get. They know how to push our buttons to get the response they want. If you are one of the lucky ones who manage to rid yourself of them, they will try to return, and it is vitally important to keep your protection up always. When we are happy, full of love, united with each other, calm, and feeling other positive emotions, they literally have no supply and will move on to where they can find it. The shock of what I first experienced carried on into the following year, and I can barely remember any of it. I shut myself away from the world, withdrew, and isolated myself. I disconnected from social media, my friends, much of my family, my life, and mostly from myself. I kept in contact with only a handful of people who kept me sane.

I stayed away mostly because I was terrified these evil forces could infiltrate the lives of others and nearly destroy them as they had nearly done to mine. It was a risk I just couldn't take. The next year, I tried once again to pick up a pen and write my story, but it was too traumatising. Every time I began thinking of it, I was suddenly sucked back into the vortex of that horrifying reality. I was so broken that I didn't think I would ever be able to put the pieces of myself back together. It was just too raw, too frightening, too overwhelming. My hand would begin to shake, and no matter how hard I tried, I couldn't get the words onto the paper. The memories would loop in my head for weeks, and then the nightmares would start again, stemming from the fear of what I had experienced. During this time, I was also trying to be a wife, a mother, study, and work as a Registered Nurse to keep our heads above water so we wouldn't lose our home.

Some days were so dark I thought I would end up in the mental health ward, rocking back and forth in a corner like in the movies. The daily impact on my own life and my family's was so painful, so brutal, so vicious, that I felt hammered to the point of utter hopelessness. That is what these dark forces do. They crawl into your mind, take up residence, and have no intention of ever leaving or letting go. They made me so miserable that I had no happiness, no joy, no peace. I suffered immensely. Everywhere I turned in my life, they filled it with struggle and frustration. Even thinking about this all over again is so hard for me to get my head around. I struggle to comprehend that this actually happened to me, that this was my life. They want to completely blow apart your sanity, your mind, your emotional well-being. I felt like my very soul had been stained with so much heartache. I was left shaken, shattered, beaten, and completely psychologically and emotionally ripped apart at my core. Yet, you can't give up. You just have to keep fighting. You don't have a choice while you still take a breath. I was told it was spiritual warfare, and it is very real.

This is why I chose not to include my husband or my children in that journey and never told them about the crippling horror that I was enduring. I needed to keep them safe from the evil and darkness that I was walking through. Gradually, with a lot of help, the right people began to cross my path as I slowly started to heal. I know in my heart that I will never be the same; my life will never be the same. But I also know that I have a beautiful spiritual team around me and receive divine guidance, which has helped me get to where I am today. For that, I am thankful beyond words. They have infused me with peace, compassion, safety, warmth, joy, happiness, and the most incredible, overwhelming unconditional love that has illuminated my entire soul. My healing is ongoing—it always will be.

I have finally reached a place in my heart where I can now put these words onto paper and relive what I went through without spiralling back down that dark, terror-filled tunnel. I believe that only by the pure grace of the divine do I now have the opportunity to share my story with the world. I began taking photos of what was happening around me because I thought I was seeing things. I honestly thought I was going mad. All the photos you see in these pages you will never find anywhere else on this earth. You can search through every book, magazine, and internet site known to man, but you will never see these images anywhere else. Why, you may ask? This is because every one of them is mine. I took them with my own hand.

I am the only one on the planet who has these photos. I originally took them to prove to myself that I wasn't going crazy. Later, I learned that the more attention you give them, the more fear they will try to instil in you. They need your fear as their energy source. After I was told this, I stopped taking photos of what was around me. I didn't give it any of my attention. I just ignored it and did everything in my power to reclaim my house, my land, my family, and my life. I thought long and hard about whether to write my story. My wish is that my book reaches someone who needs to read it, to make them understand that they are not going mad, and that there is something they can do to protect themselves and their families. If my story gives them the courage and strength to do so, it will be worth it. I asked my husband, John, as I was writing my story if he was going to read it. "No," he said. "Why not?" I asked, confused. "Because in my own way, I lived it," he replied.

I have changed the names of everyone in my story and all other identifying information purely to protect their identity. I have also not revealed where I was living at the time, to protect my neighbours who still live in that area today. It is not important that I reveal who I am. I do not want my husband, my children, or my other family members to be affected by revealing my identity—they have already suffered enough. What is most important to me is that I pray my story reaches the hands of those who so desperately need it. That is what I have been guided to do by my higher guides who continually show me direction. I have also given the name of God a "he" nature in my story, but feel free to substitute whatever you want, whether it be he, she, source, universe, the divine, etc.

My story is deeply disturbing, traumatising, and gripping in relation to the nature of the phenomena my family encountered.

People have no idea of the real danger when they cross our path. Some things I will write about will seem so foreign to your current belief systems that for some of you, they will simply not be accepted. That is fine, I understand that. I am not here to pass judgement on you—you either accept it or not, and that is your own journey to make. I have not dreamt up, hallucinated, fabricated, imagined, or lied about anything in these pages you are about to read.

I swear on the lives of my children and husband that everything I have written is all true and these events actually happened. Many people have been through traumatic experiences in their lives that are so devastating that they completely scar their souls and minds beyond belief. Some of these experiences and memories can be so painful that they erase them from their conscious memory. It remains in their subconscious, buried deep, but it will always be there, causing emotional and physical pain until the hole in their soul is finally healed.

I know unequivocally that ghosts exist, that there is another realm beyond all of us, and that spirits of the dead roam the earth. My experience with these phenomena has changed my life irrevocably. Nothing can prepare you for when a spirit with a force of malevolent dark energy makes its presence known to you. I also know that God does exist, as do Archangels, Angels, Loved ones in Spirit, Guardian Angels, and Spirit Guides, and that we are forever watched over and protected. I know there is a divine intelligence—something far greater than we could ever imagine in our wildest dreams. I know we can connect and make contact with something so unseen and so absolutely incredible as long as we believe. I knew that God had given me the courage and strength to finally put the pieces of my life back together and bring my story to the world. It is my wish that by writing this book, it will help heal my soul and the souls of my immediate family.

So, to all the non-believers out there in the world—of which I know there are millions, and yes, I too was once one of them—may my life journey give all of you who are completely spiritually blind the power to finally take off your blindfold and, for the first time, to truly see. This is my story…

MY BRUTAL AWAKENING...

"AT FIRST I THOUGHT THE FAMILY MUST BE MENTAL, BUT BELIEVE ME, WHAT I SAW WAS NOT DONE BY HUMAN HANDS." —CONSTABLE ROBERT SCOTTY CRAWFORD

"You have an entity." Those words echoed through my mind on replay. I just couldn't comprehend what I was hearing. Frantically, I got into my car and dialled my husband John's mobile number. "We have an entity!" I screamed down the phone, my heart pounding wildly. I was so dizzy I could barely see the road as my mind spun out of control. I could hear my husband, confused, saying, "Ah… ha."

"I showed the lady the photos, and she said she knows what this is because she has seen these markings before," I told him. For the first time in so long, I had validation—even if it was from a complete stranger—that I wasn't going mad.

Another lady in the group I had just met told me to get a priest and cleanse my house with holy salt and holy water. She advised me to get all of my family, including myself, to start wearing a crucifix on a necklace and to never take them off. She said to call upon my angels to stand guard around my home and to ask them to bless and protect it. She also warned that if I had any items from thrift shops whose origins I didn't know, I should get rid of them immediately, as they could be portals of darkness for entities to gain entry into my home. The same applied to playing violent video games. She suggested burning white candles for pure white light.

"Oh my God, what on earth did I just do?" I thought to myself as I arrived at the front of my house. Slowly, the roller doors went up, and I drove my car in and turned off the lights. I sat in complete darkness and silence for a few minutes, with all these erratic thoughts crossing my mind. "Those people are crazy. I just want to forget about it all. There has to be another explanation. No one ever has to know that I went."

I got out of the car, walked into the kitchen, and turned on the light. I sat down on the lounge in absolute disbelief at what I had just experienced and been told.

The phone rang, and I nearly jumped out of my skin with fright. "Karen, this is Cyndi. I want you to listen to me very carefully. You have an entity. Do you have any salt?"

"Ah… yes," I replied.

"Listen very, very carefully. I want you to go around to all your plug holes, drain holes, and toilets. This thing lives in your septic system. Keep your toilet lids down at all times. Put salt down them and all of your drains, and cover them up right now. You have my number; I will ring you tomorrow and come and see you to explain what we need to do. Do you have any rosary beads?"

"Yes, I have my Dad's," I stammered.

"Put them on tonight when you're sleeping and do not take them off. Go and do this right now."

My heart started to race. "OMG! This can't be happening." I grabbed the salt out of the cupboard and went into the kitchen. I began pouring the salt down the drains and plugged them up. My toilet, shower, drains, sinks—my heart was pounding.

Here I was, by myself in my house, not long after being told there was an entity, and I was pouring salt down drains. As I moved to the other side of the house, which was in darkness, before I could reach the light switch, all four-bedroom doors slammed shut with such force that I felt like my heart was about to stop. The terror I felt that night was pure and overwhelming, on a scale I had never experienced before in my life. I let out a scream, ran to my bedroom, and slammed the door.

Suddenly, my toilet in my ensuite began to growl loudly, and I slammed the door shut. "God, what do I do? Where do I go? What the hell is happening to me?" I jumped into bed, put on my father's rosary beads, and grabbed his Bible. I began reciting the Lord's Prayer over and over, as it was the first thing that came to my mind. I knew my friend Joy was on nightshift at my workplace. I wanted to get in the car and drive there, but my legs had turned to jelly. I was too terrified to leave my bed.

"What is this thing capable of doing? Could it cause a car accident? Would it try to attack me?" The thoughts racing through my mind were erratic. I texted Joy, absolutely terrified. "I have an entity," I began, and then suddenly my father's rosary beads broke and scattered all over the carpet. Oh my God, no, no, no… What the hell? Is this thing in the room with me? I could feel the air around me grow heavy.

My mind was spinning. "Our Father, who art in Heaven, hallowed be Thy name," I began saying louder and louder, repeatedly. Joy texted me back: "Get a sock and pick them up. Put them in there and keep them in your hand. Ask your Dad to protect you. He knows, and he will be there. You need to ask him for help."

When I was a teenager, a lot of movies from Hollywood were about séances and trying to communicate with spirits using Ouija boards. I was at a sleepover when I was about fifteen. My best friend's mother was very religious, always reading the Bible, going to church, and saying the rosary. She was horrified that these things were being portrayed. She told us that if we were ever somewhere a séance was being held and we couldn't get away—like on a ship—to go to the farthest point, cover ourselves with a white sheet, and do the sign of the cross over and over while yelling loudly, "I cover myself with the body and blood of Almighty Jesus Christ."

After she walked away, we both just looked at each other like, "Wowza, that was pretty out there."

"Sorry, my mum is a bit eccentric. Please don't tell anyone at school. Nobody will ever want to come and hang out with me," said my friend. I assured her that I never would and thought to myself, 'Your mother is absolutely crazy.' That night, I clearly remembered what she had told me. I didn't have a white sheet, but in between saying the Lord's Prayer, I was yelling out that I covered myself in the body and blood of Almighty Jesus Christ, and I think I made the sign of the cross over myself nearly a thousand times that night.

The next few hours were just terrifying. It was like being in a scene from a horror movie. What the hell was this thing? The throbbing pain in my head felt like needles stabbing into my brain.

"I'll also send you the Archangel Michael prayer. Say it over as many times as you need to," came a text from Joy. It read, Archangel Michael, please place a protection bubble of white light around me and do not allow other energies to affect me. Please use your sword and cut any cords and ties to anything and anyone who has been holding me back. Please shower white healing light over me and protect me always. Amen.

Every sound, every bump in the night was terrifying. My body was in overdrive; my eyes must have darted about a hundred times a minute at every slight sound. I was absolutely petrified. I never thought it was going to end. The adrenaline shooting through my bloodstream was just next level—my heart was pounding so fast I honestly thought I was going to have a heart attack. Sweat was pouring off me, and I could feel myself beginning to hyperventilate.

My head was aching from the pure fright, like a sledgehammer was beating down hard on it. The hairs on the back of my neck and both of my arms were charged with static electricity and standing on end. I had goosebumps all over my entire body. This thing was plaguing my mind with horrific mental anguish and causing my body so much suffering. It was driving me crazy with its malicious, taunting behaviour. My body could feel this dark, malevolent energy around me. It was like being held underwater, trying to breathe while feeling surrounded by an invisible force. It's one thing to read this, but to endure it for many hours, not knowing what is doing this to you, is a scale of terror only a few could ever imagine.

You can't switch it off or run away; I had no choice but to accept it. My body was in fight or flight mode, but I had nowhere to run. The shockwaves pulsating through my body were excruciating as I tried to deal with this intense struggle. I couldn't just turn up at my family's or friends' houses in the early hours of the morning. They had work the next day—what was I going to say to them, that I had a malevolent entity in my house? They would think I had completely lost my mind. I began to pray like my life depended on it. I endured this unfathomable terror for hours and hours.

Eventually, out of pure exhaustion, I must have finally fallen asleep. I saw the first rays of sunlight peeking through the blinds on my window, nudging me awake. I felt absolutely exhausted. "What a nightmare that was," I thought to myself. It was one of the most horrific I'd ever had. I sat up in bed, completely washed out and wiped out. As I pulled back the sheets to get up, I suddenly saw all of my father's rosary beads strewn throughout my bed. "Oh dear God," I called out in exasperation, and then I just cried and cried. I was inconsolable.

My husband John was always telling me to make sure every door and window was locked up tight when he was away. But it didn't matter. This monster wasn't outside my door; it was already locked up inside my house with me, and there was no escaping the terror.

BREADCRUMBS...

"ENLIGHTENMENT IS YOUR EGO'S GREATEST DISAPPOINTMENT"
—SWAMI MUKUNDANANDA

My first memory was being in a car seat. I distinctly remember the straps over my shoulders as I tried to lean forward. I was telling my parents about the baby that went through the windscreen and landed in the sand. I could see the baby flying through the cracked glass and the mother screaming as she picked up her baby, who was covered in blood and lifeless. I was always trying to tell them about the baby, as the sand in the river would always trigger my memory. I can still see my father, as he was driving the car, turning to my mother and asking her what I was always talking about. Every time we would cross that bridge, I would tell them the same story, but they just used to ignore it, and eventually, I would stop.

When I was a young child, I used to hear lots of voices, like they were talking to me. It was never anything bad they were saying, but I was just aware that they were always there. To try and get to sleep, as the voices were always so loud at night, I would bang my head on the pillow, thinking this would make them stop. Of course, it never did until I got older... lots of breadcrumbs.

I was told that when I was a toddler, I wandered off from my parents' house in the new town that was being established, where there was a creek outside the town. I was about 18 months old, wearing nothing but a nappy and my gold bracelet wrapped around my wrist. At the creek, which was full of water, there happened to be a bunch of kids riding their bikes that same day at that exact time. They tried to talk to me, but obviously, I couldn't talk back, being so young. A few stayed with me, and a few others rode to the police station to report that a young toddler had wandered there alone. That week, there happened to be a detective visiting, and due to the lack of phones, they couldn't ring around. My mother heard a knock on the door to find me in the arms of a detective, who had been going door to door for hours, asking, "Is this your baby?"

The entire time, Mum had thought I was fast asleep in my room. Thank God those boys were there when I wandered in that direction. If not, I most probably would have drowned. As I went through my childhood and adolescence, I had lots of flashes or hits of déjà vu.

A few houses down, I used to play with a friend who was the same age as me. Her father was in management, and they lived in a high-set house, while we were in a low block. Tina had far more Barbie dolls than I did, and they had so much money. Under their house were many different toys to play with, which is why I always went there. I dreamt that her mother, Tina, and her younger brother were crying and very distressed, but I always woke before I could finish the dream. This happened a lot as I got older, and it was always the same dream. One day, I was there playing with her cousin, who had come to visit for the weekend.

We had a great time hanging out together, but I felt really sad when I was around her. I dreamt that we were all playing together on the verandah upstairs at the front of the house. Her cousin kept slipping over and falling, and whenever she did, she would get covered in bruises and start bleeding. This happened continuously until her body and the entire verandah were both covered in blood.

I woke up in fright after having such a terrible nightmare. A few months later, when I went down to play with Tina, she opened the door crying and told me she was too sad to play that day. Her cousin had been diagnosed with leukaemia a few weeks after she had visited and had just died the night before. A few years later, Tina's father had been up on a ladder cutting down a tree when he slipped and fell. He tragically died too.

When my Aunty Pat got married, I was a flower girl in the bridal party. I never liked her boyfriend, who then became her husband, from the very beginning. To be honest, I had nothing but contempt for this man. There was just something about him that made the hair on the back of my neck bristle. When I visited my grandparents, I would only stay when he wasn't there. I just never liked that man. A few years later, they had their first son when I was about eight. My aunty had not been able to drive for many weeks, and this was her first doctor's appointment since giving birth.

I was helping carry the bassinette to the car and watching Aunty Pat put the seatbelt across it with my baby cousin asleep inside. After the visit to the doctor, we went to the shops, and she had bought me some colouring pencils and a book. Aunty Pat would always spoil me silly. It was winter and very cold, and we were all rugged up in jeans and jumpers. After getting home, my aunty decided to put a rinse in her hair to make herself feel a bit better. I was sitting quietly at one end of the kitchen with my pencils and book when my uncle came home, rotten drunk and swearing. He saw my aunty's new hair colour and went into a rage because he didn't like it. There was lots of shouting, and then he grabbed her by the hair, opened the oven door—which was at head height— and shoved her head inside. When he pulled her back out, she was crying, and there was blood visible from both of her nostrils.

In doing this, my aunty tripped over the bassinet at her feet, which set my baby cousin off, who then started screaming at the top of his lungs. I stood up in absolute fright, having never seen any sort of violence in my life, and was just petrified at what I was witnessing. I was so scared that I actually wet myself and could feel it trickling out from under my jeans, all over the floor. My uncle suddenly became aware of me watching and came towards me. He then realised that I had wet myself and raised his hand to strike me. He was so mad that his eyeballs were bloodshot, and he yelled at me, "You dirty little bitch, look what you've done!"

My aunty screamed out, "Leave her alone, she's just a baby!" He then turned back towards her, shoved her again on the side of her head with his fist, and screamed at her to make him some tea and to shut that f**king baby up now! I hated that man. He put my aunty through so much hell and trauma over the years. Eventually, she did leave him, and to be honest, I think she was lucky to get out when she did.

I had many dreams of seeing my grandmother drop to the floor of the shop she and my grandfather owned and managed back in the early seventies. In my dream, I would see her fall, and I would run over, screaming, telling her to wake up. I didn't know if she had fainted or if she had passed away, but it was always really frightening, and I would wake up in a cold sweat. My grandparents used to have my younger brother and me come and stay with them before we started school. Their house was adjoined to the shop where they lived and worked. Nan would get us to do odd jobs around the shop, like sweeping and dusting, and then give us money, always in one- and two-cent pieces. We would get so many of them, not understanding their monetary value, and we would use them to buy treats like apple turnovers and packets of Maltesers. At lunch, she would turn the milk crates over for our table and chairs, and my brother and I would get to eat our sausage rolls and drink our chocolate milks. We just loved staying there when we were little, especially during school holidays, as we were incredibly spoilt.

I dreamt a lot about Nan on the floor, but I would always wake before the dream ended. I often thought about telling her what I had dreamt, but I didn't want to upset her. One day, Nan was serving a man a packet of cigarettes when I saw her fall to the ground. Just like in my dream, I raced over to her, thinking she was hurt or even dead. Thankfully, she had only fainted.

Many years before I was born, my mother's brother and one of his mates decided to take my grandfather's car for a joyride and then put it back before he came home. Unfortunately, things got out of hand, and they ended up having a major car accident and completely wrote it off. The friend driving ended up in hospital, and my uncle was nowhere to be found.

Days then turned into weeks, weeks turned into months, and months turned into years. The police told the family that he must have run away, and due to a lack of police resources in those days, he most likely ended up in terrible circumstances. This caused my family great angst, especially my grandparents. Over time, it was something they had to endure and live with. Unbeknownst to the family, my uncle had ended up overseas and was very much alive. He eventually returned to Australia and decided to find his family again. He walked into the shop and asked for a packet of cigarettes, and when Nan handed them to him, he said, "Thanks, Mum." The shock of seeing my uncle alive again after all those years was too much, and hence she fainted. Now I understood what I had been seeing in my dreams. In the words of my mother, "My brother disappeared as a young boy and came back into our lives again as a young man."

My favourite TV show when I was a kid was *Bewitched*, and when I was an adult, it was *Medium*... mmmm, more breadcrumbs. Sometimes the premonitions would be frightening; mostly, I pushed them so far back into my subconscious, hoping they would never happen again.

When I was about 11, my best friend and I were travelling in the back of their car with her Dad driving. He had been drinking very heavily, and back in those days, there were no drunk-driving rules and no seatbelts in the back of cars. We were both in the backseat, and he began to drive erratically all over the highway. At one point, he nearly rolled the car as he went sideways down a ditch but managed to come back up onto the main road in time.

We both got down onto the floor as one of the doors flung open, and we could see the bitumen road speeding by beside us. Being kids, we were absolutely terrified. We crouched down together behind the front seat, holding hands and clinging to each other for dear life. My friend was screaming at her Dad to slow down and stop the car, but he just kept yelling back at her to "sit down and shut up" because he was so drunk.

We could feel the car swerving all over the road and hear the wheels screeching. I don't know why, but I began to pray to God to please save us, help us, and to get us home safely. As we drove into town, I knew we weren't far from their home. I could see the street lights swerving above us as he eventually mounted the curb, completely mowed down his letterbox in their front yard, and then promptly fell forward onto the steering wheel with the horn blaring loudly. We crawled out of the car, both very frightened and shaking. My friend leaned him back in the front seat, where he lay till morning, completely passed out. I never got back in a car with him ever again. Somehow, I knew we were being divinely protected. More and more breadcrumbs…

FINDING MY LIGHT...

**"IF YOU HAVE TO SEE IT TO BELIEVE IT, IT IS NOT TRUE FAITH."
—DR JAMES DOBSON**

During my primary school years, I loved wrapping my books in angel paper or cutting pictures of angels out to put on the front covers. Today, my house is filled with angel placemats, coasters, pictures, boxes, statues, calendars, notebooks, etc. I remember buying a set of cherub salt and pepper shakers and giving them to my grandparents as a Christmas present when I was a teenager. I always had toy medical kits when I was little and would pretend to give my friends injections with the toy syringes. When we played make-believe, it always seemed to be doctors and nurses. When I was confirmed, I picked Saint Catherine. When the local priest asked why, I replied, "Because she was a healer of the sick." No surprise then that when I left high school, I began studying and became a registered nurse.

My grandmother once told me I must have always had a caring, compassionate nature. When I was about three, her nephew, who was also my godfather, died in his early twenties, leaving everyone in shock. At the wake, his mother was sitting in a chair, crying inconsolably. I was told that I climbed onto her lap, wiped away her tears, and said, "Please don't cry, I can be your little girl now." I have been practising as a registered nurse for nearly thirty years.

As I grew up, I had certain dreams about different things, but I soon realised that every time I tried to tell my parents or grandparents, I was met with, "Don't want to hear any more silly stories." As I got older, I stopped telling people. Life went on as usual, and everything was fine until about age 14, when I started experiencing massive amounts of déjà vu constantly. One night, my best friend was having a sleepover, and we were having lots of fun feeding my then two-year-old sister some tea, which she was spilling everywhere.

We were laughing so much when I suddenly said, "I've seen this before, even the clothes you're wearing. Oh wow, this is out there." My best friend replied, "You can't have. I only bought this shirt brand new yesterday. I think you must be having some sort of delusion." I didn't understand what was happening to me. I knew I had already seen it exactly as it was playing out right in front of me. "I must be going mad. What the hell is wrong with me?" I thought.

One night, I dreamt I was watching a line of cars in a funeral procession. The first car had a beautiful white coffin in it. I saw it being carried into the church and there were so many white-lit candles everywhere. My good friend Marcy was standing next to the coffin with her older sisters and their grief was overwhelming. They were all crying. I went up to them and looked in the coffin and saw a young man I had never seen before. He had a distinct mark around his neck, and my first thought was that he had been in a car accident and the seatbelt had dug into his neck. I looked up, and she looked at me, just screaming with grief, and I woke in a cold sweat. The next day, I told her about it, and it upset her so badly that I swore if I had any other dreams about my friends, I would never tell them.

When I was in my final year of high school, I was selected for hockey championships in another regional city. After the championships were over, we all went to a girl's home from our team for a celebration party on the last night we were there. Later, when all the parents went upstairs, the girls grabbed an Ouija board and decided to do a seance. "Ahh, yeah, no thanks, this isn't really for me,". I told them. "What is wrong with you? C'mon, it'll be fun. Stop being such a killjoy. What are you, chicken or something?" said my teammates.

I didn't hang around. I just knew I wanted to get the hell out of there, and fast. This was not something I wanted to be a part of. I tried to convince them to do anything but that. I didn't want my teammates to be put in some sort of danger, but they weren't listening to me at all. I was chastised badly for not participating. I can remember my best friend's mum telling me that people who dabble in the supernatural can be driven to insanity, especially those who don't know how to protect themselves. She explained that to her absolute horror, she had even seen these Ouija boards for sale in shops being advertised as wonderful family entertainment, and it sickened her to her core.

Playing around with powerful energies and dipping your toes into the psychic world without really understanding it can have devastating consequences, sometimes leading people to psychiatric wards, my friend's mum explained to us. I went down to the end of the street, as far away from them as I could get. It was dark, with only a few streetlights on. There I was, a 17-year-old girl, all alone in a strange city, sitting in the gutter while I waited for my friends. I had nowhere to go, no phone—nothing in those days—so all I could do was sit there and pray to God that they knew what they were doing and were protecting themselves.

ANGELS WILL CATCH YOU...

"CONNECTION WITH ANGELS STARTS WHEN YOU RECOGNISE THAT THEY ARE THERE." —MURRAY STEINMAN

Every year, our family would travel down south to see our grandparents for the Christmas holidays. We had a unit that overlooked a river, and this year we were on the top floor. Across from it was the local park. We would often go over after tea, as it was lit up, and there were always lots of kids playing there. All my parents had to do was step out onto the balcony, and they could check on us whenever they liked.

This particular night, our curiosity got the better of us, and we decided to go for a walk. I would have been about 16, my two younger brothers around 14 and 10. We started walking and talking, and before we knew it, we had wandered into another suburb. Suddenly, everything seemed to get really dark, and I became aware of how quiet and still it was. There was nobody around; we had wandered much farther than we had anticipated. I intuitively knew we had to get back to the park before my parents noticed, and we had to get back quickly.

"Come on, boys, this doesn't feel right. We need to get back, or we're going to be in major trouble," I told them. I began to turn around and walk back quickly. "Come on, you two, pick up the pace!" I yelled. We hadn't gone far when a car pulled up very slowly beside me. My first thought was that they were going to ask for directions. I turned to see a very long yellow car pull up next to me. It kept idling, and I noticed a woman getting out of the car. I couldn't see the man, but I could see his hands clenching and unclenching on the steering wheel. On the back seat, I saw lots and lots of rope. My heart was pounding, and I could feel terror rising up. All I can remember seeing were her eyes, and in my mind, I just heard, "RUN!"

I knew at that exact moment that they weren't asking for directions, and that something very sinister going on. We hadn't exchanged any words—it was all in slow motion—and then my two brothers were coming up in the distance. I turned and saw their two shadows fall on the cement path from the massive trees they were under. At that point, you couldn't see them, but the woman turned, saw their shadows, and realised two people were approaching.

She quickly got back into the car, and it sped off at lightning speed. OMG! I knew they could possibly come back and see that we were all just kids. I needed to think quickly because I knew we were in a lot of danger, and we had to get back fast. Do we hide and risk them coming back and finding us? No, we needed to get back to our unit as quickly as possible so we would be safe.

"Please God, please let us get back in one piece. Please help us!" My legs felt like jelly, and my heart was pounding a million miles a minute. "Let's have a race!" I yelled. "Whoever gets back first will win $50." Well, my brothers took off so fast, and I was literally running for my life, thinking that at any moment that car could come back and find us. Never in my life have I run so fast. When your adrenaline kicks in, it's incredible what your body is capable of doing. I had never been so terrified, and I knew I had to get us all back to the unit safely. Suddenly, I could see streetlights and houses and knew we were nearly back.

"KEEP GOING," I was being told. "YOU'RE NEARLY THERE." The other reason I knew I had to win was because I didn't have $50 to give them, and that would be a whole other story if one of them got back first. When I saw our unit complex, the feeling of relief was surreal. I ran for that door like my life depended on it, and I remember us all crashing into the stairwell out of pure exhaustion. I did get back first, and I remember my brothers falling on top of me, and we made a hell of a noise. So much so that the people on the first floor came out and yelled at us with lots of expletives, telling us to be quiet.

We sat on the steps, bright red, sweating profusely, and dying of thirst. "We can never tell Mum and Dad about this," I said. "We'd get into so much trouble if they ever found out. I don't even know what they would do." We went into the unit and saw our parents watching TV, completely oblivious to what had just happened. I knew we had been watched over that night by some divine guidance. I still get shivers down my spine when I think about what could have happened. Thank you, God… thank you… thank you… thank you. I knew He was listening. Nearly 11 years later, at my brother Aaron's 21st, we finally told our parents what had happened that night.

SMALL BEGINNINGS...

"I COUNT MY BLESSINGS EVERY DAY, QUITE HONESTLY, BECAUSE I TAKE NOTHING FOR GRANTED." —MARIO ANDRETTI

During my childhood, every time the TV or radio was on, all I would hear about was the Azaria Chamberlain case. It consumed our lives for many years. As I kept looking at Ayers Rock, I just instinctively knew that I was going to visit it—I could see myself on top of that rock. I had many dreams about being there and could see myself climbing the rock in my dreams. For my very first holiday after I started my nursing training, I booked a Contiki tour to—you guessed it—the Northern Territory. We all had to be on the tour bus at 4:30 a.m.; if not, our tour guides wouldn't wait, and we would miss our chance to climb the famous rock. We all bundled in, bleary-eyed and half asleep, and drove off into the darkness. There were thousands of stars as I looked out my window. As we approached the rock, the tour guide began to play the theme song from the movie *Chariots of Fire* by Vangelis.

As it reached its peak, we suddenly came around the corner to see this amazing monolith in front of us, with the sun rising up behind it. It was just breathtaking—a memory that will stay with me forever. Our hearts were pounding with incredible excitement. At 19, I was about to climb the rock I had seen on the news for half of my life. As I stepped out of the bus and looked up, I was overwhelmed by how incredibly spiritual it felt to be around it in all its glory. I couldn't really express it, but I knew there was something very special about this rock and the land that surrounded it. Yes, I did climb it exactly as I had seen in my dreams, and I had a photo taken of me signing the book at the top after my climb.

The photo was taken by a young man named Nigel, who was also travelling around the world at the time. Somewhere in Scotland, in a photo album, there's a picture of me signing that book. I never saw it because Nigel never sent it to me, despite promising he would, and unfortunately, we lost contact. When we were crossing from Arnhem Land into Kakadu, we got off the bus to stretch our legs. We were told to stay close to the bus and remain in the shade. I only went as far as we were allowed to go when suddenly I felt overwhelmingly nauseous and dizzy. I just didn't want to be out there and went back to sit on the bus. My tour guide saw me and asked if I was alright. "Yeah, I just felt really out of sorts near that spot," I replied. She looked at me and asked what I felt. "I don't know, like something really terrible happened there."

"That's freaky," she said. "In that spot where you were standing, three years ago an American family was visiting with their two small children. The father got out of the 4WD and was bending over when a huge crocodile lunged out of the water and decapitated him in front of his young wife and their two very small children."

"OMG, that's horrific," I replied. I remember feeling so distressed and not knowing why—I didn't even know them. I couldn't imagine the horrific trauma and pain that young woman must have gone through. So many breadcrumbs...

In my last year of primary school, there was a girl who sat two desks away from me. She was very rebellious towards our teacher and pretty much life in general. I cannot recall the number of times she was sent to the office for her unruly behaviour. I knew she came from a very dysfunctional family and often felt really sorry for her. Some days, I could see that she was so hungry that I would buy her an ice cream or a pie so she could have something to eat. One night, I had the most terrible nightmare about her in hospital, crying in so much pain, but she looked a lot older. She had large red lumps all over her face and body—just everywhere. I could hear her screaming loudly, and then I woke up in fright.

In my first year of high school, I was working on a geography assignment and chose New Zealand as my country. As I was gluing a photo of Mt Cook onto my massive cardboard layout, Dad asked me why I had picked that particular country. "Because I'm going to visit it when I get older, and I'm going to stand at the base of this mountain," I told him. I just intuitively knew it but couldn't explain why. Seven years later, my then-boyfriend, who is now my husband, and I visited both islands on our first Contiki tour together. While standing next to a river on this trip, I suddenly began to feel nauseated and unwell. This happens randomly, but in certain places, I really feel things. As I stood there looking at the water, I couldn't understand why.

Our guide then told us that many people had drowned in that river because there was no buoyancy. Many had attempted to kayak it and had been killed, and no one had ever attempted to raft it. It was also a popular spot for suicide; many people knew they would drown and not be able to be saved. OMG! No wonder I felt like I was going to be sick—so many tortured souls had drowned there. I felt overwhelmingly sad for them all. And yes, I did get to stand at the base of that mountain.

When I was 17, I read a book about what happens to us when we pass over. It was written by a psychic who was a regular contributor to one of the major women's magazines in Australia. I was mesmerised reading it and thought it was one of the most beautiful books I had ever read. After I got married, I actually bought the book myself. Years later, a friend lost her only son in a motorcycle accident and was going through intense grief. I gave her the book to read, hoping it would help ease her pain. Unfortunately, I never saw it again. I tried to purchase another copy but was told that only a certain number had been published and that I should try bookstores or second-hand stores to find another one.

That same year, a psychic came to our hometown and set up a stall in the middle of the only shopping centre we had. I used my money from my part time job to book a reading as I was very intrigued by this other world. The only thing I remember, as it was so long ago, was that he told me I was an Aries, which was true. He also looked at my hand and told me that I would have two children very close together, and then years later, another child would arrive. He also said I would become a nurse and stay in the profession for many years, and that I had psychic gifts that I needed to develop. My first two children are only 20 months apart, and then eight years later, our third child arrived… so many breadcrumbs.

DISCOVERING MY TRUE STRENGTH...

"LIFE IS A LONG LESSON IN HUMILITY." —J.M. BARRIE

After spending six weeks in a classroom with my nursing group, we were finally going to work in the hospital on the wards. On my very first shift, a lady died of congestive cardiac failure. I had never seen a dead body before, and my nurse unit manager called the wardsmen to take the lady to the morgue, which was on the hospital grounds. Since she was my patient, I was to escort her body there with them. Upon entering, I saw a table where autopsies were performed, with various instruments visible. The place had a strong bleachy, chemical smell, and the aircon was set very high—it was freezing in there.

They wheeled the trolley into another section where there were lots of small silver doors and placed her body, already in a shroud, onto the trolley, which they then pulled out—exactly like you see in the movies. The wardsmen were a couple of larrikins who had worked there for a number of years. They knew I was one of the new recruits and asked if I had ever been in a morgue before. I was 17, straight out of high school, and completely green. "No, never," I stammered. "This is my very first time." With that, they opened up one of the trolleys and pulled out a man. His face was completely white and ghastly looking, with the shroud pulled only up to his neck. They explained that he and his wife had been travelling around Australia in their caravan when they were involved in an accident with a semi-truck and both were killed instantly.

Due to the nature of their head injuries and the circumstances of their deaths, the case was referred to the coroner, and their heads were to be left uncovered. "And here's his missus over here," they said, as they pulled out another body, showing a lady also in a shroud with her head uncovered. They were laughing hysterically at me, seeing how upset I was. Looking back now, I realise how deplorable their behaviour was. They then asked me to go into the autopsy room to grab some paperwork for them while they cleaned down the trolley. I went in, looked around, and couldn't see anything. When I walked back out, I saw that they were gone. What the?? I ran to the front door and tried to open it, but it was locked. Frantically, I began to call out and bang on the door and windows. It was then that I noticed they had pulled quite a few bodies out, and they were all on display for me to see. OMG! I was so young and started to feel like I was having a panic attack.

Suddenly, the door burst open and they were both there keeled over laughing so hard. "That wasn't funny," I said… as I ran into the toilet to cool myself down. I felt so embarrassed with what they had done to me. I was later told that every new recruit gets locked in the morgue the first time they ever go there. All the staff know about it and gets put through that… like a rite of passage. It had been going on for years. "You're not the first and you certainly won't be the last," I was told by one of the older nursing students.

I experienced so much heartache and tragedy in those three years I spent there. While my friends back in my hometown were going out to movies, B n S balls, having the time of their lives partying, going to nightclubs, I was packing pellet holes with saline-soaked gauze into a lady whose husband had shot her over 700 times with a metal pellet gun. She was in so much agony that she would scream in pain every time she tried to move.

Or was giving the gentlest sponge bath to a young girl who had been brutally and savagely gang raped in her community. Her face was so swollen from the bruising that she couldn't even put a toothbrush in her mouth and we would have to try and use swabs to clean her teeth as she couldn't even open her eyes. Or the lady who was helping her husband with the cane harvesting and her coat had got caught and she went down through a working cane harvester in torrential rain and she had survived. She endured horrific injuries and burns, but somehow, she was still alive. I was helping her put on her pressure garments and thinking how she was only a few years older than me. Or frantically removing the nail polish off the woman's fingernails, who was being rushed to theatre as she lay there haemorrhaging with her crying husband beside her holding her hand. She was miscarrying their fifth baby and wondering if their dreams of being parents was ever going to happen.

Seeing a mother being handed a stillborn baby after hours of being in labour and watching her heart break open as she and her husband cradled each other in their agony. I forgot the number of times I would go back to my nursing quarters and just cry in the shower trying to forget all the terrible, painful, raw and traumatic events that I had experienced each day. In one of my shifts, I had to hold a little four-week-old baby while they were taking X-rays as he had turned up in A n E covered in bruises and the worst nappy rash I had ever seen. The mother was on drugs, had track marks down both her arms, and couldn't even take care of herself. She was also severely beaten.

He was the most gorgeous little baby. The X-rays confirmed he had a broken left leg and a broken right arm. Being so tiny, they had to reduce his fractures with no anaesthesia due to his age; I will never forget that screaming. After finally getting his leg in a splint and his arm in a collar and cuff, I remember holding him, feeding him his bottle of formula. I just couldn't understand how anyone could do this to a tiny, innocent little baby. He finally fell asleep in my arms and I didn't want to let him go; he was so fragile and beautiful. "Come on, you've done more than enough tonight. Go home and get some sleep. You're back on tomorrow morning and you know how busy kids ward is." My night duty nurse was telling me this as she very carefully picked him up out of my arms. I crawled back to my bed that night, completely exhausted. The next morning, I walked in and saw his little cot was empty. Around 3 a.m. they had seen clear fluid coming from his ears and nose, large amounts of it, and he had started to deteriorate. The urinalysis stick showed glucose, meaning that it was cerebrospinal fluid. They had rushed him down for emergency surgery, but it was too late—he didn't make it. On his report, it showed that he had the partial imprint of a sandshoe on his liver. I cried for weeks over that tiny little baby and how his life had been so tragically taken from him. I saw some things in the children's ward that just broke my heart, especially the child abuse cases, of which there were so very many.

One case that I will never forget is a little seven-year-old girl who came to us after having a brain tumour removed. We all had to be given one-on-one handover as her injuries were quite horrific to see. As a result of this operation, she had become mute. When she was only three, her uncle had sexually abused her and had literally ripped her apart. She was permanently scarred for life and had a cystostomy and colostomy that she would have for the rest of her life so that urine and faeces could be collected in bags to be changed outside of her tiny body. Her father had actually killed his own brother over what he had done to his little girl and was currently serving many years in jail.

The police had brought him in this day in his bright orange overalls and he was in handcuffs to see his daughter. We had put her into her own isolation room. I will never forget the pain that was on the young man's face seeing his daughter lying in that bed, with her head all shaved and a massive scar down her side with staples. In just seven short years, she had endured such a horrific life, it just seemed so bloody unfair. She died only a few weeks later, which I truly feel was such a blessing for her. The lumbar punctures in children's ward were awful to watch too. I lost count of the number of times it was my job to hold them down while they were screaming and so distressed while the doctor put the cannula into their spine trying to get cerebrospinal fluid. It was such a brutal thing for them to go through. I understood why they needed it but surely there was some more humane way of getting it from them.

When I would go back to visit my friends, they just didn't understand how traumatic it was to watch a young woman in her early twenties get her breast cut off in theatre. I then had to take it to the lab immediately in saline in a plastic bag with a pillowcase wrapped around it and watching later that day as she fell apart when they told her she had terminal cancer. Watching parents crying inconsolably over their baby who is hooked up to a ventilator after drowning in the bathtub and told there is nothing more that can be done. Or trying to get a body moved onto a stretcher who was an epileptic and could feel the fit coming on. He was having a shower at the time and had managed to turn off the cold water but the steaming hot water was still on. His brother had found him underneath the scorching hot water unconscious as he was being picked up for a fishing trip. By the time he got to us, his skin was like the white flesh of a chicken when it has been cooked and cut open.

We couldn't find a vein; he died en route by chopper on the way to the Burns Unit down south. He was only 28 years old. Or there was the time I took a husband to see his five-year-old daughter in a wheelchair on Christmas Day. She was now a paraplegic after a car accident that had also killed his wife and newborn son. That same day, he had to pick out coffins for both his wife and son before I wheeled him back to his room on the Men's Ward. They had been travelling for Christmas to see his parents, who had never met their new grandchild. What can you possibly say to someone who has just been through the most devastating pain?

I witnessed such unimaginable grief and trauma in those three years, experiences that will stay with me for the rest of my life. The car accidents, the rapes, the stabbings, the child abuse, the burn victims—the cancer that was ravaging their bodies, and so much more. I absorbed all the horrendous suffering; their pain became my pain.

One morning, I was setting up a breakfast tray for a young lady who was happily chatting away with me while I looked at something out her window. Suddenly, I heard the metal dish and cutlery clattering to the floor. I turned around to see scrambled egg and toast scattered everywhere. She had grabbed her chest, her mouth open wide, staring at me in terror. I grabbed the buzzer and rang it three times, signalling an emergency. As I was only a student nurse, I was ushered out of the small room and then heard them working on her. She had been in a motorcycle accident and suffered a pulmonary embolism that had travelled to her lungs. I can still hear them confirming her time of death as they placed the sheet over her... she was only 20 years old.

Another section of the hospital was for people with severe disabilities. Some were born with such severe birth defects that it was incomprehensible how they had actually survived. Some had been placed there since birth and abandoned by their families, who never returned to visit them. I could write another book on what I witnessed in that hospital over those years. I also couldn't explain it, but every time I set foot inside that hospital, I was filled with anxiety and dread. It felt like things were always touching me, brushing over me, and sometimes my hair would stand on end. I told myself it must just be severe sleep deprivation. I just couldn't explain it. It happened every single time I was inside those walls. I saw the worst of humanity and so much horrific trauma. Seeing so much pain and devastation nearly every single day of my life at such a young age forced me to grow up very quickly. I began to lose my faith and wonder if there truly was a God.

THE POWER OF PRAYER...

"IT ALWAYS HELPS TO HAVE A BIT OF PRAYER IN YOUR BACK POCKET. AT THE END OF THE DAY, YOU HAVE TO HAVE SOMETHING AND FOR ME THAT IS GOD.JESUS,MY CATHOLIC UPBRINGING,MY FAITH." —PIERCE BRONSON

After I graduated, I worked at the local hospital where I grew up. I was on night shift when we received a call from the ambulance about a young woman who had been brought in after an attempted overdose. She had been living in a very violent relationship, and her boyfriend had gone to work on an afternoon shift. She had planned her overdose so that when he returned home, he would find her. She wrote a goodbye note, took the pills, and knew that he wouldn't be long. Unbeknownst to her, he had decided to work overtime that night. She went outside, but in her heavily overdosed state, she collapsed in the dark at the front of their house. Unfortunately, none of the neighbours noticed because they were either inside watching television or asleep.

When she collapsed, it was on top of a gigantic bull ant nest. They bit her hundreds of times, and her boyfriend didn't find her until hours later. By the time she came through to us, she was hysterical, despite the ambulance having administered medication. My heart skipped a beat as soon as I saw her. There wasn't a space on her body that wasn't covered in bites; even her eyelids and lips were swollen from the bull ant stings. It was the same girl who had been in my Grade Seven primary school class. I had seen this in a dream years ago, and now it was unfolding in front of me, just as I had dreamt... more and more breadcrumbs.

When I was heavily pregnant with our firstborn, I was staying with my parents, who lived a four-hour drive away from where my husband and I resided. One day, I was reading the local Sunday paper, which featured a story about a psychic who was planning an experiment to demonstrate the power of human consciousness. The experiment involved holding a metal spoon and, at exactly 11:11 a.m. the following day, using our minds to try to bend the spoon. The idea was that if enough people did this, the collective power would cause the spoons to bend.

I was also very intrigued with this, so the next day at 11: 11 a.m. I sat down and used my mind to will that metal spoon to bend in my hand. My mother was home with me and within a couple of minutes I used my hand and that spoon just bent in half, like butter. I was so shocked that I actually threw it when I saw it completely bent over. I can actually remember Mum telling Dad that story and showing him the spoon when he got home from work that afternoon. They both tried to bend a spoon themselves but to no avail... more breadcrumbs.

"Something is not right tonight with our baby boy," I told my husband, John. I was very concerned because, normally, when Liam was in the pram, he was always looking around, but tonight he was unusually lethargic. Since his birth, Liam had always been a very tiny baby and struggled to gain weight. After he was born, he was rushed to the Special Care Nursery and spent several days in an incubator because he was so unwell. His birth had been nearly 28 hours long and incredibly traumatic. I endured nine weeks of constant morning sickness, and then my placenta tore at 29 weeks. In the end, due to my excessively high blood pressure, I was induced. During the harrowing labour, just as his head was crowning, Liam went into respiratory distress.

I had to undergo an emergency episiotomy without local anaesthetic due to the urgency, and I nearly passed out from the excruciating pain as they worked to save his life. It took me nearly eight months after his birth before I could walk or go up a flight of stairs without being in horrendous pain. As soon as he was born, Liam stopped breathing again and was rushed to intensive care. I didn't even get to hold him until he was nearly 48 hours old, and even then, he had to have oxygen tubing over his face while I held him. I still remember being wheeled in to see him, lying in an incubator covered in monitors with an IV inserted.

As we reached the car, I picked him up to put him in the car seat, and he was burning up with a fever. Deeply concerned, we rushed to the A&E department of the hospital. Our son was transferred to a special room where it became clear that he was deteriorating rapidly. The medical team was performing ultrasounds and taking blood, and it was evident that they were extremely worried. Liam was only five months old. "What is happening to my baby?" I cried. John and I were becoming increasingly frightened. They tried to insert an IV to administer fluids, but Liam was going into peripheral shutdown.

"Your baby has a severe urinary infection that has refluxed back into his kidneys, causing severe septicaemia. We have also found that he has a ventricular septal defect in his heart, which is very serious. His heart is struggling to pump blood around his little body. We are just dumbfounded that this was never found at his birth, as he is a very sick baby. He may need open-heart surgery to fix it," said the doctor. I was shocked because he had been a bit off with his feeding that day and was unusually tired, but he hadn't shown any signs of a fever or illness.

"No, this can come on suddenly," the medical staff explained. "We have a chopper on standby to rush him to a major hospital down south, but things aren't looking good. If you would like your baby to be anointed, now would be the time."

"Anointed? What are you talking about?" I asked in absolute shock.

"We can't find a vein, and we urgently need to administer antibiotics to save his life, but his little body is shutting down. Is there anyone we can call for you?" I sat in complete shock with John, trying to comprehend what was being said to us.

Just then, another nurse came running in, saying that the paediatrician was in A&E attending to a baby who had drowned and was on his way. He immediately ran in, seeing the team around Liam's tiny, motionless body on the bed. He began yelling for specific medical equipment, and we were quickly ushered out of the room so he could work on him. The only vein he could find was in Liam's head, as the rest had all shut down. They began administering medication, and we were told to pray, as there was nothing more they could do. It was now between our baby and God.

John started making phone calls to family while I sat there, completely numb, looking down at Liam through my tears. I held his little hand and prayed like I had never prayed before, pleading with God to save our little boy. The next two hours were touch-and-go and felt like the longest of my life. But miracles happen every day. If the specialist paediatrician hadn't been there at that exact time and managed to get a line in, our little boy wouldn't be here today. Never underestimate the incredible power of prayer—it can move mountains. Thank you, God, I knew that you had been listening.

I could not explain it, but I've always known that when I pray, there's something greater than me out there in the cosmos. I don't know what it is, but I feel like they're listening. I've prayed many times, like when I was heavily pregnant with our second child and taking a nap. John and my brother Aaron were out in the lounge watching TV while Liam was toddling around. I woke up to the sound of Liam screaming. Panicked, I rushed out to find that a ceramic vase had shattered, and all the ends were sharp and jagged.

Liam had fallen backwards onto one of the jagged pieces, and it had pierced his skull. I had never seen so much blood. We rushed him to the hospital, and luckily, the doctor was there doing rounds, even though it was the weekend. He rushed Liam into the A&E. I tried to hold him still, despite being heavily pregnant, but he was thrashing and screaming in pain. Liam looked at me with such fear and terror in his eyes that I couldn't bear it. I sent John in with him, as listening to his screams was overwhelming me.

I prayed and prayed and prayed that he would be okay, especially after everything we had already been through with Liam. After what seemed like an eternity, the GP finally came out, looking exhausted, and said that Liam must have had angels watching over him because the injury had penetrated deep down to the periosteum of his skull. Miraculously, he was going to be okay, and the doctor would send him for further tests, but he was a very lucky little boy. Thank you, God… thank you, thank you, thank you.

SPIRITUAL ENLIGHTENMENT...

"THE MORE I STUDY THE UNIVERSE, THE MORE I BELIEVE IN A HIGHER POWER." —ALBERT EINSTEIN

Other times I have called on the higher realms for help, like when I was about 13 and my mother and I were on a ride at an amusement park. My mother was sitting in the front, and I was in the back. As we neared the end of the ride, we entered a dark tunnel. The ride car then began to climb steeply before hurtling out the other end at full speed. As we started the ascent in the dark, the car suddenly began making terrible noises—it wasn't on the tracks properly. I grabbed onto the sides, absolutely terrified, as the noises grew louder. All I could imagine was the car going over the sides, and us being killed or seriously hurt. I silently prayed to God in my head to save us, repeatedly.

Suddenly a man appeared out of nowhere and jumped up next to us. He asked if we were alright and used his walkie talkie to get the ride stopped. He then helped us get out and we were escorted off the premises and it was closed down for the rest of the day. It took me a long time to go back on that ride again but eventually I did. I prayed all the way up silently for God to look after me. The first time I did get back on it, I had the best time.

Another memory is when we were on holidays up north staying in cabins in a tourist park. We all had to use the amenities block, which was near our accommodation. We had been swimming in the pool for the afternoon and I wanted to go and have a shower before tea. I had just grabbed all of my belongings and had flung a towel over my shoulder and was about to walk up to the block as it was going on dusk.

My parents had hired out two cabins with an adjoining door and I was in the cabin with my younger brothers. My parents had my two younger sisters in with them. The radio was playing in the background and the announcer had said that Princess Diana had just given birth to her second child and that after the break they would announce what she had. Lots of commercials came over the radio and I sat and listened intently for what the news would be. Finally, after heaps of advertisements, we were told that she had just given birth to a baby boy and they had called him Harry. As I waited for so long to listen to the radio, I once again collected all my things and began to walk towards the amenities block.

I was suddenly aware of lots of voices and seeing an ambulance and flashing blue and red lights. My father then called me back and told me to go and wait in the cabin. I was completely unaware of what was actually happening but a terrible feeling of dread had come over me. My mother and other siblings had returned by now and I told her what had happened. Dad eventually came back and told us that a young girl around my age had been in that same block having a shower. A man had climbed over the top of the wall as there was enough space between the wall and the roof and had viciously sexually assaulted her. If I had not stayed back when I did to listen to the radio, I would have been in that shower block at that exact same time. Gives me chills to think what that other poor girl must have gone through. We packed up and left the park that exact same night.

I was returning back home as John had bulging discs in his spine and he had been sent two hours away for further tests. He was in so much agony that he could not sit upright in the car. He was lying down next to me in the front of the car after being dosed up with very heavy painkillers for the trip back home. We were only about 10 kms from home when our front tyre suddenly blew and our car began swerving all over the highway. I could feel myself losing control and honestly thought I was going to roll the car. My heart was beating a million miles a minute and I was desperately trying to stop the car from going over the high built-up shoulders of the road. It was absolutely terrifying.

John was frantic as he could not help me and was hanging onto the dash for dear life. I remember calling out, "Please God, help me," and within seconds, I was able to bring the car to a complete stop. A car behind us had seen what was happening, and a man rushed up to my window. "Are you both okay? I truly thought your car was going to roll." He called an ambulance to transport John to the hospital and changed the tyre for me. "Are you going to be okay to drive to the hospital?" he asked. "Yes, thank you," I replied, still shaking from the fright of our near accident. His wife brought me some water and tried to help calm me down. I drove very slowly to the hospital. John and I hadn't got a scratch on us… Thank you, God… thank you, thank you, thank you… xx.

John and I had travelled away for the weekend with our young son and there happened to be a baby show on Saturday morning at the main shopping centre. We entered Liam into the competition, and within minutes, he had found a new friend to play with. I watched him running around, playing with another young toddler of a similar age. I distinctly remember the pattern on his new little friend's shirt—it was so cute. The more I watched them play, the more I felt overwhelmed with so much sadness at this little boy, but I could not understand why. After the weekend was over, we made the two-hour drive back home. I told John how I felt, but dismissed it as just being tired. That night, I dreamt of the little boy's mother crying hysterically, but I could not see why. I woke up feeling so emotional and drained.

I told John what I had dreamt, and he got me a coffee, reassuring me I was just tired from the lack of sleep over the past few weeks. I felt uneasy all day but soon forgot about it over the next couple of weeks. One morning, John went out to get the newspaper that was being delivered and came back in looking pale. "What is it?" I asked. He showed me the front page. There was a big, blown-up picture of that same little boy in the exact outfit he'd been wearing at the baby show. I read that his mother had been taking his newborn sibling out of a capsule in the back seat when he opened his car door—the child lock wasn't on—and ran directly into an oncoming taxi. He was killed instantly.

My heart just broke. Only a few weeks before, he had been running around with our son, having the time of their lives playing together, and now he was gone. I just sat there and cried.

"Have you got any pains yet?" John asked, as I was already nearly a week overdue with our second baby. "No, not a thing," I replied. He had taken me for bumpy car rides that morning and was due to go back on arvo shift that same day.

The old wives' tale of taking a few mouthfuls of castor oil and sucking on an orange was his next idea to see if he could get anything happening. I took some, but nothing happened for the rest of the day.

"Well, they obviously aren't coming to meet us today," I joked. As John was getting ready for work, I started to experience niggling pains, but nothing that made me think I was in labour. "Let's get packed and head to the major hospital," John suggested. The hospital was two hours away, and because I had lots of complications with Liam's delivery and he had to go to the special care nursery for days, it had been decided by my doctor that our second child should be delivered in the regional city hospital, not in our small town—it was just too risky.

John was insistent on getting us packed and organised so we could be at the hospital by nightfall in case things intensified. But everything in me was saying, "No, do not get in that car." I didn't understand why, but I was adamant that we were not going to be travelling that day. John was livid with me and couldn't understand why we weren't getting in the car to start our two-hour trip. "You know they don't want you having this baby here. What is wrong with you? There could be complications—are you willing to risk this?" he asked in exasperation. I could hear my intuition telling me again not to get in the car. "If things get really bad, they'll chopper me out. We both know that. We'll go tomorrow when it's daylight," I told him. After he left for work, much to his dismay, I spent the next hour on the lounge as the niggles became more consistent.

I heard a knock on the door and my friend Leigh was standing there with a cake in her hand. As I opened the door, I felt like I had been really kicked in the stomach. "Oh, Karen, are you ok?" asked Leigh. "Just some Braxton Hicks, probably. They're not like the labour pains I had with Liam." I went outside to hang some nappies on the line, but every time I reached up to peg them, the pain intensified. I thought I'd better ring Mum and get to the hospital, just in case. Mum came and picked me up, rushing me to the hospital. When they checked me, I was nearly 10 centimetres dilated, and the baby was coming fast. "Where's Dad?" the nurse asked. Oh no, we completely forgot! Mum went to ring John. As I got back on the bed, my waters broke. "Well, you'd better tell him to get here fast!" the nurse called out after Mum.

Bubby wasn't waiting for anybody. Within the hour, I was almost ready to push when the midwife realised that the cord was wrapped around the baby's neck—not once, but three times. Of all the midwives who could have been on duty at that time, I had one with extensive experience who knew exactly what to do. I had to pant excessively through the intense contractions, with

Mum holding my hand. I remember panting and praying to God, asking Him to ensure my baby would be okay as they worked to remove the cord. At 7 pm that night, I delivered a beautiful, healthy 7-pound, 11-ounce baby girl. The hospital staff later told me how incredibly lucky I was that we hadn't been travelling on the highway, as there was no way we would have made it to our destination.

I would have delivered a stillborn baby as my pushing would have cut off her oxygen supply and she would have never stood a chance. Suddenly, the doors burst open and John was standing there—he had missed the entire birth. Our baby had just been put into an incubator and was being checked over. "Would you like to go and see your beautiful baby daughter?" I overheard Mum ask him as he came over and kissed me on the forehead. I was lying there, absolutely exhausted and wiped out. Thank God I listened to my intuition that day—it literally saved our baby girl's life. Once again, He was listening too. Thank you, God... ... thank you... thank you... thank you xx.

TRAIL WAS ALWAYS IN FRONT OF ME...

"WHY DO WE CLOSE OUR EYES WHEN WE PRAY, CRY, KISS, OR DREAM? BECAUSE THE MOST BEAUTIFUL THINGS IN LIFE ARE NOT SEEN BUT FELT BY THE HEART." —DENZEL WASHINGTON

John had been away contracting while I was at home with our toddler son, Liam, and our baby daughter, Taylor, who was only a few weeks old. To say things were tight was an understatement. We had to be so frugal with our money to keep our heads above water, and with only one wage coming in, things were even worse. I hadn't seen John for over three weeks, and he had finally come home that weekend to see us before heading back out for more work. The bills were coming in so fast, and I was starting to feel overwhelmed, wondering how on earth we were going to pay them.

John had withdrawn nearly his entire pay—over $2000 in fifty-dollar notes—and handed it to me. The next day, I was supposed to pay our bills and get some groceries, as he wouldn't be home again for another three-plus weeks. That evening, I was visiting my parents on the way home, completely sleep-deprived from being up most nights with our new baby. I could never sleep during the day because our very energetic toddler was always running around making so much noise. As I was strapping our children into their car seats with the help of my mother, I said goodnight and drove home.

When I looked in the car to get my purse, I couldn't find it. I went back through my bag, the house, under the car seat—my head was starting to spin. "OMG, where is my purse?" I suddenly remembered that I had put it on the roof while strapping the babies in. OMG!!! I rushed back to my parents' house in a blind panic. It was a Thursday night, so a lot of people were out night shopping, and there were cars everywhere up and down the street. There was also a sporting event on—I could hear the hooters, see the oval lights on, and people were walking everywhere near the fields. My purse must have fallen off when I drove away.

We found it out on the road, not far from my parents' house. It was completely empty—there wasn't any money in it. I burst into tears and thought I was going to pass out from the shock. Oh God, what was John going to say? How could I have been so frikkin' stupid? Then suddenly, my mother yelled out, "I found one... and another!" My younger siblings had come out to help me. I prayed and prayed and prayed that we would find that money, as we needed every cent of it to survive. As cars came around the corner, their headlights would catch the dollar notes floating in the air, dislodged by the cars in front. Thank God it was dark, and people didn't actually see what we were doing. Within half an hour, I had recovered the entire $2000. Thank you, God... thank you... thank you... thank you xx. To this day, I have never put my purse on the roof of a car again. What a life lesson that was for me that night, and one I have never forgotten.

I woke up in dreadful fright, seeing John surrounded by so much fire, looking utterly broken. I could also see a petrol station and some sort of car accident. He was in the auxiliary firefighters and was always on call. Every time his beeper went off, my heart would sink, and I would hope it wasn't anything really bad. But there was something about this dream that deeply disturbed me—I then saw people at a funeral, crying in such distress. "Oh, please let it not be about John," I thought.

Within the next couple of weeks, his beeper went off around 1 am. "What is it?" I asked, half asleep. "A car accident, go back to sleep. I'll see you when I get back," John replied. I was filled with dread. "Please be careful," I said as I kissed him goodbye. Normally, I'd go back to sleep, but this time I just couldn't settle. I stayed up, reading books and keeping myself awake until I could see the sun coming up. John still wasn't home. This is taking way too long—I thought—he should have been home by now. He's been gone for hours.

My mind was racing with all sorts of thoughts when suddenly the phone rang. My heart was pounding as I picked up the phone and heard his voice on the other end. "Oh, thank God, are you okay?" I asked. "Yeah, it's been a big morning," he replied. I let our children sleep in since it was Saturday. "A young fella collided with a petrol tanker around 12:40 this morning out on the highway near the petrol station. We had to work like trojans to make sure the whole thing didn't blow. The young fella was killed instantly, and the truck driver was sedated because he was in so much shock.

As we came up over the hill in the dark in the fire truck, there was fire for kilometres. It was a very sombre feeling, as we'd never encountered anything like that in our training before. We are all absolutely exhausted, but we're okay. We have to stay behind for a debriefing, and a counsellor is coming to see us. We saw things that we've never seen before. I'll tell you more about it when I get home. The young man was supposed to be celebrating his engagement party tonight. His fiancée is in the hospital now, heavily sedated and being treated for shock as well." She was only 27 years old… so many breadcrumbs.

Years later, when we moved to this regional city, I was in the local library when a DVD dropped to my feet. It was called

"Conversations with God" by a man named Neale Donald Walsch. I took it home and watched it, and I was amazed at the events that had happened in this man's life. Later that year, I bought a brand-new copy of the book and gave it to my father as a birthday present. I also read other books by Neale that I found absolutely fascinating... so many breadcrumbs were literally dropping at my feet. Months later, I was looking through a catalogue and ordered a series of CDs to listen to, ironically called "Awakening"... more breadcrumbs. I found myself in esoteric shops, compelled to buy certain books to read... more breadcrumbs. I joined a manifestation community on social media, something I had never done before... more breadcrumbs. I attended a workshop with my sister and her friend on how to set goals, subliminals, brain programming, how to live more abundantly, projection of the mind, and the power we all possess... so many breadcrumbs had been placed in front of me for such a long time, but I was a very slow learner. I just never realised the trail was right in front of me all along.

BROKEN OPEN...

> "WHEN LIFE PRESENTS MORE CHALLENGES THAN YOU CAN HANDLE, DELEGATE TO GOD. HE NOT ONLY HAS THE ANSWER, HE IS THE ANSWER." —TAVIS SMALLEY

We awoke to the devastating news that my paternal grandfather had suffered a heart attack and died suddenly, leaving us all absolutely heartbroken. We were shattered by the complete and utter shock. I had never really understood pain on that level until he passed away. The grief was just overwhelming. After trying to pull myself together, John organised to drop our two young children off on the way to his parents' house, who lived hours away. After saying goodbye, the tears began to flow as I became consumed with my own thoughts. We travelled for many more hours in the dark and finally reached our destination late that night. During the trip, a song kept playing on the radio. I heard the words over and over: "And I know you're shining down on me from heaven, like so many friends we've lost along the way, and I know eventually we'll be together... one sweet day."

I lost count of how many times that song played on the radio during the trip. It broke me every time I heard it. As I listened to that song once again, I suddenly had the idea to write my grandmother a poem about my grandfather that she could keep. The words came to me in the car, and that night, I wrote them all down before I eventually drifted off to sleep in the early hours of the morning. My grandmother had an open viewing so we could see Pop one last time before his funeral service. He looked exactly like he was sleeping—so peaceful and serene. I absolutely loved and adored my grandfather and couldn't imagine my life without him in it. When I saw my father look in the coffin and see him, it broke him too. I had never seen my father cry so much in my lifetime.

These are the words I penned: "I have so many wonderful memories of you, Pop, I don't really know where to start. The one thing that I do know is that I love you with all of my heart. I remember when I was small, we would spend hours in the car travelling down to see you both—it always felt so far. Your laughter, your warmth, your love, your hugs, your kisses, your smiles. I always knew when I would see you both, it would be worth all the miles. We could hardly wait to get there and see your smiling face. Just to get the first hug from you was always a big race. And I never will forget the times you would bounce me on your knee as we listened to the Christmas carols in front of the beautiful tree.

"Opening presents on Christmas morning was always such a treat. When we played our new games with you, you were always so hard to beat. Being tickled by your whiskers always made me squeal, and all of us grandkids loved going fishing with you, fighting over who got to hold your rod and reel. Feeding ducks with you at the goose ponds was always a special treat, as was arguing with my cousins over who got to sit next to you in the front seat. Having you and Nan come up for holidays was always a big thrill—who gets to hug Nan and Pop first? Not you, pick me, I will!

"Whether it was flying kites high in the sky or feeding goldfish in your pond, wiping away our tears when we cried—oh, Poppy, we were so fond of you. I will never forget you, Pop; you brought so much love into our hearts, and the thought of being without you makes me want to fall apart. Pop, I pray that you are happy with the angels up above, and may the Lord God bless you abundantly with His love. I know that God in heaven has written above your chair in letters of pure gold the words reserved for the best poppy: 'THE BEST POPPY IN THE WORLD.'"

I so wanted to read it out at his funeral, but I was overcome with sheer tiredness and overwhelming emotion, and I knew that I wouldn't even be able to read the first line. My only regret is that I didn't give it to the priest to read on my behalf or to another family member so I could share how much love I had for my Pop. I wrote it out when I got back home, surrounded the poem with pictures of angels, framed it, and sent it by post to my heartbroken grandmother.

She rang me in tears a few days later, telling me it was one of the most beautiful pieces of poetry she had ever read and had placed it under her television so that she could be reminded of it constantly. She said it would be the first thing she would see every morning and the last thing she would see every night and she knew Poppy was watching over me, just as he was to all of us. Nan told me that he would come to me in my dreams, but only when he felt that I was ready to see him as he didn't want to frighten me. He had come to Nan already in hers and she knew that he was at peace.

A few weeks after he had passed, I dreamt that I was walking in a dark forest and came across a dark pool of water. I felt really frightened as I didn't know where I was. I looked into the dark, black water, and it began to ripple. I became very distressed as I did not know what was causing the ripples, and I felt that something was about to burst out. The ripples got stronger and stronger and the water started to dazzle with the most brilliant gold light. Suddenly, there in front of me was my grandfather, smiling at me from the now calm water, and I felt so much love and happiness radiating from him all around me.

I instantly knew that he was coming to say goodbye, and I knew that he was in a beautiful place. I told him how much I loved him, smiled down at him, and blew him the biggest kiss. He smiled back at me, and instantly I woke up. I felt such a sense of calmness and relief, and I knew in my heart that he was at peace. We visited my grandmother for Christmas with our two small children, and she asked us to replace some of the plastic flowers beside Pop's headstone, as she knew we were going out to visit. John took all the screws out, and we removed the old faded flowers and placed the new ones inside the plastic container. No matter how hard John tried, he couldn't get the screws to go back in correctly.

He tried and tried, and I could see he was getting really frustrated. "Just keep trying," I said as I picked up the old flowers to take them to the bin. As I was gathering everything, an angel statue that Nan had bought for Pop fell out. "Oh no, look what we forgot to put back in!" We quickly placed the angel where it was supposed to be, and when John went to put the screws in, they went in perfectly with no issues. WOWZA! "Pop wasn't going to let you put that back on until he had his angel," I laughed. More breadcrumbs. John just shook his head at it all.

SPIRITUAL NUDGES...

"INTELLIGENCE HIGHLY AWAKENED IS INTUITION, WHICH IS THE ONLY TRUE GUIDE IN LIFE." —KRISHNAMURTI

When my maternal grandfather died, we were down at my Auntie Pat's beach house having the wake. I was just gobsmacked when she told me that there was a message on her landline phone and that it sounded exactly like my grandfather. "What??" I exclaimed in shock. She took me into her bedroom and put the receiver up to my ear. You could hear distinctly that it was his voice. He was saying how sorry he was and that he would be thinking of us all. The time and date that it was recorded were days later—he had already passed away. We just looked at each other in shock when we heard it. Even when the Delete button was pressed, it did not get deleted from the phone for many weeks after. It was just surreal.

Some days working as a manager with the company I was with were completely exhausting. One of my duties was helping disabled clients in our community get the care they needed and securing funding for this. I had been approaching various local charity organisations, asking for donations to put accessible facilities into our community. One of the presidents, Mark, called back and arranged a time to meet. As soon as I walked into his office, I felt an overwhelming sadness. He was pleasant enough and did everything he could to make me feel welcome. He gave me a big smile, was very friendly, and we talked in depth about how the charity could support various ventures in the community. We worked tirelessly together for the next five months and raised enough funds to make a significant difference in many lives.

I always felt a deep sadness around Mark as I got to know him, but our projects kept him busy. I could feel the sadness begin to dissipate a little more each time we worked together. He became so fixated on every detail and worked incredibly hard to achieve so much. We were in the local newspaper numerous times together as well. It was during this time that I discovered I was pregnant with our third child. The first few weeks were tough; I was so sick with nausea and vomiting that I could barely get out of bed. My doctor wanted to admit me to hospital multiple times, but with our other two children still in primary school and John working shifts, it would have caused too much disruption. I refused to go and promised to keep myself hydrated. My GP even made a few house calls to check on me, as he was so worried.

During this time, Mark began constantly ringing me, wanting to know if there were any other projects we could work on together. I explained that I was just too sick to do anything at the moment and that once I was over this hurdle in my pregnancy, I was sure there would be plenty more we could do. Despite this, he would contact me again within days, discussing different scenarios or funding schemes. I was too sick to care. I explained numerous times to Mark that I wasn't up to it and even began avoiding his calls. I felt awful about it, but I was so sick and just wanted to be left alone. I had enough on my plate with two other children to care for and was working from the sidelines with my actual job. I didn't need the extra stress. Finally, the phone calls stopped. "Thank God Mark got the message—it's about bloody time," I thought. I was over it all.

After nearly six weeks of being bed and homebound, I felt well enough to venture out. There was a big morning tea for cancer research at the local fire brigade. I was sitting there with a few friends when one of the team overheard something coming in from the local ambulance and police, who were located nearby. A wife had to be taken to hospital after she came home and found her husband had hung himself under their house from the bottom rafters. She was so distressed they had to sedate her and take her to hospital. Instantly, I went white, and my stomach churned. My friends asked if I was alright.

I knew I was going to be sick. I just knew in my heart it was Mark. Later that day, it was confirmed. I was devastated. I had worked so closely with that man for nearly half a year, and I was so busy with my job and my family that I just didn't see how severely depressed he truly was. Working with me had given him some sort of purpose again, and he had thrived on it. He was a lovely man, and I felt responsible for a long time, thinking I had caused this to happen. John helped me through those dark days by explaining that it wasn't my fault. This was Mark's journey, and he had chosen this path himself.

Even his own wife couldn't see the signs—how was I supposed to when I hadn't physically seen him in weeks? "If only I had met up with him or let him come over to the house, maybe he wouldn't have done this," I sobbed. "You didn't really know him that long. You need to understand that this was none of your doing," John said, giving me a hug. It made sense to me then why I always felt such overwhelming and incredible sadness around him. That event marred my pregnancy, but through lots of healing, I eventually got through it. I did miss him after working so closely with him for so many months, and I just had to pray that he had finally found some peace.

One day, I was working from home, and my head was throbbing so badly that I knew if I didn't lie down, I would collapse from sheer exhaustion. I had just placed my head on the pillow and could feel my head pounding with pain when I distinctly heard my name being called over and over. "Oh no, someone forgot to hand in their paysheet and is calling out to me," I thought. "Why can't they just slip it under my door?" I wondered, but I knew they were calling me—maybe it was important. I managed to drag myself out of bed and opened the front door. I knew I looked terrible, but I didn't care. Thank goodness the kids were at school and John was at work, so I could get some rest. As the door opened, there was nobody standing there. How odd. I looked out and saw no car, no one walking around the house. I went to the back door, and again, no one was there. I looked out into the court, and no car was driving off. WOWZA, that was strange. OMG, I really was tired, I thought to myself... now I'm hearing voices... more breadcrumbs.

My brother Aaron, who was about 17 at the time, was working on the railway when he stopped by a service station to get some food. Unbeknownst to anyone, he went home and developed the most severe gastroenteritis. For nearly three days, he suffered through it, and no one from his workplace thought to check on him—perhaps they assumed he was on days off. He was working at least an hour away and living in a house provided by the railway. Mum was home one day when she heard a car horn blaring downstairs. She found my brother hunched over the steering wheel in his car, in a terrible state. He was barely conscious and in shocking condition.

In a panic, my parents managed to get him to the hospital, where it was discovered that his organs had begun to shut down from severe salmonella poisoning, and he was also suffering from severe dehydration. The doctors told my parents they couldn't understand how he managed to drive himself all that way in such a severe condition. He replied to them as they stood around his bed, "I didn't drive the car here—Poppy did." Our grandfather had died months earlier.

My sister Jane rang me while I was driving—we had just bought a brand-new house two hours away in the regional city we often visited. The house had everything we had imagined, and we loved the eggplant purple feature walls throughout. "Where do we sign?" we both asked, so excited, we couldn't believe we had found our beautiful new forever home so quickly. Within two days of viewing the house, we had signed the papers and bought it. It felt like fate.

As I was driving on the highway with our car packed up with more belongings going to our new home, my mobile phone rang. I answered it. "You're not going to believe this—did you hear what happened to Ben?" asked Jane. This was Marcy's younger brother that I had lost contact with over the years. "He's dead." OMG! I think I nearly drove the car off the highway. What the…? Suddenly, I was back in time as a fourteen-year-old teenager and seeing the young man in the white coffin with that distinct mark on his neck. Back then, Ben was only in preschool and always running around the backyard with his toys. That's why I didn't recognise who was in the coffin—it was Ben as a young man. "He was in a car accident, wasn't he?" I asked. "No, Ben… he… he hung himself," Jane told me. I had to pull the car over and compose myself on the highway before I could drive again. I could still see that dream so vividly in my mind. It was just so surreal.

BIGGEST MISTAKE WE EVER MADE...

"EVEN THE DEVIL WAS AN ANGEL ONCE." —M. ROBINSON

The first night in our beautiful new home, we were exhausted from unpacking all day. It literally looked like a bomb had gone off inside. In the utter chaos, we all dropped into bed that night, completely and utterly spent. But seconds later, a bang on the roof bolted us all awake. "What the HELL was that?" I asked John in fright, as the kids came running in, frightened as well. "It's okay, it's probably just the roof expanding, going from hot days to cool nights," he reassured us. None of us had ever heard such banging before. This banging and knocking continued for many years. Even the children who came for sleepovers would comment on how frightening it sounded.

The knocking and banging had started the day we moved in, especially at night, and it eventually became something we all got used to. "Doesn't this happen at your house too?" I would ask the other children, and every one of them would say no. I also noticed that the toilet in our ensuite made strange noises—it sounded like a soft growling. "Can you hear that?" I would ask John. It wasn't just when I lifted the lid; it happened whenever I walked into the ensuite. "Oh, probably just the pipes. This is a new estate, remember? Maybe it's something to do with all the excavation and building going on," he told me. Unbeknownst to any of us, we were now living with a very dark, evil presence in our house, and we were about to pay for it dearly.

Not long after arriving in our new regional city, a friend invited me to a psychic expo that was coming through town. I had never been to an expo, so I agreed to go. My youngest, Jenna, was still in her pram. "You are going to be a very famous author. The book will start out very dark, but the ending will be filled with happiness," one psychic told me. Oookay, me a writer? I thought, Yeah, right. My friend also visited another psychic, who was quite old but only used a normal pack of playing cards instead of tarot. I arranged a meeting with her, and when I walked in, she had her back to me.

"Ahh, a nurse has just walked into my space," she said out loud as she turned to face me. Wow, she was good. "You are not like any nurse I've ever known before—you can actually feel your patients' pain and trauma. You need to learn how to protect yourself from this. When you work in a hospital, do you find yourself completely drained and emotional at the end of each day? Actually, don't answer; I know the answer is yes—you do, all the time. This is because you're an empath. You're so sensitive to others around you and their energies."

"What on earth is an empath?" I asked, confused.

"It means you can put yourself in someone else's' shoes, to feel their situation, understand their feelings, and see through their eyes. You can feel others' pain and anguish, but also their happiness and joy. It means you have the ability to understand their suffering, and you can bond with them. When you master this trait, it also means you have the ability to spiritually evolve if you wish to. I bet you suffer from food poisonings, digestive issues, bowel issues like IBS."

"Well, actually I do. I thought this was just because I wasn't looking after myself properly with all the shift work, lack of sleep, and not really eating properly," I replied, stunned.

"Have you ever heard the saying 'water off a duck's back'? Well, you're that duck. You need to learn to let things go—ruffle your feathers, shake all that stuff off, and keep swimming. If you don't, the water on you will get so heavy that it will eventually drown you. Please, learn how to protect yourself. Hospitals aren't good places for you to work—there's way too much trauma there, and you're very sensitive to everything that happens."

She handed me a deck of playing cards to shuffle, and a card with diamonds fell out. "Ahh, you're going to start working somewhere with the aged, and you'll be working under the stars. There's a lady with lots of colours in her hair who wears glasses. I think she runs the facility? Lots of colours? Yes, I can see blue, yellow, green, purple."

What the…? I thought to myself. "She will take great care of you. I can see white and navy. As your son gets older, unfortunately, he will be drawn into some bad company—not through his own fault, but because of the school he's in. They will pair your son with another boy to try to guide him onto the right path. Unfortunately, your son is a follower, not a leader, and can be easily influenced. When he brings this other boy into your home, you will know it. This boy's heart will be as black as his skin. Make sure you do everything in your power to keep your son away from him. You also have a lot of purple in your house—on the walls, in your furnishings, linen, etc. You don't know it yet, but in years to come, you will understand just how spiritual you truly are, and purple is a very spiritual colour. I also see a lot of red around you throughout your home. You're an Aries, and you have great leadership qualities that you may want to follow in your career, but you're not a typical Aries—you're more like a Virgo. You're humble, kind, sympathetic, thoughtful, creative, reliable, and patient. You have many traits that a typical Aries doesn't have."

Wow, what a confronting reading, I thought to myself. I can't really remember the rest, to be honest, as I believe I blocked it out, thinking this woman was just out to take my money. "Gosh, what a waste of $50," I muttered to myself.

Within the next week, John decided he didn't want to travel away for work anymore and that he missed us too much, so he promptly resigned from his well-paying job. "What the HELL did you do that for?" I screamed at him. "We have a major mortgage for the first time EVER in our life, our two eldest kids are about to start high school in a private school that costs money, and we have another mouth to feed—and you go and do this?!"

I was so upset with him. I was MAD! "That's okay, you're a nurse, you can find a job too," he told me ever so casually.

My Aunty Pat had worked in an aged care facility many years ago when I was a teenager. "Just tell the manager you're my niece, and hopefully, there might be an opening for you," she told me. I walked into a facility, and there in front of me was a nurse sitting at the desk, wearing a navy and white shirt.

"Ahh… I'm here to inquire about a job as an RN," I said. I was redirected to an office, and there, sitting in front of me, looking down at some paperwork, was a lady with glasses and hair in all sorts of different colours. I was absolutely gobsmacked—just like Flo had said. I tried to compose myself, but when she looked up and saw the expression on my face, she replied, "Oh, Jesus Christ, I'm not that f**king ugly, am I?"

"Ah… yeah, no," I stammered. I thought it best to keep that story to myself. Needless to say, I got the job right then and there, and the shifts I was assigned were afternoon shifts until 11 pm—right under the stars. Oh, wow… more and more breadcrumbs.

FEELING OUT OF SORTS...

"IN EASTERN CULTURE, PEOPLE SEE GHOSTS, PEOPLE TALK ABOUT GHOSTS... IT'S JUST ACCEPTED. AND IN WESTERN CULTURE, IT'S JUST NOT." —JESSICA ALBA

On our family holiday, we visited the Australian War memorial in Canberra. Reading all the stories and seeing all the faces of these men, women, and children was just so sad. Both my grandfathers had served in World War II, and in the archives section, you could look up their details. When I searched for my mother's father, it wouldn't let me access his files. A volunteer came over, spoke with me, and typed in a few more details. "Ah, this is because your grandfather was court-martialled—not once, but twice. His file has restricted access; you'll have to apply to open it and see why." Fascinated by what this could be about, I applied and filled out the necessary paperwork.

Within a few weeks, I received official papers, having had to prove that I was indeed his granddaughter. I could now proceed with the next stage. That night, I was sitting in my lounge room with the papers in hand, contemplating whether I really wanted to do this and what skeletons I might uncover. Suddenly, I saw a terrifying dark figure slowly coming towards me in the reflection of the glass shelves surrounding my TV. I was too petrified to move. It kept getting closer and closer, and I was unable to move or scream. It came up over the top of me, and I was about to scream in terror when suddenly it was my grandfather, smiling down at me. He leaned over me and grabbed all the papers straight out of my hand with such force that it woke me up.

I found myself sitting in the exact chair, wearing the exact nightie, as in my dream, with all the papers scattered around my feet on the lounge room floor. My heart was pounding, and I was covered in sweat. "Okay, so you don't want me to open that file then," I said out loud. I put it away in the filing cabinet, and to this day, I've never opened it and don't think I ever will.

When we were in Melbourne, we decided to visit the Old Melbourne Gaol. As soon as I walked in, I felt severe nausea. "Oh no, don't tell me you're feeling sick again. What's wrong? You've been fine all day while we were visiting the other tourist attractions," John said. "I'm sorry, I don't know why," I replied, but since we had paid for admission, I decided to push through it. Everywhere I turned, I felt sick. I hated being in there but kept pushing myself as John was interested in looking at everything. I could feel the terror and torture that had taken place within those walls. It was a debilitating feeling.

We reached a section that displayed the brutal instruments the guards used to torture the prisoners, where they were strapped down and lashed. Some of the instruments looked absolutely barbaric. After the prisoners were hanged, a death mask was made of them using plaster of Paris, and these were displayed in all the cells. You could see the intricate details of what every prisoner looked like. I remember excusing myself and going to the toilet, where I actually vomited. I was sweating, feeling hot and flushed, so I splashed water on myself to cool down. John was concerned as I had been gone for a while. "Are you okay? We can leave if you're not well."

"No… we're nearly finished… not long to go. I can do this. My heart just won't stop racing… it's like… like I can feel their suffering," I said, struggling to understand my emotions. It was the most overwhelming feeling, like I had no energy and just wanted to faint or cry. "God, why do I want to cry? This is so confusing," I thought to myself.

The tour guide explained that construction of the gaol began in 1841 and was completed in 1862. It had housed over 50,000 prisoners. After the first hanging, the body was returned to the man's wife. She owned the local butcher shop, and to attract attention and increase business, she displayed his body in the front window surrounded by flowers, advertising it as the first hanging. After that incident, it was decided that no bodies would ever be released to families again. The 135 men and women who were hanged were then buried within the walls and floors of the gaol.

"No wonder I felt so out of sorts," I thought. "I can only imagine how haunted that place must be with all those tortured souls." As we were being told this, our guide led us up to the scaffolding where the actual hangings took place, including that of the infamous bushranger, Ned Kelly. We were invited to take photos standing in the exact spot. As I stood in the footings, I thought I was going to be sick in front of everyone. "I need to get out of here and fast. I can't breathe; I feel like I'm being suffocated," I told John. He quickly took my hand and kept reassuring me, "Hold on… we're nearly at the entrance."

When I finally burst outside into the fresh air and sunshine, the relief was overwhelming. I had to sit down for a while to compose myself, and John went to get some water for me. "I can't go back in there. I'll wait for you since I know it's not finished yet. It just distressed me too much."

"It's okay, we'll go," said John. To this day, as I write this, I have never stepped foot inside there again.

I was on my tea break at work, and several new staff members, mostly from South Africa, had recently joined our team. I came into the break room to heat up my meal when I overheard them talking about voodoo, dolls, spells, enchantments, and similar topics. I listened with intrigue to their conversation. "Wow, this is really interesting but quite terrifying at the same time," I thought. They were discussing some of the experiences they or their family members had with these practices—spells involving chicken feet and people they knew personally who had died shortly after finding these items under their pillows. Okay, now this was becoming a bit too much for me.

"Trust me, Karen, the esoteric world is VERY, VERY real. Aboriginals who point the bone, witch doctors, Satanism, sacrifices, spells, witchcraft, conjuring up spirits, demonic possessions, voodoo—everything in these realms is real. People who have no idea what they're doing can end up in very tragic circumstances. This is how the other side can come into our lives. Evil is real, and evil does exist. In every faith, there is a name for the devil, for this force of evil, and if we allow it into our lives, it will completely destroy us if we let it. This can happen with the smallest of things, and very simply. Most of us will never even know what is truly happening to us. It can even be fatal. Whatever you do, don't ever get mixed up with any of that," one of the nurses warned me.

"Ahh, yeah, definitely not," I replied, but I already was—I just didn't know it yet.

One day, I was standing in the kitchen washing up. Liam and Taylor were at school, and I could see Jenna, who was about two, outside playing with our dog and her little pram and dolly. I was not really concerned as she did this every day. As I kept looking up to check on her, I suddenly noticed a lot of flies around her. I walked over to the door and watched her through the screen. She was carrying what I assumed was her dolly wrapped in a bunny rug, talking to herself, and putting the rug in the pram, but the flies were everywhere. I walked outside and was hit by the most horrendous smell. Then I saw her dolly on the ground. "What has she got in her pram?" I thought.

I walked over, opened up the bunny rug, and to my horror, saw a dead rat that had obviously been attacked and was covered in blood. OMG! "Where did you get that from?" I yelled. I immediately threw it away, grabbed her, and threw her into the bath. I think I nearly rubbed her raw trying to get the stench and smell off of her. I was brushing her teeth aggressively, all the while going ballistic with anger. She knew I was furious. "What on earth did you do that for?" I yelled. She was sobbing uncontrollably, nearly choking as she tried to catch her breath. Finally, she said through broken sobs, "The… boy… told… me… to… do… it."

Since we had arrived here, I often noticed Jenna playing and talking to someone. With her older siblings always at school during the day, she would often play by herself, as she was essentially like an only child. For Christmas, she got a tea party set, and she would sit all her stuffed toys around in a circle, pretending to have a tea party with them. She would talk as if someone was right next to her. I was in the kitchen one day, watching her play. I could hear her chatting away again, not just when she was playing but at other times too—like when she was outside in the backyard, in her room, having a bath, or watching Disney DVDs. "She's obviously very lonely and has made herself an imaginary friend," I thought. "No harm in that. A lot of young children do this."

When I asked her who she was talking to, the response was always the same. "Just the boy." When I questioned her further about who he was or what his name was, she would say, "He doesn't like me talking to you. He only likes playing with me. You're not allowed to play with us. He wants you to go away. He HATES you, and he HATES Daddy." Hearing these comments from someone so young was obviously very disturbing and made me feel very uneasy. Where could she possibly be getting this from? She was so little.

"Well then, if he hates me and Daddy, I don't want him here. You can tell him to go and find somewhere else to play." Suddenly, a door in the house would slam shut, and I would think nothing of it, assuming it was just the wind. It would distract me, and then Jenna would toddle off to play again.

As I was getting her out of the bath that night, she began to talk about the boy again. I was so drained and tired that in my frustration, I screamed at her in absolute rage, "I am sick and tired of hearing about this boy… do you hear me? Don't mention him again—I am just OVER it!" I dressed her and put her to bed, and eventually, through her tears, she cried herself to sleep.

STILL WALKING AROUND ASLEEP...

"BE FAITHFUL IN SMALL THINGS BECAUSE IT IS IN THEM THAT YOUR STRENGTH LIES." —MOTHER TERESA

The week we moved into our new home, I was busily preparing tea when I saw live on television a woman screaming as she dropped to her knees outside a house. The TV cameras had captured her in the midst of her absolute grief. I turned up the volume and heard the horrific story of how her husband, who was in politics, had taken their son and daughter—one a baby and the other only a small toddler—for the weekend and had murdered them both before killing himself. I was overcome with compassion for this woman as I watched my youngest, who was only 14 months old at the time, toddling around me. It broke me; I cried for this woman who had lost the only two things in the world that meant everything to her.

The next day, I picked up a pen and wrote the most heartfelt words to her, bought a small pink and blue teddy, and sent them to her address. She was always in the back of my mind. A few weeks later, I received a letter from her mother. She explained that her daughter was still very traumatised and unable to write properly as she was still heavily sedated. She said they had received hundreds of letters from all over Australia, but of all the letters they had read, mine was one of the most beautiful. When she read it out to her daughter, tears flowed down her face. Mine was the only letter they had responded to at that time because, as she quoted, "It was one of the only letters that had truly touched their hearts, and your words are helping us heal from this horrific and unimaginable living horror." I felt so privileged that they had taken the time to respond. I still have that letter today, filed away 17 years later.

I noticed that every night, more and more tragic stories dominated the news—because bad news sells. I wish we could have a good news channel that could be accessed at any time, day or night. All that seems to be on the news are reports about wars, guns, murders, stabbings, crimes, theft, domestic violence, famines, fires, floods, pandemics, pollution, global warming—basically every tragic event happening all over the world. This earth is a very violent and difficult planet to live on. It's one of the toughest planets in the solar system. There are so many illnesses, social exploitations, injustices, natural disasters, and staggering crimes. Life on Earth is HARD, even for those born into prestige, wealth, and privilege.

So many times, what happens in our lives just doesn't make sense—the fire-ravaged house that burns to the ground, losing your firstborn to a hit-and-run driver, hearing the terrible domestic violence next door, watching your parents and grandparents succumb to terrible diseases, or seeing the damage drugs have done to your child. You wonder how there can be so much suffering in the world and throw your hands up in the air, screaming out, "Why?" I really don't understand why bad things happen to good people—why we must endure broken hearts, why beautiful, kind people get bullied, why we have to endure so much pain, deprivation, and horrendous loss. It just became too much for me, and now I barely watch the news anymore. It's just too negative; the good, heart-warming, inspiring stories are definitely in the minority.

I remind myself that if we are not broken open, how can the light get in and remind us of the amazing people we truly are?

I had organised a play date with one of the other children from preschool to come over and play with Jenna. They had been happily playing in her room when later in the afternoon I told them to go outside and have a swing to burn up their energy. I could hear them both laughing and playing and went off to watch some TV. Within twenty minutes, I heard the most blood-curdling scream. I jumped from my chair and raced out the back to see that Jenna's little friend, Chelsea, had twisted the swing up so tight that the metal chain was completely wrapped around Jenna's throat, and she couldn't breathe. Jenna's face was turning red, and she was clearly distressed.

In absolute shock, I screamed out Chelsea's name, and she got such a fright that she let the swing go. As it was wrapped up so tight the force of it went around so fast that my little girls head hit the side of the A frame multiple times before I could reach her. "Oh my god what have you done." I screamed. I grabbed the swing and could see where the chain had started to break the skin around her neck. Jenna was grabbing her head and her throat and was inconsolable. She was just screaming at the top of her lungs. I bought her inside and began to put an icepack on her throat and was trying to calm her down and give her sips of water. Eventually she settled. I then went back outside to confront Chelsea about what had happened. "What were you thinking, why did you do such a terrible thing for, Jenna is your friend, what an awful thing to do to her." She promptly just crossed her arms, stared me down and said without blinking an eye "the... boy... told... me.... to... do... it."

I just froze and felt like everything came crashing down around me. I had never heard those words come out of anyone's mouth but my daughter's. She must have told her silly stories about this supposed boy at preschool. I was so livid with her. "That was such a nasty thing to do; you could have hurt her so badly," I kept thinking. What a horrid and cruel child she was, I thought, as I promptly took her back to her house. "Well, you can't play here anymore if you just want to do terrible things." I drove her back to her house, which was only around the corner in the same estate. Her mother had gone to the shops, and her father, whom I had never met before, was there.

I explained that there had been an accident and tried to explain what had happened, but he just stared at me in disbelief that his little girl could be capable of such a thing. I drove back home, feeling very unsettled over the whole experience. "Why did you tell Chelsea about the boy?" I asked Jenna. "But I didn't tell her; I have never told anyone about the boy," she said, and then she began to cry. The mother barely spoke to me after that, never rang to ask what had happened, and that little girl never came to play here again—which was probably a blessing for her.

"Why are you letting your little sister watch all these horror movies when I'm at work?" I asked the next morning, desperately tired. "What are you talking about?" replied my two eldest children. "Every night when I get home from work, she wakes up screaming, and I need to go in there to settle her down so she doesn't wake everyone up as you need to go to school. She's always crying and distressed about something being in her room, and it takes me ages to settle her. I'm just over it. What are you letting her watch that gets her so distressed?" They were both adamant that they never let her watch anything scary and always put her Disney movies on, but I was at the end of my tether.

Never again will I buy in an estate that is just being developed, especially when you have children and a baby. For the next couple of years, we endured so much noise—banging of hammers, tradesmen, trucks, bulldozers. The noise was deafening. My baby never slept, or if I finally did get her to sleep, she would always be woken up, even through the sounds of air conditioning. Oh, and the dust—dust went through absolutely everything. It was the worst two years. I never stopped cleaning and washing, and I was so mentally and physically drained.

One day, while Jenna was at playgroup in the local library, I decided to look around at some books. I happened to stumble upon some about Feng Shui and how rearranging furniture and adding certain elements like water could help increase good energy flow and bring positivity and money into your home. After what we had been going through since we arrived, I decided to borrow some and learn as much as I could, hoping that it might finally bring some good luck into the house instead of the constant bad luck we seemed to endure. I bought water features for both the inside and outside of the house, placed certain objects in corners, and did so many other things suggested in the books—until I was nearly exhausted. But no matter what I did—watching Law of Attraction videos, buying so many metaphysical books—the bad luck never seemed to stop for me or my family.

Every night since we had moved into this house, Jenna would wake up not crying but screaming, like severe night terrors. Now that I was working, I needed my sleep, but I was never getting any. The next day, when I would try to get some before the next afternoon shift, I never could because she always wanted my attention. It got so bad that I eventually put a mattress under her bed, lying on it while patting her back to sleep, and I would often fall asleep there myself until she woke up hours later, screaming again. This happened EVERY night for the next five years of my life.

STARTING TO CONNECT THE DOTS...

"DO YOU WANT TO BE A POWER IN THE WORLD? THEN BE YOURSELF." —RALPH WALDO TRINE

I unwrapped my birthday present from my brother Aaron—it was a small box with a pendant inside. I looked at him, puzzled. "What is this for?"

"Well, ever since you moved into this house, you've become interested in all this Law of Attraction, Feng Shui, metaphysical stuff, so I thought you might like it. It seems to be up your alley. Maybe it'll help you get some of your energy back, as you're always walking around inside this house like a zombie."

"Well, I never get any sleep," I explained. The pendant came with a brochure and a card of authenticity. It was made from Japanese volcanic rocks—lava, tourmaline, and negative ions. It supposedly produces scalar energy to enhance our biofield, promote a positive flow of energy, and help maintain energy balance. Basically, it should help your body repair itself if it's been exposed to negative energy.

I hadn't really noticed that I was becoming interested in all that, but I guess it was true. Every time we visited this regional city, I would always end up in one of the metaphysical stores, looking at everything and not really understanding why. "Thank you... I'll have to see how it works," I told him.

I had to keep pushing myself through, knowing that life goes through cycles of ups and downs. Tough times are just a phase, I kept telling myself. They don't last forever. I knew that to get my mindset right, I had to start practising self-care. I needed proper sleep, nutritious food, and regular exercise. I had to start doing activities that brought joy into my life, but with so many bills to pay and children to care for, it wasn't an easy task.

Our dog suddenly became ill with a terrible ear infection. It was so bad that they had to operate. "How on earth did this happen to him?" I thought. "Maybe he was running his ear up and down the fence and something got caught in it." I had never seen him do this, and I was perplexed as to how our dog could get so sick out of nowhere. Another nearly two thousand dollars for the operation and weeks of antibiotics. "Maybe you need to really clear out your house and declutter; it might help clear a lot of negative energy from your house since you seem to always have such terrible bad luck," my friend Elle suggested. I did this, but there was much more than just a bit of negative energy around me. Oh, if only I would wake up!

I had been up north for a three-day trip with John for work. We had a wonderful time, meeting people, going out for dinners, sightseeing. On our trip back home, I had the most overwhelming feeling of dread. I just couldn't shake it. "What is wrong?" asked John. "I don't know, I just feel so overwhelmed with so much sadness and grief, and I don't understand why."

There was nothing significant about that day, but the closer we got to home, the more the feeling overtook me. I kept thinking, "I hope everything is okay with our children." We tried a few times to ring, but the mobile phone service was terrible that day, and we couldn't get through. Finally, we arrived home, and my grandmother had been watching the children. "Are the kids okay?" I asked, worried out of my mind. "Yes, they're fine. I tried ringing you so many times, but your phone just kept saying it was out of service." "Oh no, what happened?" "Your Uncle William died this morning. He had an aneurysm burst in his heart." He had no chance; he was only 65.

I had worked with Hannah for a number of years and knew she was going through some heavy issues with her husband. She wasn't concentrating at work, was taking shortcuts, not dispensing medications properly—her work was really going downhill. I had never seen her in such an emotional state. "Are you okay?" I asked her one afternoon, becoming increasingly concerned. "I know I can tell you this, Karen, because you'll believe me. I know you'll understand. The past few days, I've been in a terrible state at work. I've barely been able to concentrate, and yes, things are really bad at home at the moment with my husband.

"There's a hairdresser who works in the facility on day shift. The other day, I noticed her watching me all the time, to the point where it became a bit disturbing, to be honest. I finally approached her and asked why she had been staring at me all day. She apologised, saying she didn't mean to upset me. Then she told me, 'You had a little girl that you lost before she was able to be born, and it affected you tremendously. She knows you're going through a really hard time at the moment and can feel your overwhelming pain. She has been holding your hand all day and has not left your side. She wants you to know how much she loves you and that things will get better.'"

With that, Hannah broke down in tears. "I've never told anyone in the facility that I lost a daughter. No one here knows that. How on earth did she know that about me? It was just incredible. I don't really believe in any of that woo-woo stuff, but I honestly believed her," said Hannah. "You're the only one I've told this to. Thank you, Karen, for listening. I knew you would believe me." … SO many breadcrumbs.

ESOTERIC DOORS BURSTING OPEN...

"IN YOUR SOUL ARE INFINITELY PRECIOUS THINGS THAT CANNOT BE TAKEN FROM YOU." —OSCAR WILDE

A few months later, that same hairdresser had a relative who became a resident. She visited on the afternoon shift, and I knew who she was. "Your son will be okay. He will walk again." "Sorry, what?" I asked, very perplexed. "Your son—please don't worry, he honestly will be fine. The doctors will be concerned that he has done severe damage to his leg, but trust me, he will walk again. Your daughter is also about to buy herself a little runaround car that she will really enjoy. You also have some sort of great-great-grandfather figure with you who is in a sailor's uniform. He is in a great position of power—maybe a captain or a lieutenant?"

I was beginning to become really intrigued with all this information when a nurse called out that her relative was now ready to see her. "Okay…" I thought to myself. A few days later, after another exhausting afternoon shift, I had just slid into bed when the phone rang at around 3 am. I was suddenly aware of John talking on the phone.

Accident, hospital, going in for surgery now. John hung up the phone and told me that the hospital had called to say our eldest son had been at an 18th birthday party. The parents had been renovating and were putting on a new roof. The old corrugated iron sheeting had been put in a corner, but our son had tripped over some that was protruding out and had torn his lower leg open, requiring emergency surgery. We were told to come up in the morning, as by the time he came out of recovery and onto the ward, he would still be out of it for quite a while.

As we had been having such bad luck for so long, a friend of mine invited me over to her place. A close friend of hers from Melbourne was visiting for the weekend, and she was a psychic. She also made her own crystal jewellery and thought she might be able to shed some light on the things that were happening. Angie was a nice lady and told me that I needed to get urgent protection around my entire family. She explained that it would be in our best interest to leave that area and sell our home. She said she could feel a lot of trauma—that the children were all withdrawn, moody, emotional—and that things hadn't been going right for us for a very long time. I asked her how she knew she had this gift.

"I used to live on a hill near a mental asylum in Melbourne. I remember as a small child that a lot of these traumatised souls would visit me, and I could see them. They would visit night and day, and being so young, I had no idea what was happening to me. There was a huge tree in my backyard, and I would try to tell my mother about it and the things they were telling me. She wasn't having any of it and would snap the branches off this tree and whip me senseless with them until I would collapse in a heap. I remember my legs bleeding all over from how many times the branches would cut into my skin."

"Oh, good God, that is just terrible. I am so sorry that you endured that."

"No need to be sorry, Karen. That was my journey. I learned very quickly to never talk about it again. My mother has never accepted that I have these gifts, and neither does my husband—he doesn't believe in it either. Hopefully, one day they will finally understand." ... MORE breadcrumbs.

I went to look at a car with John that Liam was interested in purchasing from an older woman in another suburb. Liam was very keen to buy it as it wasn't that expensive and would probably suit him for a first car. As John was inspecting it and talking with the woman, my attention was drawn to a very big tree next door. It had many branches, and all the leaves had fallen off. All the other trees in her street were lush with green leaves, but this one was barren. I didn't get a good feeling when I was looking at it and began to feel uneasy. This tree was huge, with thousands of spindly branches reaching in every direction.

The woman could see that I was beginning to feel uncomfortable as I looked in that direction. "Are you feeling okay?" she asked. "No, not really. Something about that tree overwhelms me, and I don't really know why. I think I might go and wait in the car." She looked at me and said that a few weeks ago, her neighbour's 16-year-old son had committed suicide. "Oh, I'm so sorry to hear that." He had hung himself from that exact tree.

Liam and Taylor had got their driving licences, and sometimes Liam would take my car to the shops. One night when I was finishing work, I got into my car and could distinctly smell cigarette smoke. "That bloody boy, he's been smoking in my car or picked up mates who have been," I thought. I could smell it all the way home. When I confronted him about it, he was adamant that he never did that while driving my car. "Well, how on earth did I smell that then? You know I don't smoke." He became very defensive and reiterated, "Well, it's bloody not me!"

Of course, I never believed him. Years later, I went to see a lady who reads tea leaves in our area who came highly recommended. I walked into her space, and she had different teacups to choose from. "Just take your time and choose which one resonates with you while I make a cup of tea." As we sat down, she looked right beside me and told me that my maternal grandfather was sitting next to me. "What, right now?" I asked.

"Yes, he tells me that he often rides home with you after work, especially when you work late at night, to make sure you get home safely." OMG! "He passed from lung cancer, didn't he?" "Yes, he was a chronic smoker." The penny dropped. "So, it was never my son—you're telling me that the cigarette smoke I could smell was my grandfather?" "Yes, and oh, he's getting impatient with me, telling me to change the subject. He had a terrible injury with that leg, didn't he? It caused him terrible pain for many years, and he never worked again after that, right?" "No," I replied. WOW! More breadcrumbs…

As Liam and Taylor were going to be graduating from high school and would no longer be coming on holidays with us due to work, John decided to take us away on a small holiday—our last official one together as a family. On the trip, we came across a beautiful place with amazing crystal displays and a very spiritual atmosphere. I was immediately drawn to it. I remember it was extremely hot as it was Australia Day. I had never had an aura photo taken before, but John arranged for it. I stood in front of a camera, and within a few minutes, the polaroid showed me completely covered in massive hues of gold, yellow, and orange.

"WOW!" exclaimed the lady. "You have the most amazing and beautiful aura. It's completely surrounding you." She went on to ask if I had any psychic experiences when I was growing up, to which I said I had. "You have great power within you. Have you ever thought about developing your psychic gifts again? They've been lying dormant in you for a very long time. Please think about it—you could use this gift to accomplish incredible things in your life and help others too." I was so busy working, trying to survive our financial issues, and raising three children that this didn't even seem like an option. More breadcrumbs…

The following year, an international clairvoyant visited our city. I was intrigued by all the media interest around him and heard him speak on the radio and the local television station. I booked an appointment to see if he could pick anything up. He told me lots of things about our life in general, including difficult times, and many details about our children, which were very accurate. He also told me I had gifts that needed to be developed. He was very popular, and also very expensive, so I could only afford 45 minutes with him. He told me his book would help me learn how to develop my gift more, but I couldn't afford to buy it. "I don't usually do this, so please don't tell anyone. I'm going to give this to you for free because I know you have amazing potential." He even hand-signed it for me: "Dear Karen… Enjoy my book and always trust your instincts. Lots of love," followed by his signature. I came home, placed it on the bookshelf, and never read it… more breadcrumbs.

Leaving My Door Ajar...

"WELCOME TO MY NIGHTMARE, I THINK YOU'RE GONNA LIKE IT."
—ALICE COOPER

"Ahhh, this bloody toilet—always issues with it since the day we moved in. It's always making strange noises, bubbling, running all the time, stopping and starting, not flushing properly—just never-ending," I thought to myself. John had a friend who was a plumber, and he would come over periodically to help us out as we always seemed to be having ongoing issues with it. His suggestion was to buy a whole new one, and he'd install it for us since the problems were constant.

"Mmm… we might have to do that," I thought, as once again, it was running water continuously and wouldn't stop. He was away on holidays that week, so we had to call a business and get their plumber to come around and look at it. He came out at one stage looking ghastly. "Seriously, lady, I've been a plumber for nearly 18 years, and I have NEVER smelt anything like what I just did in all my entire life. Something in there is JUST ROTTEN; I need to get some air—I think I'm going to be sick."

I went into my ensuite and could hear the usual sounds, but I could smell nothing. "Mmm… okay, I wonder what that was about." He eventually came back in after getting some fresh air, changed a part, and told me it should be working fine now. He was uncertain as to what caused that horrendous smell, but he also noted that it had gone. "Hopefully, what I've just done has flushed it away. And what's with all these noises coming out of this toilet... never heard anything like it," he said. "Really? NEVER?" I asked. "I just assumed it must be something to do with the pipes," I told him. "It's VERY unsettling—sounds like some sort of animal growling or something," he told me. "And the mould on your roof in that ensuite—it's pretty bad." "Yeah, my hubby and I have tried so many different things, but we just can't seem to EVER get rid of it."

That night, we had no issues, but the next day, it was leaking again... ahhhhhh... MY LIFE!!!!!!!!! I called out nearly in tears, "Why can't anything go right for us? WHY, WHY, WHY, WHY, WHY!!!!!!!"

When I think of all the things that have happened to us over the years since we moved here, it just staggers me. We had come to sign the final papers. After visiting the house once again and showing the children their new home, we had left in the afternoon to return. On the way back, with the car loaded up with Christmas shopping, our car suddenly started beeping, red lights flashing on the dash, and steam pouring out from under the bonnet. We quickly got out on the side of the highway with no cars in sight and no mobile phone reception. Up on a hill a few kilometres away, there was a house in the distance. "You go up with the kids and see if you can ring and get help. I'll stay down here and see if I can flag down a car," said John.

The sun was beating down on us, we had no water, and the heat was just oppressive. I had to carry Jenna the whole way as she was only twelve months old. We finally reached the house, and as I walked around the corner, I saw two Doberman dogs fast asleep near the back door. The house was all closed up, and there was no noise. OH GOD. I froze in absolute terror. I quickly got my older two's attention and put my finger to my lips, signalling them to be quiet. Jenna was squirming in my arms, with sweat dripping off her—as it was with all of us. "If those dogs wake up, they'll attack us savagely and rip me and my kids apart," I thought in genuine horror. Jenna would have no chance being so tiny. After nursing for many years, I had seen horrific injuries from dog attacks and knew of people—especially children—who had been attacked so ferociously that they died.

My heart was beating madly and John wasn't there to help me. I PRAYED to God silently for us to get out of there alive. I motioned for Liam and Taylor to start walking back down the hill again very quietly and was PRAYING for Jenna to not start crying as that would be the end of us all. We still had kilometres to walk down to get to our car and John would have no idea that there could possibly be two dogs that could come around the house at any moment and attack us.

If they did, he would not be able to even get to us in time. PLEASE GOD let me get my children back safely down to our car. At least we could all get up on the roof of the car and hopefully they would not get to us there. I had all these crazy ideas racing in my head. We couldn't get in the car as the heat would kill us all for sure having to keep the windows up if they attacked. Of all the days for this to happen it must have been well over forty degrees even in the shade. Oh God, how is this happening to us? I was trying not to cry and get distressed as I didn't want to frighten the children.

When I felt we were far enough away, I told them to run a bit faster. I didn't look back and my arms were nearly numb with the pain of having carried Jenna for so long. I dread to think what those dogs would have done to us on that property if they had woken up while we were looking for help. John had managed to flag down a car, and they said they would ring for help as soon as they got mobile phone reception. We were all literally dying of thirst. John and I started to become really concerned, as Jenna was crying with thirst from the oppressive heat, and our other children were also thirsty and tired. Was anyone going to come for us? Why weren't there any other cars? How long were we going to be stranded here?

Suddenly, we saw a car approaching in the scorching heat, and as it got closer, we realised it was a police car. The police had heard on their radio about a family stranded in 40-degree-plus heat with small children and a baby, and they were concerned for our safety, so they came looking for us immediately. The kids and I had our very first ride in the back of a police car. We were all SOOOO hot from the Perspex in front of us, as there was no air-conditioning. We had to wind down the windows, with the hot wind blazing on us, while Jenna sat on my lap. She screamed the whole hour until we got back to the regional city. It was awful—I think the police officers were glad to see the end of us. They also had no water. We were so parched and thirsty, our mouths and throats were burning. This is what happened to us after we had been to that house. Was that an omen? Oh, why didn't I wake up?!

STILL COMPLETELY OBLIVIOUS...

"STARE AT THE DARK TOO LONG, AND YOU WILL EVENTUALLY SEE WHAT IS ACTUALLY REALLY THERE." —ANONYMOUS

Numerous times I got food poisoning at occasions like engagements, weddings, and birthday parties. Our underwater camera got smashed and cost us hundreds of dollars in repairs. The number of times my car battery would be completely flat and need replacing, and cars breaking down constantly, costing thousands of dollars in repairs, needing new engines—it was endless. Due to being out of work for so long, we hadn't been able to get both our dogs up to date with their vaccinations, as we just didn't have the finances. We got a reminder notice that they were due for their shots. Heartworm was rampant where we lived, so they both had blood tests to confirm they were heartworm-free. We had never missed any vaccinations since they were puppies.

"Oh, I'm sorry, your female doesn't have heartworm, but your male does. We're going to have to start him on a two-year course of treatment if you can't afford the quicker one," the vet explained to us. The past couple of years, it has cost us close to $3,000 for treatment. "Oh, more bad luck. It just never seems to end." The number of items that have gone missing is just ridiculous. To this day, there are things of ours that I have never seen again, and there is no logical explanation for where they went.

Our son had a terrible car accident after partying excessively with friends at his mate's 21st, which he had travelled a few hours to attend. Liam had fallen asleep at the wheel on his way back home on the highway, missing a bridge, a tree, and a massive rock. As he fell asleep, his foot pressed heavily on the accelerator, and the car overturned several times at top speed. He woke up with only a few scratches. Being in a modern car, the airbags deployed all around him, and I believe this is what also saved his life. His car was a total write-off. The treating doctor in A&E told us that he must have had a big angel wrapped around him, as most people don't survive when their car leaves the highway at that speed.

Liam had unfortunately got in with a really bad crowd at school and was lucky to have survived. It was only by the grace of God that we never buried our son. I awoke and had the strongest feeling to check on Liam as I just felt that something was not right a few weeks later. I went in and turned on the light and he screamed in agony for me to turn it off, his eye was very swollen. I put a sterile dressing placed over it and rushed him urgently to the doctor who rang the specialist ophthalmologist and got him seen too straight away. Told me if I had waited much longer, he would have lost his vision and possibly that eye.

Liam never slept without the light on in that room. Many times, he would come out and say to me, "I think there is something in this house, in my room," but I would dismiss him, saying he was imagining things. I lost count of the number of times I would open his door to wake him up for school and find blood everywhere—all over the sheets, blankets, and dried on his face while he slept. It looked like a bloodbath in his room. He was having spontaneous, severe nosebleeds, and it always seemed to happen mostly when he was in that room. He did play footy and got a few knocks, so I thought that might be causing it. But after the constant bleeds, I became increasingly concerned and got him an appointment with an ENT specialist. After weeks of waiting, he finally saw the specialist, who found that the vessels in his nose were so badly damaged that every single one had to be cauterised. The ENT specialist said he had never seen footy knocks cause that much damage and didn't believe that was the cause either.

I had just finished making biscuits and, as I opened the oven door to put them in, suddenly, without any warning, the oven just died. Since it was the weekend, I couldn't call anyone until Monday. Then, when I went to put a load into the washing machine, the whole power board shorted out on me and had to be replaced. It felt like everything I touched would break down, and I started saying to John, "I think I must be cursed or something. Why is this always happening to me?" I was doing my degree on the computer, as I had been stuck in the house for years trying to complete it. One day, both landline phones went dead, and none of the receivers would work.

I was up to my eyeballs trying to complete four different modules at once, with deadlines for assignments looming. I had worked tirelessly for weeks to get everything done while also working. John was away working out west, as usual, when I got up to get a drink and stretch my legs. When I returned to the computer, the entire screen went black, and the tower turned off. What the?? I tried to turn it back on, but nothing happened. I was desperate and in a blind panic—John wasn't here to help me. In desperation, I rang our friend who owned a computer store on my mobile. I think I nearly screamed down the phone at him, I was so upset. "I think something has just happened to my computer, and I'm going to lose months of work and assignments that I've finally managed to complete." I was inconsolable when I got off the phone. WHY, WHY, WHY!!! I was screaming out loud.

I felt like picking up the computer and throwing the entire thing out the window. Ross arrived soon after as he told me that he had never heard me sound like that before in the whole time that I had known him. "Your entire system has overheated and I need to get it into cool storage to see if I can save everything for you." He could see how distressed I was. Ross unplugged everything and could make no promises but would do everything he could to help me. I remember PRAYING to God to help me and that if it couldn't be saved, I would give up my studies as I just did not have the time or energy to have to go back and do all THAT work all over again. I cried for hours that day in absolute exhaustion with the constant bad luck that just never seemed to stop plaguing my family. "It's okay," Ross later said. "Thankfully, you rang me when you did. I was able to get it into storage for cooling and cleaned everything for you. If it had been much longer, think you would have lost EVERYTHING. You should have no issues now." I think I nearly hugged Ross so hard that I almost choked him when he hooked everything back up for me. "Thank you, God, thank you… thank you… thank you," I cried.

SO MUCH DESPAIR...

"IF YOU ARE READING THIS, THEN YOU ARE BLISSFULLY UNAWARE OF WHAT IS CREEPING UP BEHIND YOU." —ANONYMOUS

The plants that were growing in my front yard suddenly started dying right in front of me, and no matter what I did, they just wouldn't come back. All these years, I had struggled to grow anything in our front and back yard, and now, one by one, they were just dying constantly. Everyone around us seemed to have beautiful, manicured lawns and gardens, but not us, for some reason. "Maybe there's something wrong with the soil on our land," I thought. One of Liam's friends, who he hung out with a lot, was down at a community park when a middle-aged man, high on ice, randomly attacked him with a samurai sword.

The attack had been so vicious that he has never been able to work again due to irreversible brain damage. I felt so thankful that Liam wasn't with him that day, as he could have suffered the same fate. Taylor broke her arm on a school trip, her earlobes got infected and had to be lanced open, and she nearly ended up septic. The visiting dental caravan accidentally pulled the wrong tooth, causing major issues for her. Then, I was publicly abused by the receptionist in front of other clients because they initially agreed to cover the cost of the necessary corrective work but refused to do so on the scheduled day.

I had to hand over more than $1,000 for the dental work they had caused, and afterward, I went straight to the Department of Health to lodge an official complaint. They reviewed my case, apologised on the spot, and immediately wrote out a cheque for me. None of my children have set foot inside that dental caravan again. Jenna had major falls all the time when she was little—falling headfirst onto cement when she was just a few months old, which required a rushed trip to the hospital. She fell out of highchairs, had things almost hit her, was nearly run over by a car, and spent half of her life unwell. Gastroenteritis, multiple tests to find out what was wrong, constant sickness, vomiting, trips to the doctor, urinary tract infections, and upper respiratory tract infections—it just never stopped.

Once a friend and I were walking down the main street in the CBD, crossing the road, when out of nowhere a large dead palm frond fell metres from above. We only heard it at the last minute and looked up to see it come hurtling towards us. Lindy scooped up Jenna and ran across the road just in time, as the frond landed with an absolute BANG exactly where Jenna had been standing. She was only two. "Oh, for the love of God, Karen, if that had fallen on her, it would have killed her for sure," said Lindy.

One weekend, we arranged to go away with the children. It was winter, and the children all had electric blankets on their beds. Just as we were about to leave, I did one more sweep of the house, making sure that all the electrical items, like the blankets, lights, power points, etc., were turned off and that all the doors were locked. Liam suddenly remembered something he had forgotten to grab. He quickly ran back inside, retrieved it, and jumped in the car as John started the engine.

We had a lovely weekend away together, but upon returning to the house, it always felt so cold and uninviting. John and I never had the feeling of relief or comfort that usually comes with returning home after being away. Instead, we always felt uneasy but couldn't explain why. When I went to open up the house, I got to Liam's room and, upon opening the door, was hit by an intense wave of heat. What the heck? Why was it SOOOOO hot in here? I opened the window and could feel the heat radiating from his bed. I quickly threw back the blankets to discover the electric blanket was on the hottest setting. "OMG, why did you turn it on?" I said angrily. "You could have burnt the house down."

"But I didn't," he stammered back at me. "Oh, what, so it just turned on by itself, did it? You obviously did it. That's it—STOP lying to me." He became so upset as I just wouldn't listen to him. "And because of that and your backchat, you're grounded for a fortnight." Ohhhhh, what a welcome home that was.

John's work had organised a weekend getaway for the employees and their partners to celebrate Christmas, as they had all done a fantastic job keeping the company afloat. We were flown down south for three days of celebrations. We had never been away from Jenna since she was born, so my sister Jade and her children came to look after her while we were away. On the last morning of our trip, just as we were scheduled to fly out that night, we received a frantic phone call from Jade. Jenna had slipped on the tiles and fallen heavily. She had been unconscious for quite a while before coming to and was still very weak and unresponsive. We told Jade to ring an ambulance and get her seen by a doctor straight away.

It was a terrible feeling to be thousands of kilometres away. We tried to reschedule our flight, but being Christmas, it was impossible. We had to wait for hours until we could board, and we rushed to the hospital as soon as we arrived. I PRAYED for her to be alright. They did multiple tests and found she had suffered a small haemorrhage where her head had hit the hard concrete tiles. They managed to stop the bleeding but were very concerned that her hearing could now be affected. I had to take her for more tests to a specialist audiologist. Jenna was given a tower and had headphones placed on her. Being only four, it was very overwhelming for her. Every time she heard a sound, she was to place a marble in the top of the tower. She was sitting on my lap, and I could see when the audiologist pressed the button. Jenna would sit there, waiting to put the marble in, but she wouldn't do it. The look on the audiologist's face said it all. Jenna had lost all hearing in her left ear from the haemorrhage. We were devastated.

John was always in and out of work, and our whipper snipper and mower were constantly breaking down. He accidentally broke the back panel of our TV while trying to plug in cords, which cost us another $500 to fix. One day, he woke up in severe pain and needed an urgent hernia operation, which, of course, got infected. John couldn't even pull his shirt down over the wound, so I rang the secretary, who assured me this was normal and would settle down. However, within hours, I had to take him to another doctor, who lanced the infection, and pus went all over the table as John screamed in agony. So much for the surgeon's advice. More time in the hospital, off work with no income, and on IV antibiotics. We've since found out that this same surgeon has multiple lawsuits filed against him for medical negligence. Of all the surgeons we could have had, it just had to be THAT one, of course.

Numerous times, our mobiles would drop out during calls or go completely flat even though we had charged them for hours. There always seemed to be a lot of disharmony in the house as the kids got older, but it seemed to be more excessive in our home—lots of fighting, negativity, and constant stress. OHHHHHHHHHH my life!

PAINFUL LIFE LESSONS...

"LIFE WILL TEACH YOU LESSONS, AND THOSE LESSONS ARE VERY PAINFUL." —ADHAN KHAN

Within weeks of starting at my new facility as an RN, I contracted a severe infection in my foot from MRSA. The pain was so excruciating that the doctors initially thought it was a white-tailed spider bite. Every time I put my leg down, the blood flow would intensify the pain, and it felt surreal—I would nearly pass out from it. In A&E, the nurse told me the doctor had ordered IV antibiotics before I could be discharged. After the infusion started, a violent, drunk man caused a major disturbance in the department. Suddenly, my arm felt like it was on fire and began to swell. I desperately tried to get someone's attention, but no one responded to my buzzer. The burning became so intense that I actually ripped the cannula out of my arm. The doctor noticed and rushed over. He saw what had happened and apologised, as the RN had inserted the cannula into my tissues instead of my veins.

I could barely walk, could hardly hold the crutches they gave me, and was high on pain medication, yet they discharged me. I was told I could drive home since I didn't live far away. I nearly drove off a small bridge that night; the only thing that saved me was the heavy chains between each post, which stopped me from going over into the river. More damage to my car. I ended up so sick that I had to spend eight days in hospital on IV antibiotics.

Our son had started playing violent video games, which I later learned could act as portals, bringing things from other dimensions into our house. He began hanging around with some very undesirable associates. I remembered that psychic, Flo, telling me that our son was hanging around with someone VERY bad. It all ended with Liam having a major car accident that nearly killed him. It was true: this other boy's heart was as black as his skin, just as she had said. He led our son down a VERY dark path.

One weekend, we managed to go away for the first time in a very long time. John and I began to feel increasingly heavy and uneasy. As we approached the sign welcoming us back, a semi-truck coming around the other side of the roundabout flicked a stone onto our windscreen, cracking it right down the middle. John went off like a cracker, shouting, "Yeah, welcome f**kin' home!" in anger. It had been raining, and the grass had grown excessively over the weekend. John pulled out the lawnmower to start mowing, but after just two rows, the mower clunked, and I saw the front wheel rolling away. Ohhhhhhhh, our life!

One day, I was rushing to pick Jenna up from school and ran inside quickly, as time had gotten away from me. As I hurried through the glass sliding door, I felt as though I had been pushed, but my mind was telling me something different. I slammed my foot into the brick wall under the sliding door, instantly breaking my second and third toes. I couldn't understand how it happened. Since it was my accelerating foot, the pain from driving was almost unbearable. I picked Jenna up in agony, got home, and could hardly walk. I had to elevate my foot on the lounge, but even the weight of an ice pack made the pain excruciating. I wondered if I would ever be able to put my foot in a shoe again, as the thought of it was just agonising. That weekend, I had to work because we desperately needed the money. Instead of taking sick leave, I foolishly went to work, thinking that with enough painkillers and resting my foot whenever possible, I could get through the shift.

Within minutes of arriving at work, I had to remove my shoe due to the intense pain and swelling in my foot and put on a boot to try and walk. BIG MISTAKE! The wheel of the medication trolley hit my broken toes like a shopping trolley, sending me through the roof in pain. I remember leaning against the wall, gasping in absolute agony, when one of my dementia residents came around the corner and saw me. She immediately came up to me, placed her hand on my stomach (yes, I had put on a tad bit of weight), and began yelling, "Help! Help! Somebody, please come quick! She's having this bloody baby right now—somebody call an ambulance!"

"Oh, gee, thanks for that, Carol," I managed to say between nearly passing out from the pain. "Just stick that knife in me and twist it around a bit harder."

"What?! You want me to stick a knife in you? I think you must be a bit bloody crazy," she exclaimed, her eyes as wide as saucers before she wandered off. I, on the other hand, didn't know whether to laugh or cry.

I remembered that Jenna had taken some Christmas photos on her iPad that we had bought her. As I was looking at them, I noticed that the front of my hair was starting to fall out. There was a big circle on top where there was literally a bald spot. I was horrified and had to cover it up with black hair dye and started using black hair spray. I went to a hairdresser to see what was wrong, only to be treated like a leper.

"I can't help you. You have alopecia or some sort of hair disease. You need medical help, and I would really appreciate it if you left my salon, as I don't want anyone in here to catch what you may have," she spat at me.

I was so humiliated. Lots of other ladies were sitting in chairs, and they all overheard what she said. They stared at me as I walked out to my car, feeling overwhelmingly embarrassed and ashamed.

A few days later, I accidentally stepped on broken glass and got shards of it in my foot.

Our border collie, Beau, was found outside one afternoon, panting and drooling heavily. We had never seen him like this. We tried to get him to stand up, but he couldn't walk. Jenna was beside herself, and we had to carry him to the car as John was on a night shift and had already left on the bus for his twelve-hour shift. We raced him to the vet, who ran multiple tests and bloodwork on him, but everything came back negative. Our poor boy was just so ill, and they couldn't determine the cause. We paid over two thousand dollars for further investigations and visited him every day at the surgery. They wanted to keep him on an IV and were trying everything they could. We got a phone call after a few days informing us that he had passed away overnight. He was all alone in a cage, surrounded by no one. We never got over how he died—it devastated all of us. He didn't deserve to die like that, and we never knew the cause. The vet asked to keep his body to do an autopsy, as they had never seen anything like it. We still have no answers to this day.

We occasionally had visits from religious people like Jehovah's Witnesses or Mormons, but they never stayed long at the front door. I could see that they felt uncomfortable and would excuse themselves and leave very promptly. Our children's friends never really wanted to sleep over—they always preferred our kids to stay at their homes. We were always struggling to find the money to pay our bills. As soon as we seemed to get on top of one pile, another would appear, and we never felt like we were going to overcome it.

Spent much of my life working weekends away from John and the kids so that we could keep our heads above water. We played tag for years—John worked during the day, and I worked in the afternoons and on weekends so that someone could be home with the children. John's job often took him away from home, so the kids were frequently left unsupervised. We both had to work to survive, to try and feed our kids and keep a roof over our heads. It was so frustrating how often our car would break down at the lights during peak-hour traffic, constantly needing to be towed away. We spent thousands of dollars fixing one thing after another, thinking each time it was the last of it, but it never EVER was. The kids had trouble at school, suffered from depression and anxiety, and struggled with their schoolwork. A woman at school made Jenna's life a living hell, accusing her of taking her daughter's lunch. They were only five years old, swapping food and drinks as little children do, but she made Jenna's life—and mine—a nightmare.

After another sleepless night with Jenna, I stumbled into the kitchen to check on my eldest two. They had also woken up late, as I had slept in after working the night before. They only had minutes to catch the bus or they would miss it. Normally, they would walk, but in a panic, I told them to get in the car. I buckled Jenna in, still in my nightie, and rushed to drop them off, thinking I would come back and get changed afterward. Jenna had a wet nappy and was hungry, but she would have to wait a couple of minutes. I managed to get Liam and Taylor to the bus with only seconds to spare, but they made it. I quickly drove back home, pressed the remote to open the garage door, and... NOTHING!!! WHAT THE!!!!!... OH no, this can't be happening.!!!!!!!

The power had gone off in my house, but I could hear the televisions from my neighbours' homes and see their lights on, while mine was completely dark. I quickly unbuckled Jenna, who was now crying loudly. I went to put the key in the lock, only to realise that the front door key wasn't on my keyring. OHHH NOO! My in-laws had stayed for the weekend, and I had given the key to my mother-in-law to use. I had completely forgotten to get it back from her, and now I was stuck outside with no way to get in. John was out west working AGAIN!

I had no phone, no purse, a screaming baby who needed a bottle, milk, and a nappy change, and I was standing outside my home in my nightie. How could my house be the ONLY one in the entire estate without power? I went to the power box and reset everything, but still NOTHING! Think, Karen, THINK! My neighbours had all left to take their children to school, and Jenna was screaming even louder. What on earth was I going to do? I quickly checked the fuel gauge; it was nearly on empty. My grandmother lived in another suburb, a good 15-minute drive away. I wasn't sure if I had enough fuel to get there, and it was peak hour, but what other choice did I have?

I buckled a very wet and hungry, screaming baby into her seat and PRAYED for God to get me to my grandmother's safely. I had no idea if she would even be home, as she often left early for shopping and appointments. Of course, I got EVERY red light on the way, and by this stage, Jenna was inconsolable. I PRAYED and PRAYED that Nan would be home and that we wouldn't run out of petrol. I was utterly exhausted, having not even had time to brush my hair or clean my teeth.

I pulled up and knocked on the door. Nan answered, finding me completely frazzled and dishevelled, with a VERY loud, screaming baby in tow. She quickly went to the store down the road, which she and my grandfather used to own, and bought some nappies and fuel. She fed us breakfast and gave me some decent clothes to change into. We called the electricity board to ask if there had been a power outage in my area, but they said that all houses had power.

By this time, I was too tired to care. I didn't want to call John, as it would just cause him more stress and worry. Nan followed me in her car to make sure I got home safely. Once again, the remote wouldn't work, and my house was still in darkness. We checked with all the neighbours around me, and they all had power. WHAT ON EARTH WAS GOING ON WITH MY HOUSE? In desperation, I had to call an emergency locksmith to break in and install a new front door lock so I could get inside.

After waiting nearly an hour in the heat, they finally arrived. Of course, being an emergency, I was hit up for that and all the labour and nearly $400 later the door was finally opened and the lock installed. I could not understand how the power was off and found the phone to ring for the electrical company to attend. As the locksmith pulled out of the driveway, my power suddenly came back on instantly. Nan and I just looked at each other in absolute shock. Ohhhhhhhh more money… It just never seemed to stop in our house.

HANGING ON FOR THE RIDE...

"THE WORLD OUTSIDE HAD ITS OWN RULES AND THOSE RULES WERE NOT HUMAN." —MICHEL HOUELLEBECQ

I remember thinking that since we moved here, all I wanted was to get the hell out of this house, out of this God-forsaken town, and move down south. Anywhere we could have a fresh start, somewhere John could find a great job—anywhere but here—but it just never happened. And so the never-ending story of our struggling life continued. I suffered from the most crippling mental fatigue.

Within a few years of us moving to this regional city, there was a terrible economic downturn in the state, and our area seemed to take the full brunt of it. I had written down statistics from the local paper: 50,000 people left town in under 12 months, nearly 100 businesses closed down, thousands of houses were up for sale, there were three times as many repossessions each week, and our city had the second-highest suicide rate in the country—22,000 people had lost their jobs. It was JUST crippling on so many levels to see what was happening to people, families, and their livelihoods everywhere we turned. After so many years of John being in and out of employment, our savings were gone, and we were being relentlessly hammered, trying to continually prove our genuine financial hardship to the banks. Why is it that when you're already down and out, people just want to keep kicking you in the guts? It was torture, a never-ending cycle of grief and despair. We were on our knees.

I imagined the devil himself playing us all like pawns in some sick video game, sending more and more evil and despair our way. It was torture. He would sit back, laugh, and rack up points every time he watched us suffer. That's exactly how it felt—he would put us through the most horrific physical and mental pain, and it seemed like he literally wanted to bury us alive. We were all just physically and mentally worn out. Hell was all I could think about. At my sister's wedding, we even lost all our family photos. I was just devastated. There was so much family discord, so much yelling and arguing, so many issues with other family members and friends.

My neighbour would sometimes come over to talk with John after work, as they both worked in the same industry at the same company. They were having major issues in their marriage, which I wasn't aware of. The next thing I know, his wife comes over and accuses me of having an affair with her husband and tells me to leave him alone. Her behaviour was erratic and so out of character for her. "Ahh, yeah, I would never touch your hubby in a fit, let alone actually find the time to have an affair," I told her in shock and anger.

When I was completing my clinical hours for uni, my car got hit while parked at the medical centre where I was working. Cars were constantly parked there, but of course, mine was the ONLY one to be hit. When our city caught the tail end of a cyclone, it caused significant devastation to many people. Our house was the ONLY one in the street to have all the air conditioners completely wiped out from water damage and the ONLY one to have both roller doors buckled and blown off their hinges. Ohhh yay... lucky us!

Another time, my car was swiped and damaged in front of a computer shop. John was buying a new monitor for my studies, and within half an hour of us walking in and purchasing it, my front bumper had been completely wiped out on the side by a four-wheel drive. A young teenager told us he had seen the vehicle hit our car and then drive away. Of course, there were no cameras, so we had to pay the $600 excess to get it fixed—again, for damage we hadn't caused. We were just sick and tired of it!

Another time, I was sitting in my car and had just turned on the ignition. Before I could even put it into reverse, I felt a big bang and was jolted forward. The lady directly behind me had reversed straight into my car. She hit me with such force that the screws holding her registration plates completely indented my rear back bumper. Her car didn't have a scratch, but she took off so fast I couldn't get her license plate. Once again, no cameras. Our insurance company told me I'd have to pay the first $600 as the damages were over $4000. Ohhhhhh, more money we just didn't have!

Our son took the second-hand car we bought for him and his sister to learn to drive a manual to a local camping area for the weekend with some mates from school. It was the first time we'd let him take the car, and from the very start, I felt uneasy about it. But John kept telling me I had to let him grow up and to cut the apron strings. On Sunday morning, we received a phone call from the local police. The car had been abandoned in the middle of a road, badly damaged, with lots of blood on the driver's side seat and window. They called because the car was registered in our name. We were beside ourselves with worry and couldn't get in contact with our son.

We had to arrange for the car to be towed—more money—and eventually, after many frantic phone calls, our son turned up. We had been worried sick. It turned out that he had left the keys in the ignition to play the radio, as there was no electricity or mobile phone service where they were camping. Another boy, who wasn't part of their school group, got violently drunk, stole the car, and then crashed it, causing major damage. Because Liam had voluntarily left the keys in the ignition, the insurance company used that loophole to avoid paying for the damages, even though the car was stolen. We didn't have the money to repair it, as the damage was extensive, and the other boy got away with it, facing no repercussions.

That very same weekend, we received the terrible news that one of Liam's friends, who hadn't gone camping with them, had tragically died. He had stayed behind to visit family who had come up from down south for Easter, saying he needed to say goodbye. He then went to the nearest petrol station, filled a jerry can with fuel, walked across the road, poured petrol all over himself, and set himself on fire. Both of his parents were head department teachers at the high school they attended. He was their only son and was only 17 years old. His mother was never able to teach again after his tragic death.

JUST NEVER-ENDING DEVASTATION...

"WE STOPPED CHECKING FOR MONSTERS UNDER OUR BED WHEN WE REALISED THEY WERE INSIDE US." —CHARLES DARWIN

In our backyard, we had a beautiful above-ground reef pool that we installed after years of saving. It came with a twenty-year guarantee, but fell apart within two years. It cost us thousands to buy and install, but neither the business where we bought it nor the company that manufactured it would take responsibility. They used every tactic and loophole they could, leaving us thousands of dollars out of pocket. After getting free legal advice, we were told we had a solid case, but due to our financial hardships, we just couldn't afford to pursue it. We endured endless meetings, phone calls, and letters for many months, trying to get it resolved, which was mentally exhausting. Taking them to court would have cost a small fortune, which we simply didn't have. We lost over ten thousand dollars on that pool, and it devastated us.

Jenna went through a phase of wanting guinea pigs, as so many of her friends had them. The only problem was they kept dying on us, one after another, over a period of weeks or months. Eventually, I had to refuse to let her have any more.

One day, I was on the home computer taking an exam when, right in the middle of it, my computer completely shut down, causing me so much distress. Thank God my supervisor witnessed what happened and was able to verify it. Then came the hassle of writing reports, rescheduling around my shifts, and coordinating with my supervisor. It was terrible.

Another time, I was driving in the CBD when a police car, in pursuit of a criminal in a stolen vehicle, hit my car with both of my girls inside. I suffered terrible whiplash and then had to wait weeks to get my car fixed AGAIN!

I was always sick in that house, suffering from horrendous heartburn. I'd walk around at night because I could never lie down, often sitting up in my lounge chair as the pain was so severe. Sometimes, the pain was so intense that I honestly wondered if I'd still be alive in the morning—I just never slept. So many people in my court had their marriages break down. There was always so much yelling and fighting coming from around me. I was trying to work shift work as an RN, look after three children, and manage the house by myself while John was always working away, never around to help. Why did we EVER come to this God-forsaken place? Ohhhhhhh my life!

The day I had to take my exams for uni, with the cut-off at 5 pm, I had booked a session with a supervisor at the local library. I arrived at 2 pm, as my exam was scheduled for 2:30 pm and would take approximately two hours. When I went to check in and take my belongings into the assigned room, I was taken aback to see a gentleman already in there with a supervisor. I approached the staff and asked when I could go in. They told me that no other person had been booked in that day except for him. My heart was racing, and I was distraught, but I had the phone message to confirm my booking. She checked her computer and, to my horror, realised that another staff member had double-booked the room. I burst into tears. "Oh, I am so sorry for this. If you can access another laptop, I'll be your supervisor if that helps," she offered.

I frantically tried ringing friends, but most were at work. Out of desperation, I called everyone I could think of, and time was ticking fast. Finally, a friend answered—she had just pulled up at home. I drove like a madwoman to pick up her laptop, but of course, she lived on the other side of the city. I hit EVERY red light on the way there and back. By the time I returned, I was a hot mess. To top it off, they then had issues connecting to the library's WiFi. I just couldn't deal with it anymore. I GIVE UP! I'M DONE! I QUIT! But as I was about to walk out, it connected. The only available room was a hot, stinking storeroom out the back, which we both had to endure. Sweat was pouring down my face; I was utterly frantic and couldn't stop shaking, let alone concentrate with all the stress. It felt like my heart was going to explode, it was beating so fast, but I managed to finish and submit the exam with just five minutes to spare.

My reversing mirror had fallen off inside my car and one morning I was so tired that I actually got in it and completely reversed into my roller doors… aarrgghhh. More damage and more money. So many times, I had to have a freezing shower when it was really cold weather as the hot water system would not work. I went out to get my uniform off the line as was about to start getting ready for afternoon shift. As I was getting pegs in my hands, I was suddenly aware of a long stick near my foot and went to kick it away. Intuitively, I then thought to myself that we don't have trees in our back yard.

At that precise moment, I looked down to see a copper head brown snake with its tongue flickering millimetres from my foot. I started to call for my Border Collie, too frightened to pull my leg away in case the snake struck. "Beau… Beau," I tried to call, but my voice wouldn't work. "Oh God, of all the times to be home alone," I thought. Suddenly, Beau came bounding around the corner, and the snake scurried away under the neighbour's fence. Another time, I went to step out into our carport and found a large black snake stretched across the doorway. If I hadn't looked when I did, I would have stepped on it for sure.

I decided to see a psychic to understand why we were going through so much bad luck. I sat across from her as she had me shuffle the tarot cards and then laid them out in a spread. "Wow, you and your husband have been to hell and back, as the saying goes. There's so much depression around both of you; I think you both need counselling or perhaps some anti-depressants. There's so much stress, especially on your husband, like the entire weight of the world is on his shoulders. If he isn't careful, I can see him having a major nervous breakdown. This stress is terrible. With all the downturns in your home city, he definitely needs a career change—he can't keep going like this; it's affecting every aspect of his life, which in turn affects yours. You've had a lot of bad luck over the years, haven't you? What happened to you as a child? I see a lot of blood and a white ball smashing into your face."

"Wow, yes, that's right. I was playing hockey in the Grand Final, just before the end, and we were only just in front. I remember hearing a whistle. I turned to see the hockey ball coming straight at me at high speed, and it hit me right in the nose. The pain was like being hit with a block of cement—it dropped me to the ground. I heard lots of voices, and blood was pouring from my nose. My white skirt turned bright red, as did my green shirt. A lady came running towards me and tilted my head back, and I thought I was going to drown as I could taste all the blood running down my throat. I was spluttering and coughing, unable to breathe properly. There was a lot of commotion around me, and I was taken to the hospital. But lucky for us, we won the Grand Final."

"And I can see a kangaroo hitting your car, did this happen to you?"

"Wow, yes it did, when our son was just a tiny baby. Thank God he wasn't in the car, though. My husband and I had just finished our shifts at the local hospital, and our son Liam was being looked after by his grandparents. It was late at night, about 11:30 pm, and we had just turned onto the highway when, out of nowhere, a massive kangaroo hit us on my passenger side while my husband was driving. I can still hear the crunching of the metal and the sound of the front lights smashing as the car swerved all over the road. It completely crumpled the entire front passenger side and peeled off the panel work like it was butter. Luckily, we had insurance, but it didn't cover a hire car. We were only a couple of years into our marriage and didn't have the money to cover that, along with all our other expenses. It took weeks to get the car fixed. I couldn't work during that time, so we lost my wage, and my husband had to buy a pushbike and ride nearly 15 kilometres in the freezing weather and rain to get to work. It financially crippled us."

"Do you have a scar on your left leg? I feel terrible pain when I see this."

"Gosh, you really are good. Yes, years ago, I was selected for the championships in hockey, and we were travelling to another regional city for the final selection trials. The night before, I foolishly decided to give my legs a quick shave in the shower. As I was finishing, I took a quick swipe at my lower leg and didn't realise I had cut out a piece the size of a 10-cent coin, which got caught in the razor. I then pulled upwards and thought I had literally cut my leg off. The pain was mind-blowing. I let out the most blood-curdling scream, and with the shower still running, blood sprayed all over the cubicle. My mother, who was near the door, came bursting in to find me in agony, completely splattered with blood, with the shower still going. Needless to say, that incident completely shattered my dreams of making it to the state championships. I never competed in those trials again."

"And you were sick a lot as a child and a baby weren't you? Were you a C-section.?"

"Yes, I was!" I answered, completely gobsmacked. "It has been reported that a lot of babies that are born Caesarean have lots of issues with their immunity as you were never exposed to your mother's flora during a vaginal delivery. This affects the immune system and the microbiome. There have been lots of studies done on this. Did you get tonsillitis a lot as a kid?"

"Apparently, I did. And when I was a baby, I was so ill and on so many antibiotics that when I was taken back to see the doctor, they were gone. The doctor told my mother they must have been so rotten that I coughed them out. I was mortified when I heard that story. The tonsils grew back since there were still buds left, and yes, I was always sick for many years of my childhood and into my adult life."

"And your mother, did she suffer any trauma when she was pregnant with you, either physical or mental? I feel like she did, and this trauma has been transferred to you."

"Physical? Like, did she suffer from a lot of nausea and vomiting? I feel like she had a terrible time with that during her pregnancy."

"I do recall my grandmother telling me that Mum did vomit for months when she was pregnant with me, and the only way they could get her to stop was to drive her around in the car, and she would sleep in the back seat."

"You suffer from terrible motion sickness too, don't you? Like on swings, in the back seat of cars—I'm even getting a vision of you vomiting on a Ferris wheel."

"Oh my God, yes, that's all true. I get violently sick from any sort of motion. I can never go on any of those fast rides you see at shows and tourist attractions. Even flying in a plane makes me vomit for hours, and I end up in bed for days until I recover. It just wipes me out."

"And what about mental trauma? I feel like your mum was told something while she was pregnant with you that really upset her and triggered a lot of emotion in her."

"I did ask her about that many years later. My grandmother had a baby out of wedlock. Back in those days, it brought terrible shame on the family if the young woman wasn't married. Nan had her baby son, and my great-grandmother told everyone she had a change-of-life baby and raised him as her own. Nan eventually married and had three more children. Tragically, her son was killed in his early twenties. My great-aunty, who is Nan's sister, told my mother when she was pregnant with me that her cousin, whom she had always believed was her cousin, was in fact her half-brother. You can imagine the shock."

"Yes, it certainly would have been, and I feel this trauma and shock has been transferred to you in some way. Was there another baby born a few months after you? Do you have a cousin close in age? I feel like he was male."

"My aunty, my mother's younger sister, also fell pregnant not long before I was born. She was terrified of what her parents would say because she was so young and not married. She hid her pregnancy from the family by wearing long coats and jumpers, but due to living in a tropical environment, it became too hot for her to continue wearing those clothes. She finally took off her winter gear and revealed she was eight months pregnant. The shock resonated throughout my family. By then, I was about six months old, and my parents had been married for over three years. My aunty decided to give the baby up for adoption as she didn't think it was fair to bring another mouth into the world that she couldn't financially support at such a young age. To this day, she has never tried to find him, and I don't think she ever truly will."

"I can see that you, Karen, are very easy going, but unfortunately, people take advantage of the fact that you're too nice. You're spreading yourself too thin, always running around after everyone else, and barely giving yourself anything. You need to fill up your own cup first before you can help everyone else around you. You're not looking after yourself, and there are a lot of underlying health issues here. If you don't address them, you're going to end up in a really bad way," said the psychic. Taylor told me that the psychic lady had expressed extreme concern for me, warning that I was doing way too much and was under horrendous stress. She said I needed to start looking after my physical and mental health, or I would pay dearly for it. Twelve months later, I nearly died…

"You need to start going for walks every day—you'll feel so much better for it. Then things will gradually start to improve, step by step. You definitely worry way too much about everything; you overthink so much. Remember, worrying is like going back and forth in a rocking chair—it will keep you busy, but it will never get you anywhere. Start listening to your wonderful intuition more, Karen. I can see that you are a very intelligent lady. I think that where you're working, they change the days and cut your hours to suit themselves and accommodate new staff. Due to your financial situation, this causes you so much stress. Leave, walk away—you have enough to deal with; you don't need any more stress and angst in your life. Go out and find better opportunities that can give you more money, but you need to actively look for them—they're not just going to land in your lap.

"Put more positivity in your life; think and speak more positively. All your kids have been through some extraordinary life challenges. Your middle daughter, Taylor, has many more ahead of her, but she will eventually find her strength, as they all will, and they will overcome everything in front of them. Get yourself a house cleansing—I feel there is so much negativity in your house that needs to be cleared. Cleanse and balance yourself and your family. It's not the right time to move; you'll be disappointed because you won't make enough money from the sale to relocate and start fresh somewhere comfortably.

"Don't move or rent unless your husband secures a permanent job; otherwise, when his contracts end, it will be up to you to be the main breadwinner, which I know you've done numerous times before. Don't be at the mercy of a landlord who can increase the rent at any time and make your life unbearable. Stay put for now. I do feel that, in years to come, your finances will improve, and you will travel overseas to at least six different countries, so don't despair—there is happiness in your future. I can also see you helping your mother a lot—something to do with your father?"

She drew a card of a man lying down with stained glass windows behind him. "Your Dad has been very sick for a while now, hasn't he? This card represents him. He's been in pain for a long time, and eventually, he will have had enough. Even though he wants to stay and be with you all, he just can't bear the pain any longer. He will go on his journey home, finally free of pain and at peace."

"Will it be soon?" I asked.

"No, not soon. Now that you know this, I can see you organising a wonderful 70th birthday for him, with so many of your relatives and friends there. Your father is going to have the most amazing birthday. He will literally be on cloud nine for months afterwards. However, he will not live to see his 73rd birthday. It would be cruel of me to tell you the exact year he will pass away, as it would cause you too much pain, but as I said, he won't see 73." My Dad was 68 when I had that reading done. Yes, I organised a surprise 70th birthday for him, and he had the most magical night. We have many videos and photos to remember that last special birthday we all spent with him. Dad died a month after his 71st birthday.

PHYSICALLY, MENTALLY, AND EMOTIONALLY SPENT...

"I FEAR NOT THE DARK ITSELF, BUT WHAT MAY LURK WITHIN IT."
—ANONYMOUS

One weekend, John and I took Jenna to the local movie theatre as a treat. We could not afford much, and we hadn't been out for so long. After the movie, we decided to take a stroll around the city centre, as none of us really wanted to go home. They both needed to use the toilet, and while I was waiting, I noticed a new esoteric shop that had opened in the main area. I went inside, and it was absolutely beautiful—so much to look at, with thousands of crystals and angels. The shop just mesmerised me. A lady noticed me, approached, and touched my arm. "Oh, sweetheart, your aura is just black. I think you and your family may need one of these." She handed me a card about house clearing of negative energy and soul retrieval. It had this written on it: "Negative energies can build up in the home, and no one suspects this is the reason for damaging emotions and incidents that take place. Negative energy can be formed by all forms of negativity brought into your home. Your home may start to feel heavy and uncomfortable to be in."

"You and your family may feel ill or unhappy on a regular basis, and this could be caused by negative energy in your home. Your children might be afraid to sleep in their rooms, hearing voices or seeing something that frightens them. Your pets may act strangely, looking around the room as if they see something you can't. These spirits may be afraid to pass on and choose to linger in the energies of your home. Spirits that hold negative energy can cause chaos in your everyday life and that of your family. They can lead to physical and mental health problems, as well as financial issues, for those living in a home filled with this kind of energy. We will come into your home and clear it. We can also lovingly help any earth-bound souls to move on."

She wrote on the back of the card that I needed to get some sage and, as I walked around my house and into each room, say out loud, "Nothing but love and light can live here. Anything that isn't love and light MUST and will leave NOW."

"Oh, um, yeah, thanks," I stammered and left immediately. She also gave me a couple of sheets of paper with all the Archangels' names on them—Michael, Uriel, Gabriel, Raphael, Chamuel, Ariel, and Metatron—with a little blog about who they are and what they do.

"What have you got?" John asked. "Ah, nothing," I said and threw it into my drawer when we got home.

John had gone out west again for work, so I said to Jenna, "Come on, let's get in the car, take the pups for a walk, and grab some takeaways on the way home." We never really got to do much together due to our financial situation, so I was trying to make it fun for her. Getting takeaways was a real luxury for us.

We parked and had a lovely walk with our dogs, but by the time we got back to the car, it was right on dark. We quickly put the dogs in the back as the mosquitoes were starting to come out and were really bad. Once they were loaded in and tied up, we jumped in the front seat, put the car into gear, and—nothing. "Come on, what now!" I tried and tried, but the car wouldn't move. I went to ring a roadside mechanic, but, of course, my phone wouldn't work. We had to walk kilometres all the way back home, getting eaten alive by mosquitoes and midges.

"Why is our life so terrible? Why do all these awful things keep happening to us?" Jenna cried. I was trying so hard not to fall apart myself. Eventually, I was able to get onto the mechanic, who came and picked me up. And you'll never guess—the shaft pin had fallen out of my automatic panel. "Wow, that's unbelievable, never seen anything like that before," said the service technician. Of course, it could only happen to us. We had to wait days for the parts to arrive—no going anywhere, as we couldn't afford taxis. We lived on tinned baked beans and noodles for a few days until we could get the car fixed—again!

Let's not even start on the appliances in the house. I think every single one we owned broke down: washing machines, dryers, microwaves, air conditioners, the big TV—it was always one after another, or sometimes three at a time, along with the car, light switches, fans, hot water system, computer, etc. It just NEVER stopped. One morning, I woke to a hissing noise coming from my bathroom ensuite. I had worked the night before and hadn't gotten to bed until about 2 am. I always showered as soon as I got home from work. John was away again, and I cautiously opened my door. There was water all over the tiles, flowing everywhere. Inside my shower, water was spraying from the hot water tap. I couldn't turn it off and raced out to the mains.

I quickly tried to mop up all the water before it seeped into the bedroom carpet—there were litres of it. Thank God I was home when it happened, and we weren't away on holidays or at work. I finally managed to call an emergency plumber to fix it, and he was baffled as to what caused it. He said the washers and other fittings were still in good condition, but he replaced them anyway. Being a Sunday, of course, the callout on the weekend cost us hundreds of dollars that we just didn't have.

One morning, our neighbour knocked on our door, very concerned, as he had observed water spraying from our roof. He was getting in his car to go to work when he saw it. "I think your hot water system has some issues and has sprung a leak. You need to get that seen to straight away." Sure enough, it was leaking water everywhere. Some part had fallen off inside the hot water system itself and had completely rusted the entire system. Once again, we were told, "Not sure how that happened, we've never seen anything like it." For Christmas one year, I bought John speakers and a surround sound system on the cheap, as it had been a display model in the store. Otherwise, I would never have been able to afford it. My son's friend came over and set it up with all the wires and cables. For the next few weeks, we got to enjoy this gift. But after a short amount of time, we noticed it wasn't working anymore.

We then observed that certain wires and cables had been literally cut off into pieces and we were at an absolute loss as to how this could have happened. They were straight cuts, the only explanation we could come up with was that there must be mice or rats maybe in the house and they had chewed the wires. How would they not look like they had been chewed? We put traps all around inside our house but we never saw any and none were ever caught. We would also hear lots of sounds coming from our roof cavity at all times of the day and night. Sometimes it would be SO loud over us in the lounge room it became a bit disturbing.

"We must have vermin or possums in our roof. You need to ring the council and get some traps up there—they could eat away at other wires and cause us even more issues," said John. I rang the council, and they came to have a look but found nothing. We set multiple traps inside, but still, nothing was ever caught.

One weekend, I decided to eat outside in the evening as it was finally cool enough to do so. It was just going to be us, as with me working so many weekends, we barely spent any time together as a family. I had just put a heap of dishes and food on the table that I had cooked. Suddenly, there was an almighty smashing noise that completely caught us off guard. WHAT THE HELL WAS THAT? I thought. We looked in horror as our glass table in the pergola shattered into thousands of pieces, smashing many of the dishes I had placed on it. We had not long bought that new setting… just unbelievable!

So much for an evening meal outside—we couldn't even enjoy that. We have spent literally thousands and thousands of dollars on repairs, money that could have gone towards holidays or paying off the mortgage, but we just NEVER stopped paying repair bills. It got so bad that the few friends we had over for small BBQs would joke as they left, saying, "We'll try not to run over any black cats or break any mirrors at your place. Must be that number 13." If only we really knew what IT was.

Even my nursing shoes fell apart one day as I was getting ready to go to work—like, seriously? I was just OVER it. John had been put off work again due to restructuring, but thankfully we had insurance cover to get us through. I submitted the claim, but they decided to reject it. Their reasoning was that John could potentially get another job with a different company down the track. Those bastards used every loophole they could to deny us money we desperately needed, despite paying premiums for years.

I was so DISGUSTED with them that I cancelled the policy on the spot. The man on the phone was so rude and full of himself, almost verbally abusive. I was at the end of my rope, and when they rejected our claim, I didn't know what to do. I HONESTLY JUST HATED MY LIFE! This wasn't living; this was merely existing, and we had been suffering like this for years and years while everyone around us seemed to be living wonderful lives. It's one thing to read these words on a page, but try living it OVER and OVER and OVER. Welcome to our life!

Friends, family, and colleagues were going away on beautiful holidays, having parties, weekends away, spending time with their loved ones, celebrating Christmas and birthdays, while we never seemed to have any of it. I became SO resentful, and the number of times I was told, "Gee, you're really being tested, aren't you," made me want to slap the next person who said it.

John pulled up in the carport driving very slowly. It had taken him hours to get home that day.

"Why are you driving so slow?" I asked with absolute dread.

"Not long after I started driving, the front wheels felt funny and started shuddering on and off. I thought I'd better pull over and have a look, but I couldn't see anything wrong. There were no indicator lights showing on the dash, so I decided to drive back a bit slower—like 70 instead of 100—but it's been a very long and unsettling trip home. At times, it shuddered so badly I thought the car was going to collapse on the highway. It's been pretty scary with so many other cars and semi-trailers whizzing past me at top speed. They were probably cursing me for not doing the speed limit, but I just knew something was really wrong with it."

Instead of taking three hours to get home, it had taken him over six, and he was exhausted. It was late Friday night, and he had to drive back on Sunday night to start work again on Monday morning. He drove the car straight to the mechanic on Saturday morning, explained the situation, and they agreed to have a quick look at it—they could see how distressed John was.

I picked him up and brought him home, and we waited for the phone call. Within the hour, they rang. I could hear the exasperation in John's voice on the phone. "You have got to be kidding me! Yeah, I think I'd better go and buy that lottery ticket." When he hung up, he literally went white.

"They checked the car and saw that the steering rod, which keeps the wheel on the car, was gone. The entire team at the shop is in disbelief that I made it home in one piece. They said even at 70 km/h on the highway, if that wheel had come off, I would most likely have been killed. They told me to go out and buy a lottery ticket because I just used up one of my nine lives. They've never seen anything like it—it has just literally disappeared."

The very next week, John's contract ended suddenly, and he lost his job AGAIN. Ohhhhhhhh our life!

FEAR CRIPPLING MY SOUL...

"THERE ARE HORRORS BEYOND LIFE'S EDGE THAT WE DO NOT SUSPECT AND ONCE IN A WHILE MAN'S EVIL PRYING CALLS THEM JUST WITHIN OUR RANGE" —H.P. LOVECRAFT

I had applied for a job online down south and received a phone call inviting me for an interview. With the last bit of remaining money we had, we bought airline tickets at full price, hired a car, flew down, and stayed in a motel overnight. The interview was a five-panel, two-hour ordeal that left me stressed and exhausted. After it was over, we drove to another suburb to view an art union home that was open for inspection. It has always been John's dream to win one. We took a wrong turn and ended up near an aged care facility on the side of a mountain with large electric gates. As we got closer, he said, "Why not throw your resume in there too?"

"No! What? No way," I replied. But suddenly the gates opened, and he looked at me and said, "Well, we're going up there now." I walked in, more glass doors opened, and I found myself in a lovely, relaxed, country-style facility. I told the receptionist that I just happened to be passing through and was dropping off my resume. Suddenly, the manager appeared, and I found myself having an impromptu interview.

We got back home that night, and I was utterly exhausted from the whirlwind trip. The next day, both facilities rang to offer me a job. I was shaking with shock, and John was ecstatic. "Oh, we're finally getting out of this godforsaken place!" he screamed, beside himself with joy. I had three weeks until my start date, and the same day, John went out and bought packing boxes, tape, and bubble wrap, and started packing. The house quickly looked like a bomb had gone off inside it.

"Where are we going to live? Where is Jenna going to go to school? What's going to happen with our pets? This house?" I asked, overwhelmed with confusion. I was in such turmoil that I couldn't eat or sleep—I was in sheer panic mode.

"You'll have to go down by yourself initially. We'll have to find you a unit, and you'll have to work full-time to pay all the bills. You need to get all the shifts you can," John was telling me. Jenna was crying because she didn't want me to leave, and she didn't want to leave her close friends. So much was happening, and the house was being pulled apart left, right, and centre. All the while, I was trying to work at my aged care facility and pick up extra shifts to help with the move. I was an emotional wreck. I hadn't slept in days.

I pulled up under the school building to pick Jenna up when a friend came over and knocked on my window. She had seen me in the car looking so dishevelled and couldn't believe it was me. She had come over to see if I needed anything because she was so concerned about my appearance.

I think I just burst into tears, explaining what was happening in my life and that I had to leave because we were about to lose our home. "Oh, Karen, the safety officer at my husband's workplace left just a couple of days ago. They haven't replaced the position yet. Go and tell John to hand in his resume, but don't let them know you're aware the position is vacant—it might be worth a shot." I was so thankful she came to see me, and I told John when I got back home. He put in his resume and got the job. It was only a few months' contract, but it was something. Now that there was an income, we didn't have to leave. I honestly felt like the entire weight of the world had been lifted off my shoulders. The relief was euphoric.

A friend of the family had mentioned to me a few times about getting an Aboriginal smoking ceremony done on the house as maybe there were lots of Aboriginal sacred burial sites on our land. Maddie had actually called and spoken to a man named Peter, who performed the "Welcome to Country" ceremonies in our regional city. She told him a bit about our story and how we really needed help. Peter arranged for his brother to come up from another settlement with different leaves from the two tribes. The morning was arranged; Jenna was at school, and it would just be the five of us.

I opened the door to let them in, and one of the brothers immediately said he could feel something, and the hairs on the back of his neck stood up. OMG! I thought, maybe there really is something spiritual here after all. We had a coffee first and sat around the table, sharing our story—things that had happened to our family and the bad luck that had plagued us over the years. They were very interested in listening and then began to prepare the tribal leaves.

We started in Jenna's room. They tried to light the leaves, but over and over again, it wouldn't light. "It doesn't want us here," they said. OMG! IT can do that? "It's okay, we'll go into another room." Within seconds, everything lit up instantly. WOW! We all went back into Jenna's room, and eventually, Peter moved from room to room, very slowly blowing the smoke throughout. The sweat was just pouring off him. I heard his brother calling out, "You need to leave these poor people alone. They've never done anything to you. You need to leave this house and give this family some peace. They've suffered enough. No more. They are not responsible. BE GONE!"

As Peter reached the kitchen, I began opening all the cupboards. I had to make sure every door, cupboard, wardrobe, and drawer throughout the entire house was open, as the energy can hide in spaces and might not be removed. I noticed Peter leaning down underneath the microwave as I was opening up the kitchen cupboards above him. Suddenly, a big swish of fire came roaring up out of nowhere, as if someone had just thrown petrol on it. Whoosh... we all just stared in amazement. We had all seen it. "Yep, there IT is," said Wal.

By now, the whole house was filled with thick smoke, so much so that you could just make out the outline of the person in front of you. But, incredibly, you could breathe normally, and your eyes didn't sting. It was so surreal. The front door was left open the entire time to move IT out of the house. After nearly two hours, it was finally over. The boys gave me the leftover leaves and told me to keep Jenna's door shut for the next couple of days and, when she got back, to take her into a small room and smoke her. They showed John and me what to do and assured us they would get back in contact if we needed them to come again.

Before the ceremony, they brought both our dogs in, and both refused to go into Jenna's room. "There are lots of Aboriginals who were burned here after they were shot and killed. There are a lot of unmarked graves and burial sites. No wonder there is so much anger and sadness here," Wal told us. Both brothers could sense that it was a very dark, angry spirit. John and I gave them a voucher as a token of appreciation for what they had done. Maddie stayed for a while afterwards, and we all had a coffee. She told me to contact her and let her know how everything went.

Later that night, I was sitting in my lounge chair watching TV, trying to process the events of the day in my mind. The next thing I knew, I had the sensation of being choked—like REALLY being choked. I could feel the tightness around my neck, and I started spluttering and heaving. John jumped out of his chair and ran to the kitchen to get me a glass of water. I could feel the grip getting tighter and tighter around my neck, and I was actually grabbing at my neck to relieve the pressure. It was ABSOLUTELY TERRIFYING! As he touched my arm to give me the water, the pressure was gone instantly, and I was left grabbing my neck, trying to breathe properly again.

"Here, have a drink. What did you choke on?" John asked.

"Nothing, I've been sitting here beside you the whole time," I told him. I was at a loss to describe what had happened, and John was a bit sceptical. "Well, you must have had something in your mouth to react like that, but anyway, you're okay now, and that's the main thing," he said.

I was so terrified by what had just happened that I couldn't sit back in my chair for the rest of the night. I knew John thought I was being a bit eccentric, but I felt so uneasy. It was truly scary, and I went to bed early that night because I just couldn't settle. When I looked in the mirror, I could see red marks all around my neck.

"That's probably just from you grabbing at your neck when you were choking on something," John said, as he could see the marks too. I knew he didn't really believe me, because how could he? It wasn't happening to him.

I contacted Joy and told her what had happened.

Joy texted me back, "I'm sitting here with my hair standing on end. Honestly, I felt more than I let on the other day when I came to visit you. Your land has a malevolent being on it that's never going to leave. I felt that malevolent dark spirit in Jenna's room as I approached it from the hallway. My vision went black, and then I had this overwhelming feeling of darkness—the same feeling I had with my sister... there is no way you could have foreseen what was going to happen to you."

I texted back, "After I finally smoked Jenna, she has been SO irritable and agitated. Really angry—you can't even look sideways at her. She was quite sick for the first few days when she got home, vomiting really badly, so I couldn't smoke her until she was well. They used Aboriginal native flora for the smoking ceremony. I put my bracelet on, which has a cross on it, and the very next day, the chain broke."

I had done some research and found out that in the 1950s, the local council decided to close the general cemetery and open a new one which is not far from where we live in our suburb. After a series of burials, it was discovered that the soil there was not suitable as after rain the bodies would wash to the surface. The council then exhumed more than 60 bodies from this new cemetery and re-interred them back into the general cemetery. This would have also caused great distress on this land.

Joy texted back, "There are beings, spirits, poltergeists, fairies, and other creatures that we live with but don't know or see, but they are here, and they walk among us. You have now experienced this, and you are a true believer, whether you like it or not. A lot of people are ignorant to things they cannot see or touch, but there is definitely something going on with your family. Look, we had the same thing happen in our family. We were cursed by a spirit that had inhabited our house long before we arrived to live there. Hindsight is a wonderful thing, but it caused devastation to five of my siblings. So what you're experiencing isn't BS—it's real. It's manifesting in negative energy. Speak to it and say, 'We're not going to hurt you,' acknowledging it or them can sometimes help. Aboriginal black magic is serious stuff, and if it has a grip on you, you have to respect it because it's powerful and it works.

"I am on night shift tonight, standing in the car park at work, and I'm sending you a white light of protection. It feels authentic because I know where you live, and I've been to your house, so I can envision your bedroom since I've been in it. I was brought up in a culture where we were taught to accept and respect these things. But there are boundaries, and they need to be reminded of that sometimes. White people smudge with sage; Aboriginals do a smoking ceremony—same thing. You're both fighting off negative energy and taking ownership of the situation. That's what's happening. This isn't your fault; you're fighting back together. Love... black man magic is subtle but deadly. Warning... then death... true story. I'm so glad that you believe.

"Beings, if I'm honest, are very strong and historical. Most white people think that being white Australians, Aboriginals are the gatekeepers of this vast landscape, having been here for eons. Your understanding aligns with the historical significance of what has happened to your family. You cannot ignore it anymore... you have to respect it... and you are doing that now. Remember what I said: get your sage, burn it, and tell them what you are doing. I truly don't think you should stay there anymore—it will just get worse, even fatal. They know you know and will not let go. OUT OF THAT HOUSE... DON'T MESS AROUND ... REALLY DON'T DELAY... MOVE!"

FINDING MY STRENGTH...

"FAITH IS TAKING THE FIRST STEP EVEN WHEN YOU DON'T SEE THE WHOLE STAIRCASE." —MARTIN LUTHER KING, JR.

The next morning, John made me breakfast as per our normal routine, I was walking out to the lounge area with coffee and toast in my hands when I turned the corner and saw the ghastliest image of what looked like a print with three claws right behind my chair. This is where I was sitting the night before. I froze in absolute terror—this had never been there before. "OMG, what the hell is that?" I screamed. Maddie arrived with a loaf bun for us to have with our coffee for morning tea. She could see how terrified I looked as I showed her the print that was on my feature wall. "My God, Karen, I think you need to get a priest, love. This is starting to get a bit scary, even for me. You need some sort of professional help."

I went into one of the local esoteric stores and saw a man at the counter. I had my youngest daughter, Jenna, with me. "Do you need any help?" he asked. My voice began to quiver. "I think I need some sort of protection around myself and my family," I told him. "Things have been going on at my house for a long time now, and I really need something or someone to help me," I said, almost terrified, and I could feel myself shaking. I showed him the photo of what had appeared on my wall after the boys had done the smoking ceremony. He asked where I lived, and I told him the suburb.

"Ahhhhh, lots of angry land there. When I was a kid, we used to draw straws to see who would do the milk run there because of so much negativity. Lots of Aboriginal sacred burial sites there—I don't really understand how the council ever approved for houses to be built there in the first place."

"Oh, so there are sacred sites there? That's what I was thinking, and so were my friends. Hopefully, we haven't made IT angry because I don't think IT is going anywhere." Another gentleman in the shop, who had overheard, told me that Aboriginals are believed to have been here on Earth for over 18,000 generations. Their mythology of Dreamtime has been woven into their lives in a very sacred way. Their creation with their spiritual ancestors, which formed the earth, rivers, and valleys, was through the slithering of the majestic rainbow serpent. He told me there are many other spirits that have formed the foundations on which this ancient civilisation exists. "You need some black tourmaline bracelets on all of you, and I would suggest that you get your land gridded."

The shop owner gave me a brochure with a lady's details and photo on it and told me to give her a ring. I knew I had to be strong for my husband and our kids—that was honestly the only thing keeping me going, and even that was being tested on levels I had never experienced before. I put the brochure away in my drawer as we were leaving in a few days for a long-awaited holiday. We had finally saved enough money to go away for just a couple of weeks over the school holidays—Liam, Jenna, John, and I. It wasn't going to be much, but we could finally have a couple of weeks away together, something we hadn't had in so many years.

Taylor and I had a massive disagreement, which ended in her leaving home and going to live with her boyfriend's parents. I did as many extra shifts as I could so we could have some spending money, and we were able to put enough aside to stay in a resort. We were so excited—FINALLY something wonderful to look forward to after all those terrible events that had been happening in our life. When we got back, I would look into ringing that lady and getting our house cleansed and gridded.

We decided to leave at night so that the kids could sleep in the back on the way down. There would be less traffic on the road, making our trip smoother, and it would be cooler than travelling during the day. We drove all night, and by morning, we had pulled up for some breakfast. John wasn't wanting to worry me but just felt that something needed to be looked at with the car. It wasn't driving right. "OH, come on, you have got to be kidding me!!" I cried out in pure frustration. "All good, we can put it into the service station here as there is a mechanic on duty," said John.

We paid to stay in cabins overnight. The next day, we met with the mechanic, who could not believe we made it as far as we did. We had the car serviced only a couple of weeks before we left on our trip, but we hardly had any brakes on any of the wheels, and the brake pads were nearly non-existent. He believed what saved us was driving at night when there was barely any traffic. He even told us to go out and buy a lottery ticket. The repairs cost us over $2,000, which wiped out most of our holiday money. I think I silently cried all the way to our unit. Luckily, we had pre-booked some of our tourist experiences, but we couldn't do a lot of the other things we had planned. Once again, we were struck by bad luck and left with no money… AGAIN!

I awoke one morning with an overwhelming feeling that I needed to have colonics. I didn't know why, but I just knew it was something I had to do. I met a lady named Kate, who was the manager, and she told me that the owner of the franchise would be coming up from another state to do training to become a colonic therapist. I talked to John about it, and he fully supported my decision to do the training. The first time I had the procedure, I felt completely wiped out, and they had to settle me with a warm cup of tea. However, I did feel that it was helping me.

The following month, as things ramped up for me, I was telling Kate my story. Stella, my national manager, was visiting at the time and was also interested in hearing what was happening. She told me that she believed my soul intuitively knew that I had some sort of parasite attached to me. "People think they can go to a chemist or doctor and get tinctures, teas, and tablets to remove them from your body, but the only thing that will completely remove them is colonics." She sent me lots of love and said, "Keep knowing with pure love and surrender, you will be okay. This is where your true power lies."

"What's your address honey?" said Sheila, who managed one of the esoteric shops where I lived. "Ohhhhh you're in that area… lots of angry land there. I normally charge $150 for a house clearing and blessing, but over there, as I may have to do a lot with the land, it might cost $300," she replied over the phone. I thought, Oh no, where am I going to find that sort of money? We had barely any income, John was out of work AGAIN, we had mouths to feed as well as two dogs, bills coming in left, right, and centre, and every time we turned around, something else seemed to break down. It was just debilitating. "Okay, no worries," I said, thinking I'd have to borrow off Mum or something. I needed help, someone who knew what they were doing, and I needed it REALLY fast.

The next week couldn't come around fast enough. On the morning of the scheduled house clearing, Sheila called to say that her mother had suddenly taken very ill and she was so sorry but wouldn't be able to make it. I was upset but understood that her mother needed her more. "Okay, we'll reschedule for next week," I said. Sure enough, the morning of the rescheduled house clearing, exactly the same thing happened. Another phone call, and her mother had taken ill again. She was so apologetic. "I am just so, so, so sorry to do this to you again, Karen." WOW—both days, two weeks in a row, that I had organised for her to be here, and this happens. "I promise we'll make it work next week and finally get things settled."

Things were ramping up at my house, my nightmares were becoming more brutal and graphic, and I was desperately in need of professional esoteric help. I was tidying up the house for the third time the night before the house clearing when my phone beeped. I read the text: "I'm sorry, it's me again. You're not going to believe this, but my mother has taken ill again… I'm so sorry to do this to you again, Karen." Now I was REALLY angry. Three bloody weeks I had been waiting for this to be over and done with, and it just kept dragging on and on. I was FURIOUS. For goodness' sake, can't someone else help your mother? This is supposed to be your business, and you keep letting your clients down OVER and OVER again! I felt like screaming at her. I was just SOOOO mad. I hadn't told her my story, as I wanted to see if she could sense anything, so to her, it was just another house cleansing. But I REALLY NEEDED her, and she was constantly letting me down. I picked up the phone and texted back that I didn't need her help anymore, as I had dealt with the situation myself and wouldn't be needing her services.

"No worries, honey, well, if down the track you do, you know how to find me," she texted back. …Yeah right, I've been needing you for the last THREE BLOODY WEEKS, and what a waste of time that was for me… I won't EVER be contacting you again for ANY HELP! Obviously, she wasn't the person who could truly help me. I would just have to find someone else. Later, it was revealed to me that IT was making sure she never set foot on my property so I could get no help from her whatsoever.

Print that appeared behind my chair the next morning after Aboriginal smoking ceremony performed on my house.

MY HOUSE BLESSING...

"THERE IS NO DEFINITION OF BEAUTY, BUT WHEN YOU CAN SEE THAT SOMEONE HAS THEIR SPIRIT COMING THROUGH, SOMETHING UNEXPLAINABLE, THAT IS BEAUTIFUL TO ME." —LIV TYLER

"Anne can do it," one of the nurses told me where I was working as a registered nurse. "She smudges houses and is also a forensic healer. She's incredibly gifted."

"What is a forensic healer?" I asked.

"It's regarded as the deepest and most effective way to release trauma, stress, and pain. It can answer longstanding questions and help clear stubborn blocks related to your health, finances, and relationships. It can also help with chronic physical, emotional, and spiritual conditions. A healer finds clues in your energy fields as to why you have certain conditions and helps release them using over 90 healing pathways. Just as we are what we eat, we are what we experience in life. A person's current state of energy, health, spirituality, and emotions can directly result from their past experiences. It's stored in our DNA, cells, and energy fields. Over time, accumulated abuse, stress, and trauma can cause major dysfunction until it's healed. This healing can profoundly cleanse your energy field, leaving you feeling less stressed, less in pain, and more connected emotionally and spiritually. They also place a blessing on you at the end of the healing and much more. I'll give you her number. She'll do it, and she won't charge you if you have genuine financial issues."

I had been looking after Anne's mother for years at the facility where I worked, so I knew of her. Anne always visited during the day, and since I worked permanent afternoon shifts, we rarely crossed paths. Only when her mum had a turn did I get to talk and spend some time with her. Anne remembered me and turned up the next day to do a house cleansing. She told me to have some matches, sage, white candles, and several pieces of natural black tourmaline ready. She was due to arrive around 10.

That morning, I woke up feeling nauseous and started dry retching. The pain around my sides and abdomen was like I had been set on fire—just the most severe burning sensation. I remembered a few weeks earlier when I had felt unwell and went to the doctor for a check-up and blood tests. Before seeing my GP, an RN took all my vital signs and asked if I wanted to get my hair tested. She also offered to measure my fat mass, muscle mass, body mass index, basal metabolic rate, bone mass, etc., and calculate my actual metabolic age. After being so run down and suffering from extreme sleep deprivation for so many years, I decided to find out. Although I was only in my forties, it came back that my BMR was barely a blip on the screen—it hardly existed. Most shocking was that I had the actual metabolic age of a 60-year-old woman. I looked in the mirror and saw that all around my mouth was green, and I felt horrific. My head was spinning, and I just wanted to vomit, but I couldn't eat any breakfast.

John and Jenna were at work and school, and I had waited over three weeks for someone to come and help me. I knew I had to drive to the esoteric shop on the other side of town. I got in the car with a bucket in case I vomited, and to be honest, it felt like it took nearly an hour to get there. I was just SO sick and kept feeling dizzy while driving. The pain was horrendous, but I couldn't cancel again—I had been waiting too long for this. I somehow stumbled into the shop, and the lady took one look at me and said, "You need to get to a hospital; you're so ill."

"I just need to pick some things up, and I need to drive back home and do this smudging."

"OMG!!! You drove here in this state? Are you sure you can drive home? I feel like I need to ring an ambulance for you."

"Gosh no, I'm fine, just really tired," I lied. "Can you please just show me what I need? I have to be home asap." After getting my supplies, I somehow made it back home in one piece. I remember lying on the bed, but no matter what position I got in, I just couldn't get comfortable, and the pain was increasing. I took some mild painkillers, as that was all I had, and waited for Anne to come.

Anne finally arrived, and when I got up to answer the front door, I felt so sick I thought I was going to pass out. "Oh, Karen, are you up for this today? You look really terrible."

"Yes, yes, I'm fine," I lied once again. I wasn't going to let another opportunity slip through my fingers. By now, the pain was so unbearable that I excused myself to take off my bra, hoping it would relieve the pressure, but it didn't. Anne explained that every door, wardrobe, cupboard, and drawer in the entire house needed to be opened, which was excruciating for me to do in my state.

I then had to go around with her holding a white candle and she said a little prayer in each room, as she did her thing, I was so grateful that she was there but it was the longest two plus hours of my life. I could feel myself burning up and the pain just wouldn't stop. Anne said a smudging prayer in every room that she went into while I held the white candle. "Negativity that invades Karen's sacred place I banish you away with the light of my grace. You have no hold or power here for I stand and face you with no fear. Be gone forever for this I will say, this is

Karen's sacred place and you will obey." The very last part of it I distinctly remember was when we were in the kitchen and she called on all these angels to come and be around us to protect us. Suddenly there was a whoosh and all this energy just seemed to come out of nowhere beside and behind and swirl all around me. I remember all the magnets and papers flew off my fridge and she looked at me and said, "It's okay, they heard me—they are here with you, Karen." ...WOWZA! As soon as I laid down afterward, I think I practically passed out.

BIGGEST CHALLENGE OF MY LIFE...

"I'M EVERY NIGHTMARE YOU'VE EVER HAD, I AM YOUR WORST DREAM COME TRUE. I AM EVERYTHING YOU WERE EVER AFRAID OF!" —STEPHEN KING

We gave Anne a voucher to say thank you from one of the local esoteric shops and she used this to buy herself a generator for her healings. "Thank you so much for helping me and my family," I told her.

"You are always very welcome. I admire you so much, Karen," she replied.

Anne went to visit her son interstate and got the Hamsa tattoo—a hand with the all-seeing God's eye, full of protection and representing all religions. "I just love it; it's so beautiful," Anne told me. I bought some protective bracelets for John and Jenna. He had broken out in small boils over his stomach, was getting bad headaches, and had become so irritable. The worst was when he woke up screaming at 4 am with horrific leg cramps, something he'd never done in over 30 years. The next day at work, he had an accident, ripping open the back of his calf muscle and ending up on crutches. The lady at the esoteric shop told me something was happening to him and to sage him immediately. "Your husband needs urgent and massive protection," she cautioned. So continues our never-ending story.

Mum had been at the markets and bought me a beautiful silver necklace with a cross for protection. She also gave me Dad's rosary and Bible. She told the people she bought it from that it was for my protection. "OHHHHH that's not good," they said. Within days, the chain had snapped, and I was unable to wear it. I gave it back to her, and she returned to the markets. When they saw her, they said, "We knew you would be back. My husband has made this so strong that it cannot be removed—there's no way the cross can come off. Get her to put this on and never take it off."

That night, I had a terrible nightmare of webs all through the house, with dangerous black spiders trying to bite me. Feral, vicious cats were trying to attack me, and I could actually smell the most foul-smelling urine. The nightmare seemed to go on for hours until I finally woke up in a cold sweat. I had never experienced anything like that before in my dream state. I was throwing holy water on the spiders, and when the water hit them, it was as if they were being fried. More would disappear, but others kept coming. I couldn't keep up, but thank God I woke up.

Oh, happy days. I looked up a website and read that dreaming of cats running around your home indicates a lack of direction, protection, and freedom in your life. It reveals the rage of enemies planning to attack you in your home. The site also said that cats in your dreams indicate you are in the wrong home and that in a bad environment, symptoms of death, sickness, and demotion will be a major attack. It also indicated that the powers of darkness are fighting among themselves because of the glory of God within you. "Well, at least God is on my side," I said out loud to myself.

I was so exhausted from these terrible nightmares. Anne had told me to buy a book to use as a dream journal and to write down what I could remember each morning before starting my day. I have had such horrific, brutal dreams over the years and nightmares for such a long time. I can't recall how many times I've woken up in a cold sweat. It got so bad that John stopped us from watching programs after 8:30 pm because most involved violence, death, or trauma of some kind, hoping it would ease my nightmares. We started watching comedies and listening to tranquil music, but still, the nightmares continued, and I didn't know why.

Some of these nightmares used to affect me for days, especially the ones where something was trying to kill me. I could feel myself being chased and stabbed; I could see people in hoods with no faces, and rifles being aimed at me. I could even see down the barrels of the shotguns pointed at my face. I would always wake up, but somehow I was never killed or died in my dreams—something was always trying to hunt, hurt, and kill me. I have endured these nightmares for many years.

Joy asked, "When you go to bed at night, which side is closer to the toilet?"

"Oh gosh, my right side."

"Do you always turn and face that ensuite door?"

"Well, yes, I do, and the door is always open, and the toilet lid is usually up... I never really thought about it. I could hear those sounds but always assumed it was the plumbing... WOW, that is unbelievable and really frightening!"

"Oh, this isn't good," said Anne. "I really wish you could get out of that house. It's a terrible place for you all. Hopefully, the bracelets will help. Ask Archangels Raphael, Michael, Gabriel, and Uriel to stand guard over all of you and at the four corners of your house. It seems like things are really ramping up and attacking your husband too. Stay strong. Blessings and strength to you all—may the angels cover and surround you with their wings of protection."

Jenna had started having terrible nightmares and was getting constant nosebleeds after waking up, just like Liam used to have. Before we realised what was happening in the house, after Liam had moved out, Jenna had pleaded with me to move into his old room. Anne told me that Jenna needed to wear an amethyst bracelet when she goes to bed. We put pieces of natural tourmaline, which looked like pieces of coal, above each door on both sides of the frame, one in each of the four corners of the house, and small clusters of it in front of all the phones and TVs.

I was told that natural tourmaline is far more powerful than polished stones. I lost count of the number of black tourmaline bracelets I went through. I would be getting up to do something, and they would just break, shattering and scattering all over the floor. "That's good, Karen," Anne reassured me. "They're taking the hits for you, keeping the negative energy away. They're doing their job. Always keep them on you."

John had to go out west to work after being unemployed for months, and he had to take our car. Our eldest daughter Taylor was getting married interstate, and we were desperately saving up the money to get there since Jenna was also a junior bridesmaid. It was going to cost over $3000 in airfare alone, which was extremely difficult as I was also in the process of completing my degree, requiring hundreds of clinical hours for which I wasn't paid. We had started saving like mad, but then John pulled into the carport swearing and was just so angry.

The steering column of the car wasn't working, there was no air conditioning, and he had driven back three hours in the most stifling heat. The windows wouldn't work because they were electric, so he couldn't even put them down for some air. He nearly passed out from the heat, sweating profusely and bright red when he pulled up. It cost us over $3000 to fix, so we were unable to attend our own daughter's wedding. During the past few years, we had to claim financial hardship on our home not once, not twice, but five separate times.

We called the bank to see if we could use our equity to at least buy the materials we needed to paint and fix up holes, etc., since we had no choice but to sell. They refused to help us, telling us to just sell the house as it was and that it wasn't their problem. "Our safety nets are all gone now. I can't stress about it anymore. I've done so much of that over the years, and it literally nearly killed me," I sobbed to Anne.

"Yes, banks can be so unfeeling in people's distress. They don't really go out of their way to help people get their lives back on track. I always keep you and your family in my prayers and protection. Love you all; I think you are wonderful for what you've endured. May the angels always be beside you, protecting and guiding you to a better life," Anne said, giving me the biggest hug.

Each time, we waited for the application to be approved, we could barely function, always fearing it would be rejected and that the bank would repossess our house at any moment. The stress was, at times, just incapacitating. Jenna had just bought a second-hand car that was in really good condition. We signed all the papers, made sure the insurance was up to date, and I travelled in the passenger seat since she was still on her learner's licence. We were only a couple of minutes from home in peak hour traffic when the car suddenly wouldn't drive. Panicked, I got Jenna to pull into a barrier off the main highway and put on her hazard lights.

The car came to a complete stop. She had just paid over $3000 for it and had only been driving it for 10 minutes when this happened. Jenna burst into tears as cars surrounded us in every direction. I called John, who was driving up behind us, and explained what had just happened. He arranged for a tow truck to take the car to the mechanic. It turned out a rock had become lodged somewhere in the engine, causing it to completely stall. The mechanics had never seen anything like it before—of course, more bad luck.

After four years of doing my degree, due to our financial situation yet again, I couldn't afford to attend my own graduation down south. All those years of study, assignments, examinations, hundreds of unpaid clinical hours, and so much hard work, and I was the only one who couldn't be there. Life just felt so unfair, and we never, ever seemed to catch a break. We were brought to our knees.

BEING PROTECED BUT JUST NEVER KNEW IT...

"PRAYERS OF APPRECIATION ARE THE HIGHEST FORM OF PRAYER."
—ALANIS MORISSETTE

I was feeling unwell and couldn't get out of bed due to severe nausea. John was so concerned that he rang the house call doctor. They said they'd arrive within 90 minutes, but we waited seven hours for him to show up. He was there for less than 10 minutes, didn't do any observations or examinations, flicked a wafer beside me, told me to take it, wrote out a script, and promptly left. He said if I got worse to, quote, "get to the hospital." I was too sick to really care by this stage, but John was livid.

The next day, John was supposed to go away for work, but I was still very ill. I didn't want him to worry, so I pushed myself to act as if I was feeling better. If he didn't work, being on casual wages, he wouldn't get paid, and we desperately needed the money to cover all our bills. I was getting ready for work and had just put on my uniform when an incredible wave of nausea hit me. I quickly sat down and grabbed a bucket as I began to vomit.

"Oh no, what is happening to me?" I thought. I needed to get to work, but it just hit me out of nowhere. I must have vomited for 10 straight minutes and felt completely wiped out. I quickly cleaned myself up as I needed to drive to work—it was the weekend, and they probably wouldn't be able to find a replacement at such short notice. I took some Stemetil, ironed another clean work shirt, and drove to work with the windows down to get some fresh air. By the time I got there, I was feeling so dizzy and just wanted to lie down. If I could just lie down for another half hour, I was sure the nausea would pass.

That weekend, my second-in-charge (2IC) was there, which was unusual, along with a lady who was doing some extra work for the facility. The lady took one look at me lying down and said very loudly and rudely, "NO, NO, NO, GET UP! YOU SHOULD NOT BE HERE!"

I was trying to explain, but she just talked over me, and I couldn't get a word in. By this time, my 2IC had come into the room and could see that I was unwell. "I'll start ringing around to get someone to cover for you—you look terrible." I went to grab my bag and keys when the lady said again, quite rudely, "And where do you think you're going?"

"Home, aren't I?" This woman was annoying the hell out of me.

"You can't drive home; I'll take you."

"OH GOD, NO!" I thought. I'll see if I can ring some friends, but she was SO insistent. I just wanted to lie down before I vomited everywhere as I could feel it coming on again. She did drive me home, and I could barely talk as I was trying not to be sick in her car. I could only imagine the reaction if I did. By the time I got home, I was nearly retching. I thanked her and went straight to bed. Within the next minute, I vomited everywhere. It didn't stop for nearly four days.

I couldn't eat; even trying to sip water made me vomit. Jenna went up to the local store and bought some flat lemonade, hoping that would help, but nothing did. Even slowly rolling over from side to side made me so dizzy that I would start vomiting. When I had to get up to go to the toilet, I nearly passed out. Jenna, by this stage, was frantic. "Mum, you haven't stopped vomiting for days. I think I need to ring Dad or an ambulance or something. I don't know what to do, but you're really scaring me. This should have stopped by now."

Being the stubborn nurse that I am (trust me, doctors and nurses make the worst patients), I kept telling her I would get better, that I had just caught a virus and it would be over soon. I didn't want anyone contacting John, as he was three hours' drive away and I knew he would just worry. I must have started going in and out of consciousness because I couldn't remember a lot. I vaguely recall seeing Liam come in with his face covered by a tea towel, as the smell of the vomit nearly made him sick. "Quick, Jenna, help me get Mum in the car. We're not going to wait for an ambulance—you're going to the hospital," I overheard John say.

"God, I feel like I'm dying," I muttered under my breath. Even the seatbelt was painful to have across me. We got to A&E, and there were so many people and screaming kids. I just wanted to lie down. I suddenly realised that John was home.

"Yes, Liam rang me, distressed about the state you were in. He told me that you were so ill and that you urgently needed to get to a hospital but kept refusing an ambulance as you didn't want to worry me. I told work there was a family emergency and drove straight here without stopping to get you there myself," John explained.

They took me into a room where I was triaged, had my observations recorded, and had a cannula inserted into my arm. I do remember moaning because I was in the most horrific pain when I overheard the doctor say, "Get her out of here. I can't do my job with all that moaning and groaning going on—it's driving me crazy."

I thought to myself what a bombastic prick of a man and a doctor he truly was.

I was trying to sign my name, but I was so sick I couldn't even do that and nearly collapsed on the floor in front of the emergency nurse. After many hours of waiting, I was finally put onto a bed, hooked up to machines, and given a Fentanyl injection, which I can only describe as heavenly. No more pain. Bloods were taken, and then I was wheeled into a room for a CT scan. "What am I being put in here for?" I thought as wardsmen lifted me on and off some sort of bed. It felt like I was floating. A female doctor came to tell me that my white cell count was off the charts and that I was one VERY sick lady who needed urgent surgery. What the...?

I began to argue, insisting they had the wrong blood results and the wrong patient. I heard John apologising, telling them that I was an RN. "Ah, well that explains it," I heard someone say. I was in and out of consciousness when a male doctor appeared in front of me, smiling down and telling me he would be performing the emergency surgery. "What? NO, NO, NO! I don't need surgery. You've got me mixed up with someone else."

"Come on now, Karen, what are the 5 Fs for gallbladder issues? You should know," he said. Slurring my words, I responded, "FAT... FAIR... over FORTY, FEMALE... and you forgot FABULOUS. You definitely forgot FABULOUS." I heard him laugh so hard, and he said, "Well, I've just worked nearly 16 hours straight, and I really needed that laugh, Karen."

"What, you're going to operate on me, and you haven't had a break for nearly 16 hours? NOOOOOOOOOOOO..."

NEAR DEATH...

> "GREATNESS LIVES ON THE EDGE OF DESTRUCTION AND THE REASON SOMEONE IS GREAT IS THEY SURVIVED DEATH."
> —WILL SMITH

I could feel hot bile running out of my mouth while my head felt like it was spinning a hundred miles an hour on a merry-go-round. I was just praying for it to stop. Every time I vomited, the horrific taste of that bile nearly made me pass out. "My wounds, please, just someone splint my wounds while I vomit; the pain is just horrendous. Why can't anyone help me? Oh god, what is happening to me."

Every time I vomited profusely, it felt like I was being stabbed repeatedly. Even to this day, I cannot listen to any news story about a stabbing, as I know what that pain must feel like. I remember thinking, "Well, if this is what I lived for, just let me die—I can't take this horrendous pain anymore."

After what seemed like an eternity, I saw a dark room. I heard the room fill up with urgency and cries of "Come on, guys, we're losing her!" I saw white light in my eyes, heard trolleys, running wheels, people moving around my bedside. I was thinking to myself, "My God, that woman next door to me must be REALLY, REALLY sick."

I was then suddenly aware that I could feel myself rising up out of my bed and looked down to see people all around a bed. It was like being in 3D, and everything was just swirling around me. There didn't seem to be a ceiling or walls, just a mass of different colours. I could see the lights right next to me and could hear the humming of the fluorescent lights.

There seemed to be such a sense of urgency around the bed, and I was aware of many voices all at once. I could see where they were all standing and had no desire to go back down. Suddenly, a tunnel appeared around me with all these beautiful colours, and I felt so at peace as I slowly moved through it. I felt so free—there was no pain. I felt my whole body becoming infused with the most overwhelming sensations of love, calmness, and euphoric bliss. It was like being embraced in the most incredible warmth. I didn't even think about all my loved ones I had left behind. I knew they would all be fine—I had no sense of loss leaving them at all.

The white light swirling around me suddenly widened to engulf my entire body, and I remember it being SO bright, yet it didn't hurt my eyes at all. I have never felt so much contentment, serenity, and just absolute pure love.

Within a few seconds, I found myself in a dark room, and my Dad was lying down. He then sat up, smiled, and said ever so casually, "Hello." The shock of seeing my Dad alive was just emotionally euphoric. "Oh my God, Dad, you're alive, and you look so well… and you look so… so… young. I need to let everybody know that you're ok; everyone thinks you've passed away. I need to let them know… OMG! I need to let Mum know."

With that, he walked out of the room onto a tarmac and climbed into a small plane. Dad was a pilot in real life, and I went to get on the plane with him, but the doors wouldn't open. The propeller started up, and I could feel the plane slowly starting to move.

Desperately, I began lunging at the door as the plane started to get faster and faster. I began banging frantically on the window—why wasn't Dad looking at me? Dad, can't you see me??? Can't you hear me??? Open up the damn door!

My heart was racing, and my legs were moving faster and faster. I could feel myself becoming more distressed. "Just open the door!" I was screaming. The plane was going so fast, and I was practically running now. I could feel my heart absolutely pounding in my chest, and I was banging frantically on the door with my fist. "DAD, DAD, PLEASE!" I was crying hysterically now... "OPEN UP THE DOOR!"

Suddenly, Dad stopped the plane and looked down at me. "I can't let you in."

"But why not?" I sobbed.

"Because it's not your time—you need to go back."

'Go back? Go back where?' I thought as he looked back down at the tarmac.

I looked down to see what he was looking at, but there was nothing there. When I turned back around, the plane was gone. I looked up into the sky and saw it flying off into the distance. There was the most dazzling display of a kaleidoscope of radiant, brilliant light and colours, accompanied by the most serene, peaceful feeling—pure exhilaration and calmness. I just knew I wanted to go with him. I felt so drawn to it, everything swirling around me in a sensation of profound peace. I felt complete euphoria—no stress, no anxiety, no fear, no pain, no sadness. Just overwhelming happiness. NOOOOOOOOOO! Come back, you can't leave me again!

Suddenly, I became aware of myself sobbing inconsolably. I remember feeling so angry with him, dropping to the ground and pounding my fists into the tarmac. "Karen, that wasn't you dropping on the ground—that was you dropping back into your body," a spiritual friend later told me. I had no memory of going back into my body. "If your Dad had opened that plane and taken you with him, trust me, you wouldn't be here today. Your Dad was protecting you. Your husband and your family need you more, and you have a story to tell the world. We are all eternal; death is nothing more than an illusion. Our true birthright is simply stepping through the veil between dimensions, which brings us the most incredible joy and peace," Elle told me.

The next few days in ICU were a blur. I was just SO sick—no energy, could barely walk—and the PAIN!!! OMG! The pain was crippling. I had an IV, drains, a catheter, wound dressings, nasal prongs delivering oxygen, and could feel the pressure of something wrapped around my legs that was pumping blood to prevent clots. Every few minutes, there was some sort of beeping noise—no time to sleep or rest. As I was coming around after my surgery, I had the sensation of someone kissing me constantly on the forehead. I couldn't move or talk. I thought it was John but later found out it was Liam, who had rushed to be with me when he heard I was having emergency surgery.

So many doctors and nurses, so many beeping machines—it never seemed to stop. I just wanted to go home and rest, never feeling so sleep-deprived in my life. Finally, I was given the all-clear to go home. The assistant surgeon came to see me and told me that my surgeon had persevered for over six hours to remove my perforated gallbladder and clean my abdomen as I was so septic. I was really lucky to still be here. During the operation, I also haemorrhaged and lost a lot of blood. They told John that if he hadn't gotten me to the hospital when he did, I wouldn't be here today. I was just so incredibly grateful that I survived.

John sat beside me day and night for eight hours a day and never left my side. He would get up early, get himself organised, and be there as soon as the ward opened at 8 am. He bathed me, helped feed me as I was so weak, dressed me, and eventually helped me walk as I got stronger. The nurses looking after me were doing such an exceptional job but were so busy and understaffed. John helped shower and dress me before all my wound dressings were attended to. He helped me with everything. Honestly, I don't know how I would have gotten through it all without him. It must have taken a big emotional and physical toll on him, but he never once complained and went out of his way to do everything he could for me.

John would get the nurses when my pain was excruciating so I could get relief. He was truly a Godsend. His love and support were unwavering. Visits from family, phone calls, text messages, flowers, physical therapy, and the nurses constantly checking on me and taking vital signs—so much happened in such a whirlwind that, to be honest, I didn't even know night from day.

I was so sick that the hospital only allowed immediate family. I thought I must have been hallucinating from all the anaesthesia I'd been given. I also knew that I had experienced something mind-blowing. I couldn't get out of my head what I had seen, and to be completely honest, my experience transformed me. I was no longer afraid of death. I did not fear it in any way. After what seemed like an eternity, I finally got the green light to go home. As we drove around the corner, I saw our house. "Ah, our home… my sanctuary," I thought as we pulled into the driveway. "It's so good to be home." I had no idea of the TRUE horror that was about to be unleashed in my life.

ABSOLUTE SHEER TERROR...

"SON, THE GREATEST TRICK THE DEVIL PULLED WAS CONVINCING THE WORLD THERE WAS ONLY ONE OF HIM." —DAVID WONG

Driving home and seeing our house felt so good. The roller doors went up, and in we went. John came around to help me out of the car, as I was still so weak and exhausted, and every step seemed to hurt. As he was helping me inside, I looked up at the carport walls and saw the ghastliest-looking hand prints. "OMG! What the heck is that??" I asked. I had never seen them before. "Oh, probably just kids," John replied. "Oh no, I thought we had moved those Aboriginal spirits on. Is it from them? How long have they been there? Did it happen the day of the smoking ceremony?" I asked with dread.

John was more interested in getting me inside. I was very unsettled by those marks and couldn't stop thinking of them, but yes, he was probably right. But what kids would have been in our carport? Eventually, due to tiredness, I drifted off to sleep. My friend Jenny had a daughter around Jenna's age and had offered to have Jenna stay with them for the next few days until I felt well enough to drive again. School was closer for them to walk to, and it would allow me to actually get some sleep and recover.

Since the air conditioners had all died on the night of my emergency surgery, the heat was just terrible. At least she would be in air-conditioned comfort over there until we could afford to get ours fixed. John helped me down to her room and said, "You pack a few overnight things because I don't really know what to pack for a 16-year-old girl." I laughed and began to open her drawers. "I'm just going out to the shed; take your time. You're still very weak and lethargic. If you need me, just yell out."

I had only just started to move around her clothes and open drawers when I felt something slither over one of my arms. I then saw the most dazzling rainbow colours, and it took me a few seconds for my brain to register what I was seeing. OMG, it's a snake! I got such a fright that I jumped back in shock, and right behind me was her chest of drawers. The corner hit me right in the spine, and I lunged back in absolute agony. With that, I burst one of my wounds open and could feel blood trickling from it. OH NO! I grabbed myself to try and stop the bleeding and began to call out to John, but I couldn't scream loud enough. Eventually, with my muffled cries of "Help, help… there's a snake," he came tearing back inside to find me upset, shaking, bleeding, and absolutely distraught about a snake with the most dazzling colours.

"Are you sure you saw this?" he asked. I think the terror on my face said it all. He helped me outside and put a towel down in front of the closed door. He rang wildlife rescue, who told us they would send someone over as soon as possible, and to keep the door closed and not go in there until they arrived. A knock on the door came quickly after, and we answered to find a little old lady who must have been over eighty. The net she was carrying was bigger than she was. John and I nearly had a coronary as we watched her get down on the floor, lift up sheets, and open drawers without any concern.

"If it had colours, it was probably just a python. Can't hurt you. Still, I can't use this other arm at the moment as I'm having an operation shortly for carpel tunnel, so I'm a bit disabled at present."

With those comments, we nearly fainted. After searching through nearly everything, she concluded that maybe I was seeing things, as the room had been torn apart when something moved behind the wardrobe. Sure enough, out came a spotted python. "Gotcha!" she exclaimed loudly.

"But that wasn't the snake I saw. My snake had colours—beautiful colours all over it."

"I'm sorry, love, snakes don't travel in pairs. This is the only snake in here."

I argued with her, telling her to please keep looking, as THAT was not the snake I saw. After ripping the room apart even further and showing me every hidey-hole in existence, I had to conclude that maybe, with all my surgery and sleep deprivation, I hadn't seen it after all. She had the snake and had got it out of our house—what a welcome home present that was for me. I collapsed on our bed in absolute exhaustion, in pain and bleeding heavily.

The next few days were a blur of visitors coming to see me—lots of phone calls, flowers, chocolates, lotto tickets, and crystals. I felt overwhelmed with love, knowing that so many people were thinking of me. My mother had been interstate when I went in for my emergency surgery and had now come to see me. I was sitting in the lounge when she arrived. I was still very weak, and my vision was not the best. She brought me some flowers and began to tell me about how Dad had come through a psychic medium when she was away visiting my sister Jane. I listened intently to what she was saying, trying to take it all in.

Mum told me that Dad had said my name and that I had been through some horrendous trauma. "Karen has a hell of a fight ahead of her. There are going to be some very difficult times ahead for her and all of her family. He knows what is happening to her, and he is protecting her," the medium told them. "He knows how hard things are going to be and will be helping Karen through it." At the time, I truly thought it was about my surgery and getting me well, as I had been so ill. I had no idea that he was talking about the malevolent spirit in our house that we were all completely unaware of.

Mum continued, explaining that my Nan sits in a chair in a big lounge area that isn't hers, but she has claimed it. There is a man who comes and sits beside her every day, holds her hand, and he is wearing an Akubra hat. He will be coming to take her back home soon. We all knew that was my grandfather, who had passed many years before. The medium also mentioned that my sister Jade has a little sausage dog and that when Dad comes to visit, the dog can see him and starts barking madly, going around and around in circles on their lounge chair. Dad often goes out riding with our brother Aaron on his motorbike.

Dad saw his own funeral and was absolutely overcome with emotion when he saw how much had been done in such a short amount of time and all the people who had come to show their respects. He just said it was incredible. We buried my Dad within 48 hours of his passing. He visits my sister Jane, who has squeaky floorboards, and often sits near their black stools while they are having tea. Dad thanked Mum for nursing him and knew it was hard for her, telling her how much he loved her. He watches Mum crocheting in her chair, sees her kiss his photo every night and day, and notices her lipstick marks on the glass frame. Dad went on trips with Mum and my sister Jane interstate. He loved sitting in the back seat with Mum and listening to the music she was listening to, and he watched her play solitaire on her iPad.

He started talking about happy hours on the road trip and loved doing different things than what they did. He wished Mum a happy anniversary, as he knew a special one was coming up—it would have been their 50th, but he had passed seven months prior. He leaves feathers and flickers lights to let us know he is around when he visits. He was with my mother and sister when they were discussing whether or not she was going to have another child, as he had overheard the conversation and told Jane that if she did, it would be a boy.

When Dad was passing, the washing machine and the microwave decided to go on the blink within days of each other. Mum ended up having to get both replaced when Dad was still in hospital. She would often say that Dad must have done this too. "Your husband often tells me that since he has passed, he overhears you telling family and friends how he blew up the washing machine and microwave on you. He just wants to let you know that he didn't do either of these things; it must have just been their time to go." Dad said he saw the tickets on the fridge where Jane had put them and knew they were going to be there that night to communicate with them both. These were just some of the messages the medium passed on to them from Dad.

Jane said she was spot on in every way, saying all of their names correctly without any hesitation. She even started talking about my paternal grandfather, who had come through and said his name too. She said that Dad and all of the family who had passed over in spirit were all sending their love, and the medium commented on what a big family we were. Jane told me that this lady is truly so gifted and amazing, and she was so glad that Dad had come through and made contact with them; she would never forget how it made them all feel. Jane said it definitely helped our mother too since making contact with Dad. It has given her life purpose again as she knows that Dad is with her through her new journey and that she will be okay. It was just so surreal to listen to this.

I contacted Taylor, who had moved down south with her husband because they couldn't find any long-term permanent work and were also experiencing a lot of bad luck. Taylor had gone to speak to an Aboriginal elder. "Mum, that snake was a warning. They pick the most vulnerable person in the house, and if the warning is not heeded, they will come back and take the next person permanently." Like, what the?? That is NOT what I wanted to hear. Suddenly, living here started to feel really frightening.

Prints that appeared in my carport after
I arrived home from the hospital.

FIRST EVER EXPERIENCE...

"YOU HAVE GOT TO BELIEVE IN YOURSELF, YOU HAVE GOT TO BELIEVE IN GOD. IT DOESN'T MATTER WHAT YOU FACE, YOU KNOW THAT YOU'RE GOING TO WIN AT THE END OF THE DAY. KNOW THAT HE IS GOING TO GET YOU THROUGH IT." —KELLY ROWLAND

We were so grateful when the people who came to fix our main aircon told us that it only needed to be gassed, and it cost us just $700. It was such a relief, as it was just SO blistering hot. The day John was to go back to work for the first time, he had arranged for a friend to come over and spend a few hours with me, as I was still very unsteady on my feet and my vision was not good. Jenny came and sat with me, and we talked for ages. I got up to make us coffee, but she said she would do everything for me. I was determined to do it, as they said the more I walked, the more I would get better. I noticed that when she was talking to me, she would always look over my shoulder, as if she were looking at something in the distance. Eventually, I asked her what she was looking at.

"Karen, I'm not really sure I should tell you this, but I think I need to. There is a big, black, dark shadow behind you, and it is following you everywhere you go. I think there is something in this house with you."

"ARRGGGHHHHH! WHAT THE!!!!!! That's a bit unsettling. Are you serious?? OMG!!! That is really VERY distressing."

"Please protect yourself, Karen. I am feeling really frightened for you."

I sat there in absolute shock at what I had just been told, trying to look behind me. She then went to the toilet, and when she came out, she asked me if I heard that music.

"NO, what music?"

"Like in a jewellery box. I could hear it being wound up, and then I heard a few chimes. Did you honestly not hear that?" she asked me.

We went around to all the windows and listened, but there was nothing. Wow, that's a bit strange. To this day, I have never heard it.

The next morning, after yet another brutal nightmare of being stabbed in the ribs with a large hunting knife, I began seeing more marks in the carport. They hadn't been there yesterday. More were appearing, and I knew it wasn't kids, as the roller doors were down most of the time. Surely no kids are coming in here and doing this—and why would they? I went to turn on the air-conditioning, and nothing. What the? We had just paid hundreds of dollars, and we only got one day of it working. I rang back, only to be told that they were booked up for weeks and couldn't give me a definite day for them to come back. I was livid; I was trying to recover, and the heat inside the house was stifling. In desperation, I rang another company and must have sounded so distressed.

A technician came over a few days later. He explained there was a leak somewhere in our system, and instead of the other company finding it, they had just re-gassed it. I showed him the receipt, and he just shook his head.

"This is just terrible. They should be hung out to dry and quartered for what they have done to you. Not only did they not find and fix the leak, but they also re-gassed it with the most expensive gas on the market. This is just ludicrous."

I wanted to cry. Why were all these terrible things constantly happening to us? What a waste of nearly $700—it was all for nothing, and it was money we really needed to pay other bills and try to survive. I wasn't working and didn't know when I would be able to work again. After he left, I sat there and cried for hours.

The next day, John took me for a drive to the beach to see a bit of nature and let the ocean water run over my feet. I was still very weak and could not walk properly. I had to hold onto him the entire time as I was so dizzy. We only took a few steps, as I was not up for walking long distances, when a white feather suddenly appeared at my feet.

"Oh, that is beautiful," I said as he bent down to pick it up for me. My mum rang at that exact moment and asked what I was doing.

"I am at the beach," I replied. I told her about my white feather.

"That is in your path for a reason. Probably Dad looking after you. Pick it up and take it home; they are messages for you."

That afternoon, I couldn't stop feeling dizzy. My head was swirling like I was on a merry-go-round going a million miles an hour. Oh no, I must have pushed myself too much today. The next thing I knew, I was vomiting profusely and just couldn't stop. John came in, so worried, and said, "I'm not taking any more chances with you. I'm ringing an ambulance."

"No, no," I pleaded, "I only just got out of hospital. I don't want to go back."

"I nearly lost you once, Karen. I'm NOT risking this again. This is not right; you've only had a bit of soup."

I was trying to talk, but the vomiting was abhorrent. "Oh, what was happening to me?" The ambulance turned up, put me on a stretcher, and loaded me into the back. I cannot begin to explain how dreadful it is to be in motion in the back of an ambulance when you are profusely vomiting.

It felt like the driver went over every pothole from my house to the hospital—it was just horrific. John was following behind in our car. By the time I got to the hospital, there were no beds for me to lie down on. They put me out in A&E in a wheelchair, gave me a bag to vomit in, and told me to put my head against the beam supporting the above floor while I vomited profusely in front of everyone waiting to be seen. John was still trying to park the car. The ambulance officer bent down in my ear, in between my extreme nausea and vomiting, and whispered, "For God's sake, wake up to yourself. You know how this works. Stop carrying on with all your crap. Talk about an attention seeker… you're an RN; start acting like it," and walked off.

I was just in shock that he said that to me, but because my vision was so distorted, I couldn't make out who he was, though I knew his voice. I spent the night in the EDSU, hooked up once again to machines and being monitored 24/7. I never got an ounce of sleep as there was so much noise and other people being brought into A&E. The IV was going again; please, no catheter this time. PLEASE PLEASE PLEASE!!! My arms were so bruised from the number of IVs that had tissued from all the IV antibiotics I had. My veins had collapsed multiple times. Sometimes it would take over eight attempts before they were finally able to get a cannula in, and it was excruciatingly painful. It looked like I was a drug addict if you didn't know me. My face was gaunt, my skin and hair looked terrible, and I had big black circles around my eyes from the extreme sleep deprivation.

The doctor who had seen me in A&E originally came in that morning to see me again. "You look familiar to me."

"Yes, I'm the one you told the nurses to get out of triage because I was moaning in agony from the excruciating pain I was in. You were complaining that listening to me apparently 'carrying on' was disturbing you and you couldn't do your job properly. I was rushed for emergency surgery."

He had a female beside him. I just looked at him with contempt. I could tell he was very taken aback.

"Oh, I'm sorry to hear that," he stammered back.

'Yeah right, I'm sure you are,' I thought as I just stared at him.

"Well, we are sending you for some more tests. The physio will be here later this morning to see you," and then he promptly left. Later, Mum came to visit, along with John, before he left for work. They put some big goggles on me, and I had to watch certain things on the screen while they recorded my eye movements. They did a lot of other tests, and I had horrific nausea throughout. I had to stop multiple times as I knew I was going to be sick.

They told me that normally, when people experience this sort of vertigo, the crystals in the inner ear are not aligned, and they can fix it. But in my case, my crystals were in perfect alignment. They were baffled as to what was causing this, as every time I would stand up to walk, I would go sideways to my right and crash into the wall, and my vision was terribly distorted. They said they would do more tests and get back to me. Eventually, after more investigations, they discovered that I had right-sided vestibular damage from the amount of gentamicin and other antibiotics I had to save my life. I was diagnosed with severe gentamicin ototoxicity. I suffered from extreme vertigo, dizziness, and profuse vomiting, and I was deteriorating badly to the point where I couldn't even stand up.

"Well, how do I fix it?" I asked in disbelief. 'This can't be right; you must have the wrong patient,' I was thinking.

They got me to put on goggles and recorded my movements. "This is someone with normal vestibular function, and this is someone with damaged function," said the physio. They then showed me mine, and I realised that it matched exactly.

"Well, how do I fix it and make it all come back to proper functioning?" I asked.

"Karen, you can't fix it. You may never walk again, drive again… or even work again. You will need intensive rehabilitation to get through this, and then we will have to review. We are going to look at sending you to a vestibular specialist down south who will put you through more extensive testing, and then we will be able to see where we are at. I am sorry; there is nothing more we can do for you. You may have to look at going on a permanent disability pension. We are truly so very sorry."

After they left, I think I just stared at the wall in the hospital in absolute disbelief. This nightmare just won't seem to end… I want to wake up. My heart was beating so fast… this is not happening, and the tears just began to flow again. Why is this happening to us… I cried myself to sleep that night. Why didn't you just let me get on the plane, Dad… why is this happening to me… why, why, why?????

I rang John with the news and told him that they were looking to transfer me down south for more extensive tests.

"For how long?" he asked.

I did not know; I was still in shock. "I will ask Mum if she can come with me, as I know you have already lost so much pay being a contractor with all that time off that you spent up with me in ICU and EDSU."

When he came to visit me in the hospital that afternoon, he looked absolutely broken. Someone had overheard his conversation with me and that I was being sent for tests down south at another major hospital. They went to management and told them, who then thought that he was going to be away for more extended time. The manager then called him into his office, said that there was no more work available and not to come back on Monday. As if we weren't already down and out on our luck—no air conditioning in this stifling heat. I was off sick with barely any sick leave to cover. Bills were once again piling up around us, and now my husband had lost his job on top of it. How on earth were we going to get through this? I think I cried again for hours. I was starting to wonder why I had honestly survived.

Road to Recovery...

"I GIVE ALL THE GLORY TO GOD. IT'S KIND OF A WIN-WIN SITUATION. THE GLORY GOES UP TO HIM AND THE BLESSINGS ALL FALL DOWN ON ME." —GABBY DOUGLAS

The next few days were a blur. I do remember the Specialist telling me that when things become overwhelming "just remember Karen that you are still alive." John was now out of work, and he was determined to get me better. He arranged for me to have Bowen therapy with my aunty, colonics with my manager, massages, and intensive rehabilitation with the physios. He bought so much healthy food and organised for me to have forensic healings with Anne. He drove me around, taking me for very slow walks down the beach and to the gardens. I remember that during colonics, I was so sick I couldn't even lie down on the table without help.

My manager, Kate, gave me a variety of products and did a few treatments all for free, as she knew we had no money. I was incredibly grateful to her, as I truly believe that this removed a lot of terrible toxins from my body, which dramatically aided in my recovery. The first time I went to see Anne, I had no idea what a forensic healing was. John drove me there, and Anne was waiting at her front door for us. She had some lovely meditation music playing in the background. She gave me a big hug and took me into her treatment room.

There was a massage table in the middle of the room, and all around it were angels, crystals, candles, Buddhas, spiritual pictures, and sayings. It felt very calm and peaceful. I was still not walking properly, and John had to help me lie down on the table. Anne went around and lit a lot of candles and then saged the room before she commenced. I had to hold her hand while she said certain things, and I could feel her fall back to a corresponding number. This number then had a message for me. Anne was like a conduit to the angelic realms. I do remember that at the end of my sessions, her arm would swing back and forth really fast.

"Wow, I wonder what that is all about," I said out loud.

"Karen, this isn't me; this is you," she replied.

"Oh wow, okay," I said.

"Yeah, you are REALLY wanting your power back," Anne told me.

A few times during my sessions, I remember she would nearly hit the cabinet behind her as she seemed to almost fall backwards with a lot of force. "Oh, I am so sorry," my arm would swing that forcibly, and I didn't seem to have any control over it.

"That is okay; that is your higher self coming through. You are definitely wanting to get your power back." It was all such an incredible experience. After my very first healing, I suddenly had the urge to go to a church. So many weekends working, I never got the chance to get there, and on the odd occasion that I did, I would always feel unwell not long after arriving and want to leave, without really knowing why.

When we arrived, I put the holy water on me as we entered, and immediately, I felt ill. The nausea was terrible, and my head began to swirl. I could actually taste vomit in the back of my mouth. I was terrified that I was going to be sick in the church, and people would be arriving soon for the Sunday night mass.

"Quick, I need to get out of here," I told John.

"But we have not long got here," he said, confused.

"I know, but I can't be in here; it is making me sick."

I had seen so many movies over the years of people between two parallel bars learning how to walk again. Never in a million years did I ever think this was going to be a part of my reality and recovery. Now, I was here too, holding on to both bars, trying to learn how to walk without going sideways. I had so many other activities to do, and some days, I would push myself so hard trying to recover that I would vomit for hours afterwards. I had to get back to work, or we were going to lose our home. After everything that John and I had already been through, I was just not going to let our home be ripped away from us. We had worked too damn hard for so many damn years to keep this roof over our heads. I was JUST not going to let that bastard bank do this to us.

My vestibular specialist was gobsmacked at how well I was recovering and asked what I was doing. He called me his "Miracle Girl," and I was determined to overcome this terrible predicament. He had never seen so much recovery in a person with so much damage. My workmates were amazing—they turned up at my house with so many gifts, money, flowers, gift vouchers for food, Christmas hams, Christmas cakes, and a beautiful card with all these lovely messages written in it. This is how we actually survived. If it wasn't for them, I don't know how we would have got on. I sent a private message back to work, telling them all how blown away I was by their overwhelming generosity in helping me and my family.

I shared that I had been having intensive rehabilitation and that I knew, with everyone's love, support, gifts, money, food vouchers, flowers, visits, gift cards, Christmas gifts, beautiful messages, cards, texts, phone calls, thoughts, prayers, and healings, that all of this had definitely got me through so much. It literally brought tears to my eyes at how caring, loving, kind, and thoughtful everyone had been. I felt so incredibly blessed; they were all JUST amazing. Thank you… thank you… thank you… all so much xxx. I was just overwhelmed that my workmates cared so much for me and felt so blessed in so many ways. The day I finally walked back into my workplace felt surreal. The love, support, and hugs that I received felt so incredibly humbling.

UNFATHOMABLE FEAR...

"I AM NOT AFRAID OF THE DARKNESS OR THE NIGHT. I AM AFRAID OF THE SILENCE WHERE THERE IS NOTHING TO HIDE ME FROM MY OWN TERRIFYING THOUGHTS." —ANONYMOUS

I bought three black obsidian bracelets—one for John, Jenna, and myself—and was told not to get them wet and to always wear them. John was at work, having picked up some casual shifts, and Jenna was on a sleepover. The markings around the house were starting to increase. The growling in my toilet was getting louder, and the night before, while I was in the kitchen washing up, I saw a large, tall black shadow moving from the hallway to the toilet.

"What on earth are you wearing?" I said to Jenna. It looked like she had multiple layers of clothing on—or at least that's what my mind thought. Suddenly, I remembered that she wasn't even in the house. My heart began to beat rapidly, and I could feel terror welling up inside me. I saw it move slowly across the hallway, and at that VERY moment, I knew I was really in trouble and needed urgent help.

I had only just started driving again. This is all just a bad dream. There's got to be an explanation for what is happening. I found the brochure I was first given months ago and texted the lady whose number was on the back. She gridded land; she would definitely be able to help me. She told me her meditation class started at 7 pm and to just bring a water bottle and an open mind. I went to grab my car keys but couldn't find them anywhere. I always left them in the same place, but for some reason, they weren't there. I desperately began to search through my house, tearing things apart. I need to go tonight. No one is home… it HAS to be tonight. Just when I was about to give up, they appeared. I grabbed them and raced to my car. Then I couldn't get the roller door to go up.

"OH, YOU HAVE GOT TO BE KIDDING ME! WHAT NOW?!" I screamed in frustration. I went to the locking mechanism and kept pressing the handle, but nothing would work. Over and over, I tried. Finally, I let out a massive scream of frustration, and with one more push, I got the door to open.

I started the car, and on the way, I hit EVERY red light. "NO, NO, NO," I was thinking, "I am going to be so late. I can't walk in there; what will they think? I'm so late… I can't do this… just turn around and go home. This is just crazy. What is happening to me?" All these erratic thoughts were going through my mind. I finally saw the shop and ran to the front door. I was already 20 minutes late, and the shop was all locked up. I knocked a few times and realised that the group would have been out the back. I'm too late. I began to walk back to the car; by now, it was pitch black when I heard a voice call out, "Karen, is that you?"

Cyndi had been waiting for me and was about to start the meditation session. "I have been waiting for you."

"Thank you," I said, looking very dishevelled. "What a journey it has been to get here tonight."

"Come out the back and meet the other people in this group," said Cyndi. I was so dizzy from trying to get there on time and was feeling so stressed when I walked in. There was a small group of men and women all sitting around in a circle. We passed around a large pack of cards and had to draw one card. When it got to me, I pulled a card that I couldn't see clearly... SECURITY, the ability to feel secure in one's life and in one's home. I was just gobsmacked. OMG!!! That is incredible.

When it was my turn, I was asked for my name and why I was there. "My name is Karen," I stammered, "... I have security." I could see everyone looking at me, and I felt my heart beating wildly. What was I going to say? Just say the truth. You don't know these people. You probably won't ever see them again. "I think I have something in my house. I was given your number, Cyndi, for you to help me, so... here I am."

I honestly thought everyone was going to burst out laughing, but instead, another young girl in the group said, "Yes, so do I. I am a beautician and have clients in my house every day. There is definitely something in my house too." Suddenly, I didn't feel so out of my depth. Someone else was going through exactly the same thing—or so I thought. We went on to do a meditation, and after the session was over, I went out to an area where you can have a cup of tea and talk with other people. I could hear another woman talking about seeing something jumping out of her bathtub, and with that, I bolted. "This honestly can't be happening; gosh, these people are all crazy. Never heard so much rot in all my life," I thought. But then I was there too.

That same night, Cyndi rang me to tell me to put salt down all of my drains, and I endured the most terrifying and harrowing night of my life. I have NEVER known that amount of sheer, pure terror in ALL my life. Cyndi came around at 11 o'clock the next morning and asked me for a ceramic bowl—it could not be plastic. I was trying to stay focused, as I had literally been up most of the night, but I did not want her to know how terrified I was truly feeling. With that, she got pink Himalayan rock salt and poured a small amount of oil onto it. "This oil is pure Egyptian oil... you need to mix this through; you only need a few drops... and this needs to be put down the pipes and drains. Don't EVER use normal table salt; it has to be either rock salt or Himalayan salt. Keep the lids down; the drains need to be covered at all times. I'm looking at you and can see that you are completely broken. Mentally, physically, emotionally, financially, the only thing that I can see that is still in complete alignment is your spirituality."

She walked around my entire house and seemed to spend a lot of time in Jenna's room. Due to all of our financial issues, we had decided to sell, as we couldn't see how we were going to be able to keep the wolves from the door—they were circling and getting closer and closer.

I had started packing up the house and putting a lot of our items into cardboard boxes and had placed them in one of the rooms. "While IT is still here, this house will never sell," she told me. "You need to get rid of this energy if you want to leave. Who knows maybe after this is all over with, you and your hubby will decide to stay?"

"Where will this energy go?" I asked.

"Say sorry to your neighbours," she told me.

"Oh, what? I don't want this going there; I need to tell them," I said, mortified.

"NO, you never can. No one will believe you anyway; they will honestly think that you are mad, Karen."

Cyndi kept looking out the window towards the shed in the rear left of our backyard... "IT'S out here. I can feel it... where are your sewerage pipes?"

"Ahhhhh, I have no idea," I told her.

She also screwed up her face a few times.

"Is everything okay?" I asked, concerned.

"I can just smell vomit. IT has been vomiting all over you, your family, this land, and this house for such a LONG time. It is just nauseating to me. Horrific smell."

"Oh no, how many others could smell this too?" I wondered. Just great! She also gave me two crystal geodes that were to be placed in my two toilets and placed other items throughout my house. Cyndi also put a heap of crystals I had never seen before on a coffee table with a triangle-type piece of wood and asked me if I had any pictures of my Dad. On one of the crystals, she placed a necklace with the evil eye amulet on it. I had been given a photo last Christmas of Dad and our family priest, who had been a large part of our lives. I put the framed photo of them both on the table as well.

"When you are feeling overwhelmed, just come over here and sit and talk to your Dad; he will help you," Cyndi told me.

After Cyndi had walked around slowly, both inside and outside my home, she came back and told me that I had three dark entities here. She mentioned that she thought I had a shape-shifter, which was very dangerous and vile too.

"WHAT THE... THREE? AND A SHAPE-SHIFTER? LIKE, WHAT THE HELL IS THAT?" I think I nearly screamed in fright at her. She told me that she must get access to certain crystals as they are very powerful. She said I had to get Jenna out of that room and shift her into another bedroom. She also instructed me to use that concoction she made with salt and oils and put it down all the toilets and drains every single morning and night, and that all the toilet lids were to be kept down. All the drains had to be covered up, but not with plastic—it had to be glass or ceramic.

She told me that she believed nothing Aboriginal was here anymore and that the smoking ceremony would have cleared and moved them on. She said that these terrible dark entities were always here and were attached to this land. There can be entities that are very sinister and live in the lower astral realms. Sometimes, they have been referred to as "the hells." They are not like what you see on TV with images of hell with fires and burning lakes, but they are filled with some of the most disgusting filth and dregs of humanity. They could have indulged in the most incomprehensible of immoral activities like paedophilia, murder, rape, robbery, etc., and have suffered from severe alcoholism and drug addiction, which caused them to do horrific things.

John was still struggling to come to terms with all of this. I think if she had told us that it was definitely Aboriginal, he would have believed her more. He was just struggling beyond comprehension with it all, and to be honest, so was I. It was suddenly UNFATHOMABLE! She said that neighbours would not believe us, and we had endured enough over the past 15 years, with these entities relentlessly taking their wrath out on my entire family. We needed to start thinking of ourselves for a change. There was now a very unpleasant smell coming from our toilet, and there was a big crystal geode facing our toilet. "I hope that smell doesn't get any worse," I was thinking. I asked John if he could smell it, but he could not smell a thing. That was most probably a blessing for him, as it was nearly making me sick. Hopefully, fingers crossed, whatever she has done is working. Cyndi told me I have to keep my protection up around myself at all times, as I am the main target since I am the one trying to get rid of them. Jenna has not been sleeping well for a long time, and now she is barely sleeping at all, which was understandable. When Cyndi walked into her room, she said out loud, "OH MY GOD, this is VERY powerful."

Crystals placed in my house by Cyndi,
who did a house clearing and gridded my land.

INFESTATION AND OPPRESSION...

"SOMETIMES I FEEL I AM REALLY BLESSED TO BE BLIND BECAUSE I PROBABLY WOULD NOT LAST A MINUTE IF I WERE ABLE TO SEE THINGS." —STEVIE WONDER

"This thing is the King Scumbag of ALL scumbags!" Cyndi told me. "We will organise to do an extraction."

"A what?" I asked, completely perplexed.

"It is attached to the land. Once this is done, everything will be fine. It has oppressed you for so long like a moth to a flame. Have you felt anything happening to you?" asked Cindy.

"Sometimes I feel the mattress beside me go down, and I think John is there as I can feel movement. When I turn on the lamp no one is ever there. I have walked out, and he is sitting in the lounge chair, and I have asked why he didn't answer me, to which he replies, 'I haven't been in there. Think you are more tired than you even realise,' he says to me."

Cyndi then asked, "Has it pinned you down in the bed yet?"

I was absolutely terrified when she asked me. I think my eyes nearly popped out of my head. "No... I have never had that happen to me," I said, my voice shaking. I sent Jenna out to stay with Mum for a few days until the extraction was going to be done. I heard sneering right next to my right ear after I got John off to work the next day, and it was really frightening.

"Just keep doing what I told you, and we will do the extraction soon," Cyndi reassured me. I took her out to John's back shed, and there was the most revolting smell coming from it. Inside, the roller doors were covered with prints made in the dust.

"Oh no, I think you might have another shape-shifter as well. We need three people, as it will take the trinity to eliminate it. Your husband needs to be a part of this, and we need to explain to Jenna that this energy is NOT Aboriginal. Not sure that she doesn't have empathy for it."

What the?? Now Cyndi didn't think it was Aboriginal. It was just too much for me to comprehend. What the HELL was this, then, and why was this happening in OUR house? John had the major manager coming in a couple of days, and there was no way he would be able to get time off. When he got home that afternoon, I asked him where the sewerage pipes were.

"Out behind the shed in the back left of our yard. Why do you want to know that for?"

I think every hair on my body stiffened when he told me.

I had been feeling so out of sorts that John rang Anne, concerned for me. Anne did a healing on me and was shaking after what came through. Now she is ill with shingles, and these appeared in my carport in the last few days. Ahhhhh, am I EVER going to get any peace? Maddie had a frightening experience too. She was driving her car not far from my house when, out of nowhere, she said a crazy man stood in front of her car, waving his arms around frantically. She had to slam on the brakes. He then began pounding on her bonnet and was swearing at her to give him her car. He opened her passenger door and was about to climb inside. She was so frightened that she slammed her foot on the accelerator, throwing him off balance. She was so shaken up that she stopped at the servo and got them to ring the police. Maddie had to make a statement, but she didn't press charges. It really shook her up badly; she had never experienced anything like that before. It just terrified her.

I told Joy about it, and Joy was frantic with me. "GET OUT OF THAT HOUSE... DON'T F**K AROUND... REALLY, DON'T PAINT... MOVE!!!!! I HAVE ALREADY TOLD YOU THAT ONCE BEFORE. Get those Aboriginal boys back, mate, ASAP. It is their spirits/people. Or move out. You can't stay there anymore. It will just get worse. Please get the f**k out of there. People forget that this land was inhabited by a nomadic race whose culture was suited to this harsh landscape and have disrespected them from the get-go. Unfortunately, you and, no doubt, others around you are feeling the wrath of the restless, if not angry, spirits because of the atrocities dealt to them long ago and the cheek of our society to build houses on top of them unbeknownst to you—a clash of the living and the dead. Unfortunate but so true, as you've discovered belatedly. Moving is your only option now. This thing is not attached to the house; it is attached to the land. And because you are so open and gentle, that is why it is JUST SLAMMING YOU!!!!!"

I could hear my dogs outside digging again at the drain next to my toilet. They had been doing this for so long, and now I finally realised why. For many years, I always had this sensation that I was being watched and could never really put my finger on it. When I would spend most nights awake, it felt like I was being brushed or touched, or my hair was being pulled, but I just thought that due to severe sleep deprivation, I was imagining so much of it.

"Oh, mate, maybe this is a blessing in disguise to get you off that land. Well, really, if he hadn't dug around in your abdomen to retrieve that toxic gallbladder that had perforated and basically bleached your organs with Genta, we wouldn't be having this conversation. You and hubby are both fighting off negative energy. Please get the HELL off that land," Joy said in exasperation.

OUR NEVER-ENDING NIGHTMARE...

"HELL IS EMPTY AND ALL THE DEVILS ARE HERE." —WILLIAM SHAKESPEARE

My brother Aaron thought it was all a bit of joke originally and sent me a video to watch. It was by a lady who delved into this world and described about stage one as Infestation--how these negative energies can come into our lives in many ways. Through satanic rituals, wicca, witchcraft, Ouija boards, even just asking for proof that they exist. I have never done ANY of that, so how was this relevant? She then went on to explain that they can also be attached to houses and even to the land that you are on.

Stage two is called Oppression, where they pick the person of least resistance. They can also pick more than one person. That the person or persons can experience bangs, knocks on their house, scratches, sometimes in threes, as this is mocking the trinity of the Father, the Son, and the Holy Spirit. You can hear voices, growling, objects moving, get sudden cold chills, have electronics break, smell rotting eggs, and have terrible nightmares. They want to make the victim feel that they have no way out of their hell. They want to cause sheer terror; they know everything about you, and they will focus on what scares the hell out of you. They focus on the power of your fear.

Usually, it is through your dreams, so people can start having the most terrifying nightmares and wake up in a cold sweat, screaming and not actually knowing why. This is another way that they target you. Well, no wonder all I ever dream about is drowning, spiders, and snakes. I am absolutely petrified of all of them. Millions of people all over the globe become victims of dark entities simply because they are unaware of the warning signs. They are real; they exist; they are not imaginary. They can come in many forms; they have their own agendas; they know who they want to attack. So many of these people are told that they are crazy and that they are going mad, but they are not. These entities are vile, disgusting, cunning, and have no empathy for humankind. No words can simply express just how ugly, menacing, evil, manipulating, and grotesque these entities are.

They drain you of your power, energy, and life force, weakening you in every way possible. A constant lack of energy is often an indication that you have a spirit attachment. They draw so much energy from us so powerfully without our awareness that we lose the desire to do anything. Even one attached spirit is a heavy burden on our energy system. When there is more than one, we can become so utterly exhausted that we cannot even make ourselves a cup of coffee in the morning, let alone get out of bed. They can target people of strong faith, those who are close to God, close to love, close to heaven. They want to destroy their faith, break them, and turn them away from God. You must ensure your own safety if you feel a presence in your home or work environment.

The moment the entity knows that you are aware of IT is when the true impact will hit you, and the terror may escalate. But do NOT stop. Do not show any fear in your voice. Remember, this is your home, your environment; they do not belong there. Sage, Dragon's Blood, and Frankincense are very powerful—burn them around your home. Say, "Only love, light, and positivity may reside here. All negative entities must leave the premises now in the name of God and love." Stand your ground. Call on the higher realms to assist you, call on your spirit guides, angels, guardian angels. Sprinkle holy water over yourself and your house. Confirm this in the name of love. Sprinkle rock salt around your entire home—your windows, your doorways—to create a barrier of safety. Say out loud, "Only love may cross this barrier." Healing and protection practices must become routine. Believing that you have conquered your demons and are strong enough to ward them off is a HUGE mistake. Entities will make your home life miserable.

They will invade your relationships with your children and your spouse to break bonds. They will cause arguments, fighting, and communication breakdowns between parents and children, between husbands and wives, between different family members and friends. They will cause whatever devastation they can. They are also responsible for electrical problems, plumbing issues, large appliances breaking down, and declining health for you and your family members. The list can go on and on. They can cause severe mood swings, poor memory, unexplained fears or phobias, disturbing nightmares, sudden onset of physical problems, especially around the neck and back, sudden onset of panic or depression, anxiety, inability to focus, hearing voices, and problems with addictions. Unexplained outbursts of anger, emotion, and sadness, impulsive behaviour, confusion—your pets may suddenly shy away from you, growl, or become wary of you.

Most activity is around 3 am as this is when the highest velocity of psychic energy is in the universe. They will make their victims feel that they have no way out of their living hell and make them feel trapped in their existence. They have no empathy for humankind. They are deceiving and cunning and have strong abilities. They can make things appear and disappear and also move around a room. You could also have the feeling of being pushed and shoved. Some have even been pulled out of their beds. They want to break their victim's spirit and faith and make them feel abandoned by God. Some signs that they are attacking you can be a sudden onset of depression, thoughts of self-harm or harm to others, and becoming argumentative towards family, friends, or work colleagues. When they are psychologically attacking you, it can feel as if a dark cloud has literally wrapped around you like a wet blanket, and you just cannot get it off, no matter how hard you try. Some people even talk about constantly feeling watched by something they cannot see.

They will continue to exist as long as humanity sustains them with collective ignorance and uncontrolled negative thoughtlessness and energy. If you are fighting with negative spirits, they will find ways to attack you even more, and you will lose EVERY time. The entities that have spent a long time here within this earthly plane have lost all morality and sense of humanity and could be labelled as demonic or even evil. They move from host to host, leaving a trail of emotionally traumatised and used-up bodies and people in their wake.

Apparently, the most common place to pick up a parasitic entity is in a nursing home or a hospital. This is because it is where people have died, and also because these buildings are full of weakened immune systems. Someone with a healthy immune system can fight off a mild parasitic attack, but someone under anaesthetic or distracted by trauma is like having a house unlocked while thieves roam freely. A combo entity—not an actual conscious being—can be implicated when someone has a troublesome spirit attached to them. This entity can give them a very rough time with their physical body, including movements and functions, often causing serious health issues or even early death. These entities can cause diseases, illnesses, bad luck, bite marks, scratches, and can cause people so much depression that they take their own lives. Three scratches and three knocks mock the Holy Trinity. Call on the Almighty and say the Lord's Prayer three times, followed by three

"Amens" at the end of the prayer. Keep protection around you and your family at all times, and never EVER give up.

I pressed stop. I just could not watch anymore; it was just too much to deal with. I shut my phone off; it was just TOO disturbing. For the next few days, I had the sensation of doors slamming and sending me backwards. I would stand in front of the mirror and could see my hair being lifted up right in front of me like it was being played with. I would go to put on pieces of clothing or use my toothbrush, and I could actually smell vomit. Other times, my computer would turn on by itself, or after I had turned off my tap, it would turn back on again. Another time, I was walking into my bedroom, and I felt like I was being shoved in the back. I turned around, but nothing was there. Every time I walked into my ensuite, my exhaust fan above the toilet would just go ballistic, even when there was no wind outside.

Personally, I like to think of these demonic and negative forces that are at work in the world not as the Devil, Satan, or Lucifer, but as Hatred, Deceit, Corruption, Jealousy, Fear, Wrath, Sloth, Envy, Vengeance, Lust, Pride, Vanity, Greed, Gluttony, Violence—to name but a few. These are all monsters of which we, the human race, have created for ourselves.

I personally believe by using energies like love and light, we can transform our world. There will always be a perpetual war between the powers of dark and the light. Every time evil is committed by a soul, it helps to strengthen the dark side. Every time good acts are done, so much light is brought into our world. Negative dark energies will try to put temptation in our path to allow evil to flourish around us and sometimes within us. The purpose of pure divine energy is to guide us towards and see the pure light of God. I believe people cannot fight darkness with darkness; only pure divine light can overcome darkness.

TAKING BACK MY POWER...

"HISTORY HAS SHOWN US THAT COURAGE CAN BE CONTAGIOUS AND HOPE CAN TAKE ON A LIFE OF ITS OWN." —MICHELLE OBAMA

I was standing in the kitchen washing dishes when I heard a bang. I looked around and saw that the necklace with the evil eye amulet had been thrown off across the room in front of me. I think my heart was beating that fast that I nearly had a heart attack. I slowly went over, picked it up, and placed it gently back on the crystal. "Oh God, I need to get out of here!" I cried out loud. I went for a drive to clear my head. Only a couple more days and this will be all over, I was thinking to myself. What the heck was I going to do?

"Is there anyone else you can think of, someone who can deal with this, and someone you can TRUST that will keep your story private and help with this extraction?" asked Cyndi.

My friend Joy was the one who originally got me thinking that something was wrong. I rang her and asked what she was doing at 10 am Thursday morning. "Would you like to come over for a coffee and help me with an extraction to get some dark malevolent entities out of my house?" I laughed, as if I didn't laugh, I would have cried.

"Yeah right, what are you going on about?" said Joy.

"No, I'm serious. This is actually happening." I texted her the photos of what had been put in my house by Cyndi.

"Holy shit! This is really going down. OMG, of course I will, see you Thursday."

I made sure Jenna was out of the house at school and John was at work. That morning, Cyndi texted me: "What time is Joy arriving? Open your Bible to Psalm 23 and read it softly but using your voice. Say it three times—the King James Version. Joy needs to also. See you in a couple of hours. Not sure if you are feeling anything, but if you are, put your rosary on. Oh yes, we are VERY active. Been at me since 0600. DICK. Big mistake to that energy. Do not challenge me. Ask Joy to bring any Pounamu she may have. I already have my warriors in place. She may recognise a couple. See you soon. I may be early as I am already pacing. And ask Joy to bring her warriors. See you soon."

Anne texted me as she knew the extraction was happening that morning. "Stay in your power, blessings and strength to you all. May the angels cover you all and surround you with their beautiful wings of protection."

I was trying to find the King James Version, and suddenly my phone would not connect to Google. What the!!! Oh no, I can't find it, I have to say it. Oh gosh, NO, NO, NO! Anne kept me sane and texted me through the verses. "Here it is. Will be thinking of you today, will say some prayers to help you through this xx." The night before, I had been talking with her on the phone and could hear growling and hissing so loudly.

"Wow, can hear your dog or cat, what is wrong with them? They sound upset with all that hissing and growling especially," I said to Anne.

"Karen, there are no animals beside me. I can't hear anything."

My mind went blank. What the hell was in my ear? What was I hearing? My heart began beating so loudly I thought my ears were going to explode. Oh my God, what is happening to me? My mind went so dizzy; I needed to get off this phone. I told Anne what I was hearing, and we finished the conversation rapidly. I slammed the receiver down in absolute fright. That same day, I finished work at colonics and, upon arriving home, went to the toilet. As I approached my ensuite, which was off my main bedroom, I could hear buzzing noises. I cautiously opened my ensuite door and, in disbelief, there, right in front of me, were hundreds of blowflies. They were all suspended inside some sort of bubble, flying around and around. I had never seen anything like it!

The black mould on my ensuite roof was terrible to look at and seemed to be spreading so rapidly that it was about to cover the entire roof. We had tried so many different products to remove it, but no matter what we used, it just never stopped. I immediately went to grab the fly spray. I walked in and sprayed them all, and as I was walking back through the kitchen, John arrived home from work. He opened up the door to come in.

"What are you cooking? I can hear all those flies."

I looked at him completely puzzled. "I'm not cooking anything; I've only just got home myself."

We heard it coming from near our dining room window. "There must be a hole somewhere." I pulled back the curtains, and INSIDE our house, climbing all over the screens, were hundreds more flies. OMG! I sprayed like mad. Quick, where was the hole? John went around the entire perimeter of the house, but I knew there was no hole. This wasn't something from our dimension; there was nothing to attract flies into the house. I KNEW it was something very bad. I texted Cyndi what had happened, to which she replied, "I knew it was going to do something to you. There is always lots of activity before an extraction. Won't be long now; hang in there."

Joy had decided to take me out for lunch to a tavern near where she lived the day before. "Get all your black tourmaline out of your house, and we will go down to the ocean and cleanse them and cleanse you, and I will shout you lunch."

I met her there, and we ordered our lunch dishes. Within seconds of the meals being put in front of us, flies appeared out of nowhere and completely covered us. The waitress got the cook and pointed at us both from the corner of our eyes. We suddenly became aware of a few people sitting outside who were also watching us. We were just swarmed by flies. They were so bad that we couldn't even get the food into our mouths.

OMG! We both looked at each other, gobsmacked. We couldn't even finish our meal, and the waitress was so apologetic. "I... am... so... sorry," she stammered. "We have never seen anything like this before." We got the meals put into takeaway containers. So much for a nice, relaxing lunch. Joy and I walked over to the esplanade.

"Here, you hold our meals, and I will go and wash your tourmaline for you. Next time you're down at the beach, come and walk in the ocean. The salt water is very cleansing for you. I am praying for you, Karen. We will get you through this; so will your Dad. You have no idea how much I love you, and I know how loved you are by your family too. I pray for you every night. Stay strong, you are very loved and very protected. I know you have the power to get yourself through this too. Please always remember how very loved you truly are."

I thanked Joy for her lovely words, and she gave me a great big hug. Deep down, I was absolutely petrified. I cried all the way home.

THE EXTRACTION...

"THREE, FOUR, BETTER LOCK YOUR DOOR. FIVE, SIX, GRAB A CRUCIFIX. SEVEN, EIGHT, GONNA STAY UP LATE. NINE, TEN, NEVER SLEEP AGAIN."—WES CRAVEN

I was thinking repeatedly, "What the hell did I do to deserve this?" I was pacing around my house, the sweat pouring out of me was unbelievable. My mouth was so dry. I put on Dad's rosary beads and cried out, "Oh please, God, let this be over with." My mind was still trying to process that this was actually happening to me. Why me... why me?

I heard a car pull up. It was Cyndi. She gave me some items to bring in. I was on remote control; my mind was just numb. She set up a tablecloth on my table and placed certain items on it. I saw a photo of an older woman and heard her telling Joy that it was her grandmother who helps her. Joy turned up with her Pounamu warrior symbol around her neck. She hugged me and said, "Come on, girlfriend, let's do this."

We had to put a protective oil on ourselves and I overheard Joy saying, "Wow, I can really feel that it doesn't like that at all." Another man turned up at the front door, and we were introduced to Kyle. He sat in the corner near the crystal vortex and photo and went to shift the cushion.

"What is this? This is REALLY heavy," he asked.

"That is a cushion that Mum got made for all of us children and all the grandchildren for Christmas. They are made from my father's shirts that he used to wear," I replied.

"Oh, okay, so that is why I can't lift it up. Your father is here with us and is letting me know."

"WHAT!?! My father is here right now, at this very minute?" I asked, completely perplexed.

Just then, my salt lamp blew, and Kyle looked straight at me. "He sure is, Karen. He doesn't want me touching his cushion, so I will leave it right where I found it. He is here and wants to help you."

I looked at him in complete exasperation, my eyes wide open in disbelief. "Hello, Dad, so glad that you are here," I said as I hugged his cushion. It didn't feel heavy to me at all. Kyle then began to do some sort of meditation.

Cyndi began going around the house with bells and sage. I had to clean all the mirrors in my house.

"It's gone in there!" Cyndi suddenly yelled out. It was a room that we were using as our packing room, and it was a complete mess. I went to use my toilet as my bladder was spasming from all this terror, and I could hear that thing as loudly as I had ever heard it in my life. It was like a drowning, guttural groaning sound that put chills right through me.

"That is the death rattle," said Cyndi. *I will never forget that sound for the rest of my life*, I thought to myself.

We came out into the lounge area where IT had choked me in my chair.

"It was coming up over the top of your chair and enveloping you. It was attacking all your right side, as this is where the claw mark is. Then it would have moved to your left and completely wrecked you, even taking your life. After it was done totally destroying you, it would have started on your husband, then your children. When there is nothing left to destroy, IT will move on to find its next victims," Cyndi told me.

I sat there with my mouth wide open in complete shock at what was being said to me. This just can't be real; please let me wake up from this nightmare!

"Where is all the damage?" Cyndi asked.

"Oh my God, it is all the right side of my vestibular that was damaged… and my right vision is worse than my left. Are you telling me what I think you are??"

"Oh, absolutely, I am."

Cyndi sat in my chair and began to wriggle and slide around, saying something like in tongues that I had no idea about. Joy had to ring the Tinksha bells, and I had to ring a normal bell back and forth while this was happening. I couldn't move my legs and just stood there, dumbfounded by what I was witnessing. It seemed to go on for so long.

Suddenly, as quickly as it had started, it was over. Joy then had to go and put the salt all around my front and back yards, and I had to follow her with the hose to ground it into my land. When Joy got to the back shed, the wind whipped up suddenly, and the chicken wire behind her began to move forward. I thought she was going to get caught up in it as the strong wind came out of nowhere. Around the side of my house, the drain next to my toilet began growling, and I saw Cyndi take the hose. She placed it down inside and, with it running at full speed, said, "Good riddance to you and NEVER come back." Eventually, the growling got softer and softer and then stopped altogether. Cyndi then placed my plastic owl over the top of the drain and turned off the hose. "It's all over, Karen. It's gone."

I think I just stood there for a few minutes, completely numb. I couldn't talk, I couldn't move, I couldn't function. This was like being a star in a Hollywood horror movie that I never wanted to be in. I could feel my heart beating so fast. We all went inside and said a special prayer, all holding hands together in a circle. With that, everything was packed up, and goodbyes were said. Joy and I just sat there together at my dining room table, both trying to come to terms with what we had witnessed.

"Come on, let's go to the local club near here, and we'll have a drink," said Joy. I went up there a completely different person. I finally realised this esoteric world WAS truly real on levels I had never experienced before.

Cyndi texted me the next morning to see how we all were.

"Yes, it's almost surreal, like something is wrong with the toilet as there are no sounds after SO many years listening to them. The first night after you did the extraction, everything was great till about 10 pm. Then, out of nowhere, I got that choking sensation in my chair again. Not as strong, though, like previously. Lights flickered. Got myself a drink. Felt unsettled and couldn't sit back in the chair. Had a really bad nightmare afterwards. Maybe just anxiety after everything that has happened. Our dogs have been barking mad, literally, for the past couple of days. Not sure why. Apart from that, everything seems okay. John told me I should write a book. I have been writing down dot points about our family and what we have been going through since we moved into this house. Just so much devastation. Lots of things we tried to forget about. Just wish we could have found you years ago. Ahhhhh, we have found you now. You truly must have been heaven sent xxxx," I texted back.

My Dad's cushion that Mum gave to all of us after he passed,
made from the shirts he used to wear.

THE RESURGENCE...

"DEMONS ARE LIKE OBEDIENT DOGS; THEY COME WHEN THEY ARE CALLED." —REMY DE GOURMONT

"Remember what I said about the holographic echo. It will dissipate. After so many years, it will take a little while. Each echo will be smaller, though. A little bit like aftershocks following earthquakes," Cyndi texted.

The next couple of days felt so good. I was the first time in years that I would go into my toilet and there were no sounds—no gurgles, no growling, nothing after all these years listening to those sounds and truly thinking that it was always the pipes. Everything felt so light, no heaviness, no bangs or bumps, it just felt so wonderful. And I slept. After all these years of the most horrific, brutal, graphic, terrible nightmares, I actually slept. Mostly, I think that I had been wired up on such high levels of pure terror that my body was just physically and emotionally exhausted.

I had to stop being so hard on myself. To take a moment, to breathe, to sit back, and to look at all the suffering that I endured that gave me the courage and strength to not give up. For the mistakes that gave me so much wisdom to keep me going. I was still moving forward despite everything that I had gone through. I had to keep going, to keep enduring, to keep persevering, and to keep remembering that through all my darkness, the sun was going to one day come out again for me. I had to remember that after being in the middle of a horrendous storm, there were now clear skies ahead for me and my family. I had to stop underestimating my resilience and remember how strong and capable I truly was. Inside me was an inner strength. It was my purpose to discover it and my destiny to master it. Slow and steady always wins the race. I knew that I was not alone in this journey. I had to fight for myself and never, ever let myself give in. While I hadn't been looking, I had allowed these lower and negative entities to enter through my door into my house and into my life. I know I will NEVER leave the door ajar ever again as long as I take a breath.

A few days later, I went to bed and swore that I heard the toilet growl. Just ever so slightly. I froze in absolute fear. No, my mind was playing tricks; that didn't happen. I just imagined it. Cyndi told me in her text that it would take a while to dissipate due to being here for so long. I went to bed and had the most brutal nightmare. I woke up in such a cold sweat; it felt so very real. I went to the basin in our ensuite and could smell the foulest odour, and my mouth was bleeding. I felt so ill.

No, this was just my imagination at such a heightened level that my mind was playing terrible tricks on me, I thought to myself. I went and had lunch with Anne and told her what had happened to me.

"You need to let Cyndi know; that doesn't sound right, Karen. Something is going on again; please get in contact with her ASAP. I'm really worried about you."

John had to fly over to the other side of the country for work and told me to play some angel music in the house and to constantly wear my black tourmaline. I honestly didn't think he truly believed what was happening to me, but after talking to him, I think he was finally starting to. At night, I would lie in bed in the dark, and I swore I could see black figures swirling around the room and all over me. *I must just be so severely sleep-deprived*, I thought to myself.

That night, I had another terrible nightmare about swimming in dark water with the most gigantic tarantulas around me. They were falling from the sky, and I was trying to get to safety, but I just couldn't see where there was any land. I woke up again in a cold sweat. Before I left for work, I sent Cyndi this text message:

"Hi Cyndi, just about to leave for arvo shift. Feeling a bit uneasy, so just wanted to touch base with you. Not sure if it's the holographic echo, but I've had blowflies in my car. It won't start at all now, so I've been using John's car. There are what look like scratch marks all over my mirror. Dead birds at my front door covered in ants, and the stench was overwhelming. Most disturbing are the nightmares I've been having. The last one left me with such a terrible taste in my mouth. Still can't get rid of it. Didn't tell my husband… God, I think I'm going mad. Is this all part of what happens? Just feel so out of sorts. Will check my phone on my tea break and hopefully you'll get this message."

When I returned from my break, I opened my phone and read this text back from her:

"BLOODY SHIT!!!!!!! Ok, sounds like a resurgence. I am putting guardians in place above your house now. Be at yours at 0830. Get more salt. Will bring more oil. No wonder I have been burping all day. Had hoped to have seen you last night. You also need to learn how to fight back. Will bring more Pieter lite too. Had to get more supplies on Sunday as I had run out. The scum bag went to the car; we will beat this. Have sentries in place, and the grid is activated. Am pulling in my global network of friends, and I believe we will have to repeat next Thursday. It is going to take the trinity to eliminate it completely."

Within the hour, another message arrived:

"So, lots have been installed since your message. You should have contacted me sooner, or I should have checked back sooner instead of trusting. I am now trusting that I will be able to get to town in the morning and that you will be home. Did we get all the drains around your home, Karen? Did we miss one? Please go around inside and outside your home and double-check that every one of them had salt and oil put down them. Love and light."

I checked every drain and pipe inside and outside the house. Suddenly, I thought of the dishwasher. As I opened it up, a whole swarm of flies came barrelling out at me. "Oh no, quick, get the fly spray!" I yelled. We managed to spray them, and I put holy salt and water down the drain outlet. That night, I could barely sleep. Every time I did finally get some rest, it was always terrible, brutal nightmares.

When is this all going to stop... I just want my life back... haven't we been through enough? I thought. "Just leave me and my family the hell alone... do you hear me, you f**king vile disgusting scum? Get the HELL out of my house... get out!" I screamed out loud in so much agonising frustration.

As I walked past the spare bedroom, my heart stopped again. All over my purple quilt cover were prints like claw marks. I walked into the room slowly and saw more claw marks all over my roof. They were JUST everywhere. It looked like my entire roof had been attacked, like a battle had gone on in there. That was the room that was hardly saged, and it ended up being the room that was attacked.

I then noticed, as I was walking up my hallway with the light on, that there were scratch marks all over my purple feature walls. When I turned on my lamp in our bedroom, I could see scratch marks inside the outer fabric of it as well. There were even scratch marks on my salt lamp in the lounge area. I could see them all over my windows and glass sliding doors. It was like IT or THEY had gone on a complete rampage throughout our entire house.

Cyndi arrived the next day with some other friends and told me that she had to bury something and needed a small metal trowel or teaspoon. We went into my backyard, and she showed me a necklace made from a red-bellied black snake and lots of snake fangs. It had belonged to James and was one of his favourite necklaces. He had passed away the day before I nearly died and had come to either Cyndi or his mother (I couldn't remember which one) and had told them that there was a beautiful lady with a beautiful family who needed urgent help.

The first time Cyndi had come to my house, she looked straight at me and said, "James must have been talking about you, Karen. You can see his family's mango tree from your front yard, You are THAT lady."

I had never met James but was extremely grateful for any help that he was also giving me from the esoteric world. His mother had given permission for the necklace to be buried here to keep us protected. We had to stand in a formation and Kyle began to dig. As he was doing this, Cyndi once again made comments about the stench of vomit that she could smell. The necklace was buried with some crystals and Cyndi started singing some song in tongues that I could not understand. I'm pretty sure I heard a big bang again and knew that was my neighbour Paula falling off her chair in her pagola hearing this all happening.

A prayer was then said, and the teaspoon was thrown down the front of my drain which was at the front of the house. I awoke the next morning to find the mirror in my bedroom had some bizarre pattern all over it, like it had been scratched in the condensation from the air conditioner being on all night. When I showed Maddie, she said, "Look, Karen, this is just incredible; there is a lady in there and she has long dark hair. Can you see her?"

"Well, sort of, maybe," I replied.

I showed Cyndi, and she said she definitely could and believed that the figure had come through from either the fourth or fifth dimension.

Ohhhh this was all seriously way, way toooooo much for me. Other dimensions? I got up to go to my toilet in my ensuite and not only could hear the growling again but when I would turn the light on it would just flicker like crazy. More bizarre images were appearing throughout my house, on my walls, mirrors, shower screens, pantry cupboard. Even the material on my lounge chair where I lay my head had a skull and some weird face looking like it was screaming coming out at me.

My son was coming to stay for a few days for work and that was the room he was staying in. I can't have him in there. What if this thing attacks him? Oh God, this just can't be happening. Cyndi told me to get the big piece of black obsidian and place it on the bed, say the King James version of the Lord's Prayer three times, and get rid of the marks.

My son arrived, and by this stage, I was like a deer in the headlights. All these things had been happening to me—at the house, the sounds, the bangs, the prints. As you can imagine, trying to explain this to my son was like trying to explain that the sky was actually pink with polka dots. He didn't believe a word I was saying and thought I was completely and utterly crazy. We ended up dragging the mattress out into the lounge room, as I just felt that being in that room was not safe.

Cyndi texted:

"Good morning, activity from the multidimensional lightworkers over your area early this morning. From creeks to Bruce Highway and from creeks into rivers and out to sea. How was your night? My guides are adamant that I don't work from your house in a healing capacity with the crystal bed, but to set it up here in my space for you."

I was told about a crystal healing bed that had come from Brazil. Kyle had been visiting and had brought one back with him. I had never heard of it, but if it was something to help heal me and my family, I was all in.

"Where do we have to go?"

"Out to my place. I have a special healing room, which is where my guides want me to help you and your family."

Ah, okay. I did have to really encourage Liam to go, as I knew this was also frightening him to a degree.

"Your family has been through horrendous trauma, and you need to heal from what was done to you all. We have a special crystal bed that would really benefit you all. Please come out and try it and bring your family too," Cyndi explained.

Our middle daughter, Taylor, had been living away for a few years now and was unable to attend, but the four of us all went. Cyndi was going to put us on it for half an hour at a time, as she didn't want to overwhelm us too quickly. I was lying on this bed and saw all these crystal lights above me that changed and were all different colours of the chakra.

"Just lie down; I'm going to put this small covering over your eyes whilst you listen to this very soft music and just see what happens."

Within minutes, I felt so relaxed and could see this purple indigo light spinning towards me. I could always see one eye. As it got closer and closer, the purple would suddenly explode all around me. WOW, that was impressive. It would happen over and over, just the same thing—no other colours—then my time would be up.

Cyndi asked me what I had seen, and I described it to her.

"When you have your complete spiritual awakening, Karen, it truly is going to be EPIC!!" Cyndi told me.

Like, okay??? I went for a few more sessions. It was always relaxing—just the same thing repeatedly, nothing different—but it was obviously helping us with our healing. I was very thankful to Kyle for letting me and my family use it all free of charge. I was the only one who used it a few times. I started playing "Invoking Angels to Your Home" for love, peace, and protection. Cyndi also sold me pure Egyptian oils to burn in my home. It did smell beautiful. "Put some on you too," she told me. I did, multiple times.

Scratch marks all over my mirror.

Marks that appeared all over my blanket.

Prints that appeared on my roof.

These were taken in the room that was barely saged when Cyndi was performing the extraction. She focused more on my house but barely touched this room, which is where many occurrences later took place.

COMPLETELY BROKEN OPEN...

"MONSTERS ARE REAL, GHOSTS ARE REAL TOO. THEY LIVE INSIDE US AND SOMETIMES THEY WIN." —STEPHEN KING

The trauma of what I had experienced was overwhelming. I was NEVER going to look at the world in the same way EVER again. I was NEVER going to be the same person EVER again. My life was NEVER going to be the same EVER again. You can't unknow what you now know, you can't unsee what you have now seen, you can't unexperience the things you have now experienced. I felt so unbelievably alone. These things weren't happening to anyone but me. People were trying to help but they could never truly understand what I was honestly going through. How could they understand the terror?

My friend Elle said to me, "People don't understand that if they don't set proper boundaries and protections and do not invite in beings that are aligned for their greatest good, they can cast a wide net and then get the shock of their lives when they get some pretty evil things inside it. If you only want high vibrational beings that are for your highest good then you have to say it out aloud and clearly and firmly. Only ask for your loved ones, angels, true spirit guides, and guardians with only the intentions of being benevolent to come through. As you are asking this, envision a beautiful beam of brilliant white light beaming down and swirling all around, completely protecting and shielding you. Say and state with intention that all other entities with any sort of harmful intention are FORBIDDEN.

So many people start to delve into spirituality and think that when they begin, everything is going to be peaches and cream—fluffy and harmless, like rainbows and unicorns. Then, they get the complete shock of their entire lives. For anyone starting this journey, you need to do proper research, learn how to protect yourself, and always assert your boundaries and power." I was SO confused. I NEVER asked for any of this; I NEVER started any spiritual journey. I NEVER wanted any part of it, but for some reason, I was being SLAMMED left, right, and sideways by IT, and I truly didn't understand why.

I would go down and sit in my local church on the pew and just cry. I would think silently in angst so no one would overhear me. *Why was this happening to me and my family? Please, God, Angels, help me. I don't know what I am fighting or why IT had picked on our family. I just want some peace back in my life.* I didn't know where to go or where to turn. I was so scared that if I talked to other people about IT, they would think I was crazy, or worse still, that I would bring this terrible thing into their life. I had never honestly felt so alone in all my life.

The absolute disbelief, the loneliness, the true horror of what I was experiencing every single day of my life was debilitating, and I was beginning to wonder if this terror was ever going to stop. Even when I was at work, it was like my senses were in overdrive. For the first time, I could see scratch marks all over the walls and on the ceilings in different rooms around the facility where I worked. I grabbed the pups to go for a walk near my local park. I had to get out of the house. I was just hysterical—why won't this thing leave me alone? I was walking, sobbing uncontrollably. No one can help me. What if this thing never leaves me alone? What did I do to deserve this? No one on this planet could understand the sheer terror that I was feeling. I walked along the pathway and was so thankful that no one was around, as everyone was at work.

I just cried and cried, sobbing uncontrollably, when in the distance I could see something spinning from the sky. It didn't float but actually spun so fast. I took a few more steps towards it as I had no idea what it was. I was in an open area, and there were no birds flying over me. To my absolute astonishment, it was the most beautiful white feather. I looked around to see which bird it had come from; there was nothing around me. *OMG! Is this a sign from my angel? From Dad?* I was thinking. Suddenly, I felt like I was being watched over and protected, and that everything was going to be okay. The sheer relief I felt that day was just indescribable. I went home and placed it on my duchess, and the feather still remains there today.

My son was in the room with me at my house when he pointed to the wall and said, "How long has this lady been on the wall for?" All these thoughts began to fire rapidly in my head. *What... OMG! I had never seen it before. When did that appear? The same night the marks appeared all over my room? Had she always been there… what did this mean?* There also seemed to be a male figure appearing beside her and a hand with bracelets on it. What was happening now?? I went to work again in a complete and utter daze. How I was able to function and do my work properly was just beyond me. I was so completely and utterly sleep-deprived on levels I had never known.

My work colleague, Campbell, believed what I was going through. I had worked with him for many years. We had clicked from the moment we met; there was never a bad or harsh word exchanged between us in all those years we worked together. Doing shifts with him was so easy—the left hand always knew what the right hand was doing. If it hadn't been for him, I don't know where I would have been mentally. Campbell was listening intently to everything that was happening to me. He was probably the only person outside of my family who truly knew all the terrible bad luck we had been enduring over the years. That night on evening shift, I was showing him some of my photos.

He sat with me during our tea breaks and listened to my stories as I showed him all the photos that were appearing all over my house. Having someone to talk with through this terror helped me to function to a certain degree at work, as Joy was always working permanent night shifts. I asked him if he really did believe me, as maybe he was thinking that I was going mad. He answered, "Yes, of course, I do. You have never been an attention seeker in all the years that I have known you, and secondly, I KNOW you. I have listened to what you and your family have been through over all these years, and even I was starting to think that something just wasn't right. This was just too much bad luck for one family to be constantly going through."

Joy rang to let me know that she was bringing her husband Steve with her that morning to get a chest of drawers that I told her she could have. Campbell was about to leave at the end of his shift that evening when he noticed that his mobile phone was showing lots of different colours, which it had never done before. "That's a bit strange," he muttered and left. The next day on shift, he told me that night he had a dream and could see the words "DANGER DANGER" and woke up. He then realised that the power box outside his home was sparking, and flashes were going everywhere. The next morning, he got an electrician around to fix it and also saw that the bush near it was completely covered in flies. *Did IT follow him home? Was it a coincidence? Were there other entities there???* I thought to myself. I told him to go and buy some sage and cleanse the hell out of his house and himself as well.

That morning, John had to fly to the other side of the country for work. He needed to be at the airport by 6 am. I was jolted awake by him screaming at me at 5:30 am because his alarm clock didn't go off. "I bloody well set MY alarm; what the HELL is going on?" Oh, what a morning that was. I dreamt my neighbour Molly came over to see me, distressed, talking about all these growling sounds coming out of her pipes. She mentioned getting plumbing work done, having nightmares, and fighting with her husband. It was a very intense dream, and she said she just couldn't deal with the bad luck that was happening to her.

A few days later, I was walking my dogs, and Molly was getting her mail. I noticed she had a wound dressing completely covering one side of her face. I hadn't seen her in a very long time. She told me how she had been bitten on the face by some sort of insect—maybe—but she wasn't really sure what it was, and neither was the doctor. She thought it might have happened during her sleep since she had no memory of being bitten. When she awoke, it was already there, and the pain had intensified. The infection kept getting worse, despite a plethora of antibiotics. Nothing seemed to stop it. Molly eventually had to undergo surgery under general anaesthetic to try and clear up the terrible infection on her face. OMG! What the HELL was on this land!

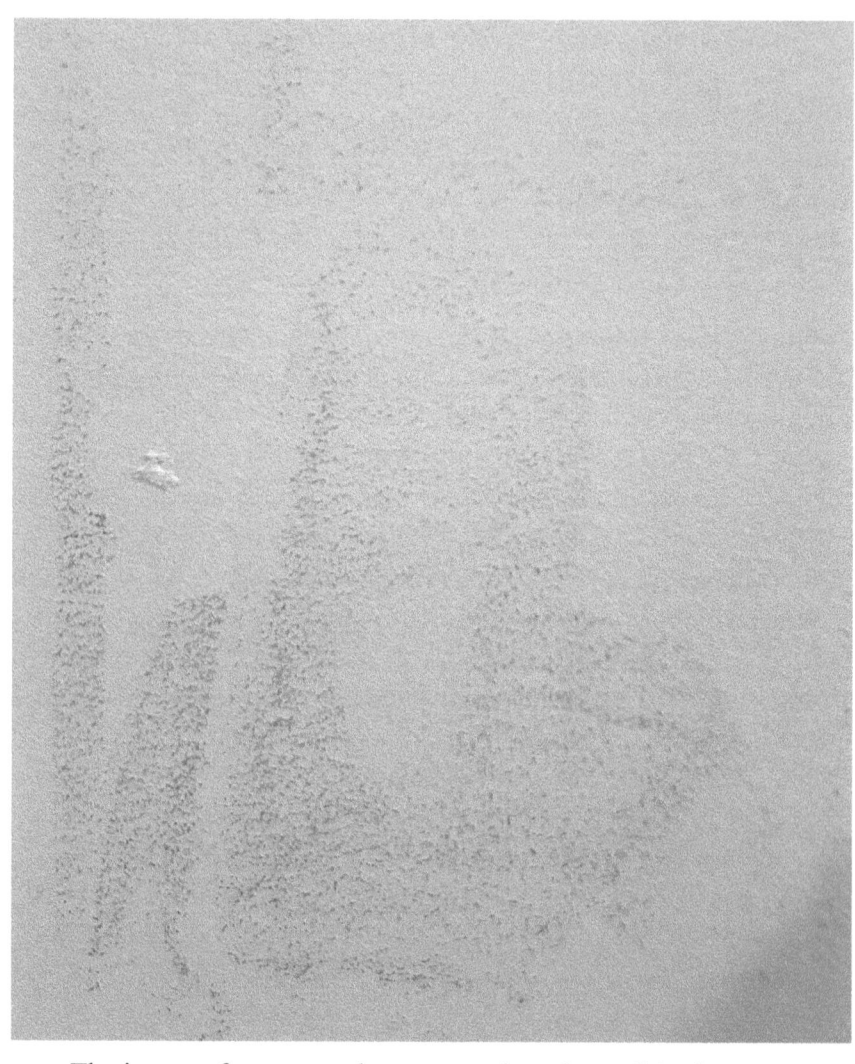

The image of a woman that appeared on the wall in the room that was barely saged.

MY DARK NIGHT OF THE SOUL... I MEAN YEAR!

"NEVER GIVE IN, NEVER GIVE IN, NEVER GIVE IN." —SIR WINSTON CHURCHILL

Words cannot even begin to describe the horrific loneliness that I was feeling. My new reality began to seep into my consciousness. I felt so utterly hopeless with absolutely no way to protect myself from just how brutal and vicious it truly was. I was living in so much horror and I just couldn't mentally overcome it. There simply was no escape. I had no choice, I thought, but to succumb. My life just seemed to be crumbling around me. It was like the entire earth had been ripped out from under my feet and everything came crashing down around me. I felt so empty and so alone. I needed to escape this nightmare.

I walked into a shopping centre and saw people walking around, trolleys everywhere, people doing their shopping. Children were laughing, friends catching up for coffee in cafes, talking, completely oblivious to the other world that was around them. *WAKE UP!* I was screaming silently to myself. They had NO idea. I wanted to turn back time, to never have moved into that area, to have gone to another suburb. To have never left the town where we lived previously. We were so happy and content. We only moved here to give the children a better start in high school and it had been one of the biggest mistakes we had EVER made.

"You are experiencing a spiritual awakening, Karen; you have finally woken up to what is actually happening to you," said my friend Elle.

"What is an awakening?" I asked, curious. *Oh, why did I ever have to wake up?*

"Because it was your time. The doorway has been opened for you, and now there is no turning back. It's where you basically feel such total spiritual disconnection, like you have been completely abandoned by God. It is, in a way, a severe spiritual depression. Some say they feel betrayed by life, feel like they have no solid ground to stand on. They lose all meaning for why they are living and for their actual life. You have woken up to your new consciousness. A spiritual awakening is exactly that… waking up. Most people in this world, even though they don't know it, are asleep. They are born asleep, they live asleep, marry in their sleep, have children in their sleep, and pass away in their sleep without EVER waking up. They never understand the loveliness and the beauty of this thing that we call being human.

"It's like when a snake sheds its skin; you are shedding the old you and awakening to the new version of you. It can be so traumatising for some that you may feel emotionally and spiritually numb, as the pain can be so crippling. It's like you are glued to one spot and can't take your next step forward.

"You feel like every single day is a struggle. You lose who you are, what life is actually all about, and you feel like you have been reduced to the mode of just barely surviving. Your soul is maturing, growing, and expanding. If you stayed the same, it would be like stagnating. Once you come out the other side, you will feel so much more connected to everything. I know the process is extremely painful, and you start to understand that the only person who can save you is actually yourself. You will find your life purpose and fulfil your destiny of what you are actually here to do. You will get through this; you will find your way along this path, and you will find the light at the end of the tunnel. Your soul will light the way for you to find yourself out the other side.

"Not everyone has them—most are caused by some life-changing event like a car accident, divorce, death of loved ones, betrayal of some kind, life-threatening illnesses, or lots of major life changes or trauma. I think yours was caused by your near-death experience. Lots of people can feel completely detached and disconnected from everything around them. For many, it can be very frightening and confusing. You can experience a wide range of emotions—from grief, sadness, depression, anxiety, frustration, and anger. It is also very lonely, extremely uncomfortable, and a VERY challenging time because you are undergoing an intense period of incredible spiritual and personal growth. They say that there are four different stages of an awakening. The first one is when you emotionally hit rock bottom. You feel so much pain, frustration, and complete confusion with every aspect of your life. You will start to question just about everything. In the second stage, you will develop your awareness.

"You will start to understand all the behavioural patterns and childhood conditioning you went through. You will begin to recognise that voice in your head, which is called your ego, and realise that none of this serves you anymore. The third stage is when you will want to hide away from the world, almost cocoon yourself—a time for you to be alone and reflect on everything you have learnt. This is essentially the beginning of the birth of the new you, your true self. Lastly, it is known as the rebirth. As your consciousness expands, you will experience so much of the divine. You will want to share this with others, almost creating a ripple effect of awakening. Please always remember that despite everything you go through, you are NOT going crazy—you're just awakening and evolving into the new you.

"You may feel completely alone and lost; you start questioning everything about your life. You just want to be alone. You may want to quit your job. You basically want to purge your life. You start to crave some sort of meaning and purpose to your life and see through the illusions of society, wanting to understand on a deeper level who you really are. Your senses are heightened, and you may get physical symptoms too, like insomnia, chronic fatigue; you may change your habits and begin to spend more time in nature or start to meditate. Part of this is called a Dark Night of the Soul."

"A what?" I asked, completely confused.

"The Dark Night of the Soul and the spiritual awakening process are intertwined; you can't have one without the other. It's like an enlightenment; you're awake to a world of which many others have no idea."

Elle continued, "We are all spiritual beings down here in this third dimension, in this Earth school of life, so to speak, having a human experience. We also need to understand that we are human beings who can have spiritual experiences. What you are feeling now is a complete disconnection from the divine. Do you feel utterly alone, lost, hopeless, like you're completely empty, and it feels like you will never be the same again?"

"Yes, sort of. The only way I can describe it would be like if you grew up in a family with your parents and siblings, and then you wake up one day to be told that you were actually adopted, and everything you had ever known as truth was, in fact, made up—just one big fat lie," I replied.

"This is all completely normal, and it will eventually pass. The shock of it is so distressing to even process, and it just shakes you to your core. It makes you question every part of your existence. There is a lot more information on it on the internet and in books—way more than I can ever really explain to you. Putting it simply, Karen, it means the beginning of your initiation onto the spiritual path. It comes into your life like a volcano and explodes everything around you that you always thought was reality. The hidden gift buried deep within this is that it always occurs at the precise moment you need it.

"Please understand, Karen, this is part of the process, and there is a purpose behind it. You are going to shed everything that no longer serves you—habits, relationships, feelings, beliefs, and so much more. The reason you are in the dark is so you can go through this process and finally step out and be in the light again. The reason you feel so lost is so you can find the right path and then find your way back home again. Don't be surprised if you don't want to go out and do things you once enjoyed doing; you will just want to be on your own. You will start to notice that your circle of friends will change too; you will start to find your tribe. It will teach you many things, including that you don't have to live your life trying to accomplish so many achievements and earning all the best degrees.

"You are worthy, just because you are here, and you are worthy just as you are. You've heard about the Clairs, right? There are different ones—Clairvoyance is the ability to see, Clairaudience is the ability to hear, Claircognizance is the ability to know, Clairsentience is the ability to feel, Clairtangency is the ability to receive information by touch, Clairgustance is the ability to taste, and Clairalience is the ability to smell. From the things you have been telling me over the years, you have the ability to do some of these things, but one will be your strongest.

"You may start to have more intense dreams. You may start to purge lots of pain that you've tried so hard to bury, and it will bring it to the surface so that you can heal and move forward with your life. Some people also experience lots of physical symptoms too that they have never had before—things like anxiety, not sleeping, digestive issues, and many more—but you will find the strength in yourself to keep going. Deep down, you will understand that everything you are going through is for your highest good.

"Basically, first you suffer, then you awaken, and finally, you ascend. You find your true gifts and power. Some ascending symptoms you might encounter are headaches, mood swings, feeling emotional and anxious, heart issues, palpitations, lethargy, and exhaustion. High blood pressure, hot flashes, ringing in your ears, intense dreams, vertigo."

"Wow, that sounds exactly like ME. Gee, the universe isn't making this easy."

"No, it's certainly testing a lot of people. It's all about stripping us of our old 3D ways and opening us up to the Fourth and Fifth dimensions. You will never learn to evolve and grow if you don't go through this. You have to trust, to know that the universe has amazing plans for you, that this amazing transformational process you are going through is going to help you find your true self and bring your life into the most phenomenal alignment. Trust, Karen; the universe knows what it is doing. A lot of people find that their own family and friends just cannot accept what is actually happening to them, and this can make you feel so terribly isolated and alone. Some even begin to treat you like you have some sort of social disease."

I even know of some families who have actually called to have their relatives locked up in psychiatric wards because they think their family member is going completely mad. You will start to question who you really are. You'll also begin to understand that there are only a few people you can really trust and confide in without being treated like you are incredibly insane. You have to, in a sense, realise what is important to you, find your strength, and discover YOUR own inner truth. Everyone around you who isn't capable of truly seeing, so to speak, should not make you doubt your belief in yourself. Always honour your own inner truth. Every one of us on this planet is gifted, but most people will never open their package.

"I truly think that where you were living, this was eventually going to happen to you, Karen. This was always part of your destiny—your soul contract, if you like. We all have a spiritual team that is here for our own development and growth. They know what your soul has chosen to explore in this lifetime, what lessons and purpose you are here for. This is already in your soul's blueprint. You were never going to escape it. It has happened, and now you know your power, and you will be so much better for this. You have been picked for this spiritual journey for a reason. It is now time for you to remember who you REALLY are.

"There is such an adventure waiting for you; just trust your own wisdom that your life will unfold in ways that will be mind-blowing. You don't have to do this alone, either. You have so much support on this journey with your own spirit team. They know why you are here and what you are meant to learn. They are like a team of high beings that will guide you, but on a vibrational level, not a physical one. They can't talk to you directly like we can speak to each other; rather, they will speak to you through your intuition and guide you through your development and growth. Listen to them when they are trying to communicate with you.

"This divine life you were truly meant to live is waiting for you to go and find it. Let it show up on your path. There have been many lessons, experiences, healings, karma, growth, and learning that have been set for you by your soul to fulfil. Clear your mind and let the universe support you, and get the heck out of your own way. You felt like your world was crumbling around you, but through everything that happened, you and your family were being divinely protected. Your purpose is to be here, to appreciate, feel, and experience this amazing thing called life," Elle explained to me.

It was definitely a lot to take in and try to understand—Soul contracts? Soul Awakenings? Soul Blueprints? This was just all WAY too much.

MIRACLES FALLING ACROSS MY PATH...

"SOMETIMES THE BAD THINGS THAT HAPPEN IN OUR LIVES PUT US DIRECTLY ON THE PATH TO THE BEST THINGS THAT WILL EVER HAPPEN TO US." —ANONYMOUS

Jenna and I had come back from our afternoon walk with our pet dogs, Bella and Beau, when I could see something coloured sticking out of the letterbox. It had been hand delivered and had my name on the front. When I opened it, it was a beautiful butterfly card, and inside were written the words, "Expect a miracle," nothing else. I was baffled as to who would have given this to me and rang heaps of family and friends. They all saw it and said how lovely it was, but it wasn't from them. I went around to my neighbours, but they too denied that they had done it. To this very day, I still do not know who placed that beautiful card and message for me in my letterbox, but yes, the miracle was definitely coming.

I was washing up the dishes early one morning, knowing everyone would be arriving soon. I suddenly felt very cold, and the air around me got really heavy. I moved over to the drawer and heard a noise behind me. I turned to see, on the mat, just seconds after I was standing there, a pair of scissors that had been in my knife block, opened and lying on the floor. "REALLY? Is that all you've got?" I screamed out. Then I thought I had better not provoke IT anymore. "Please, angels, come and protect me." Within seconds, I heard a knock at my front door. I opened it to find Joy and her husband.

Steve was a huge man...so many muscles. I wondered if he was going to fit through my door frame. He definitely worked out. "Come in," I ushered. Joy had told me how her husband Steve was also spiritual and had the gift of astral travel. *Wow, maybe he can feel something when he comes over*, I thought to myself. I was in the process of making them both a coffee when Cyndi and Kyle arrived. I noticed that Steve was starting to squirm in his seat and was beginning to sweat. He started to go increasingly red. Everyone else was talking amongst themselves, but I could see how uncomfortable he was becoming. The redness and sweating continued, and I took him his coffee. "Are you okay?" I asked, very concerned.

"No, not really," he replied. Joy suddenly became aware of it herself. It was also starting to rain.

"We might have to go now," she said, "before this rain really hits so we can get the chest into the trailer and get it home." I agreed. Later, when I rang her, she told me that IT was attacking him. "OMG, is that why he was sweating and going so red?"

"Yes. We had to drive straight down to the ocean, and we had to splash him all over with the salt water to cleanse him," she said, Steve told Joy "and we're f**kin' saging those f**kin' drawers too. There is nothing evil about your friend either."

Oh gosh, did he think I was! I thought.

Cyndi came around in the second week, and Kyle once again sat in the corner. I had sent her photos of the images that had come through the wall.

She told me she was coming over to see me that afternoon and was bringing someone with her. It was the mother of the young man who had passed away. A few others that Cyndi knew came in and took photos of the image. "Have any of you ever seen anything like this lady before?" I asked. Cyndi replied, "No, never in all my years. I think it might be Queen Isis, and the male figure appearing could be her husband, King Osiris… or maybe it is Mary, and the male figure could be Jesus Christ. These images are meant for me, Karen, I don't think they are meant for you." Like, what the...?

It was Valentine's Day, and they were all coming back to finalise everything and collect all the crystals. The big black protective stone had a massive crack down the side of it. *Oh no, Cyndi might think that I've dropped it and cracked it*, I thought. I was so worried and told her that I only noticed it before she arrived, which was the truth. "It's okay, Karen; it was doing its job, it is fine. It is taking the hits. Black tourmaline is a VERY POWERFUL PROTECTIVE CRYSTAL."

This was to be a celebration that everything was over and had moved on. I was told I had to have yellow flowers and some morning tea to share with everyone who had helped me through it all. That morning, I got my daughter to school, and do you think I could find any yellow flowers, being Valentine's Day? Everywhere I went, there were red roses. I was beginning to get frantic as I knew they would be turning up soon at my house. I saw one last shop as the traffic was madness. I couldn't believe it—there were some yellow roses. I quickly went in, bought them, and drove home. I literally just got everything set up in time when they turned up. I could hear them all talking amongst themselves as I was making them all cups of tea and coffee. Some of it was just too out there for me to comprehend what was being said. I just sat at the end of the table, trying to take everything in.

Eventually, one of them looked at me and could see that it was just too much for me. "Ahh guys, this is all a bit overwhelming for Karen." Suddenly they all stared at me. "You are not on the same level as us yet, Karen, but trust me, you will be coming."

"Oh, that's okay; I'm quite happy to stay where I am. I have no desire to go anywhere else," I told them.

"Mmmmmm, yeah, doesn't work like that... you're coming whether you're ready or not. You can't stop what is going to happen to you, Karen. You just have to accept it and go with it. You are an empath, Karen; you can feel the energies and emotions of others around you immensely. The more you resist, the harder and more challenging it will be for you." With this, they were all looking at me. I didn't really know how to respond, so I just took a breath and lifted up a plate.

"Anyone for a biscuit?" was my reply. It was just WAY over my head.

As I walked into work that afternoon, I was honestly still in a daze. I could not get the thoughts out of my head about what was happening to me. They just kept self-looping over and over in my mind. This is like something out of a horror movie. Surely this cannot be real, but I knew in my heart that it was. I bought some angel cards for the first time and asked for some divine intervention. I drew three cards. The first one was "battle," the second was "home," and the third one was "Archangel Michael protection." WOW! This particular afternoon, I had to swap ends of my facility, which very rarely happened. I walked into a resident's room, and there was a woman sitting on a chair opposite her mother, who was dying. She immediately put me at ease when she smiled and said, "You look exhausted; are you okay?" For some reason, even though I had never met this woman before, I said, "I don't think you would believe my story—it's pretty diabolical."

"Try me... I'm a good listener," she replied.

I instantly felt a connection with her and began talking. She made me feel so at ease, and before I knew it, we were talking about the esoteric world, and she pulled the hugest crystal out of her pocket. I told her that I—wait for it—had a malevolent entity, honestly expecting her to laugh at me. "I don't doubt it; there are hundreds in here, you know." What! "Well, this is where people pass away. Every hospital and every nursing home on the planet is jam-packed with entities; they are infested and just crawling with them." I honestly nearly fell over. I couldn't believe what I was hearing. She believed me, and she knew more about this esoteric world than I did.

"So, you believe me?"

"Yes, I can feel terrible trauma around you."

I felt so at ease in her company, and she was so easy to talk to. I told her that I had photos of what was happening to me and that images were now coming through my walls.

She asked if I could send them to her, and she would send them through to a man called Cameron who lived down south. He was very much into spirituality and would let me know what was happening. Suzannah became another one of my God-sends to help me through. I invited her to my house the next day with her young teenage daughter. She came to have a look and took photos of what was happening. I took her out to John's shed to show her the prints that had appeared all over the door. Suzannah came and gave me a piece of a crystal called Shungite and told me to keep it on me for protection.

"One of the best visualisations for protection for yourself, your family, your home, and possessions is to create a white light that cocoons your entire house and land. This protective cocoon, I believe, gives you great and amazing power. I always create a mental picture in my mind before I go to sleep of my house, land, pets, and possessions, and of my husband, myself, and family all surrounded by this amazing white light. I know this cosmic energy will surround us all and keep everyone safe while we sleep," Suzannah explained to me.

"This always works well when you do it with positivity and faith rather than in fear. They are tools; they have little power in themselves, but you can concentrate and energise them with the power of your mind. This can then help you take back control of your life and environment, like your house and land. These tools will help to defend your home, your family, and your life."

Many messages were shared between us, and I was so blessed to have met this amazing lady. Suzannah was at my place having a coffee with me, and I explained that the week before, I had called and spoken to a nun about getting my house blessed, and that she and a priest were finally coming over soon to do it. "You what… OMG!!! Karen, you need to cancel… you are poking the bear; that will just make IT angry, and you will feel ITS wrath. This thing is extremely malevolent. Seriously, get on the phone and cancel it now. Do they know what they are doing... have they got any experience with malevolent entities? This can be really dangerous if they don't truly know what they are doing. I wouldn't be doing this. Few clergymen and women are really educated about the paranormal. Most of them, to be honest, except for a select few, will truly not understand. Most of them will do WAY more harm than they ever will do good," Suzannah explained. I was terrified. I hurried to find their number and called the parish to cancel, but it was too late—they were already on their way over.

"Oh God, what have I done," I said, frightened.

"It's okay; we will deal with it. I will go now and ring you after. Just tell them as little as possible and get them out of here as quickly as you can," Suzannah explained. I suddenly heard a car pull into the driveway, and I was left wondering what on earth was going to happen. I just knew having them in my house was going to be a big mistake, and I was going to pay dearly for it. Believe me, that night, I definitely did.

ONE HELL OF A FIGHT...

"IT IS BETTER TO CONQUER YOURSELF THAN TO WIN A THOUSAND BATTLES, THEN THE VICTORY IS YOURS. IT CANNOT BE TAKEN FROM YOU, NOT BY ANGELS OR BY DEMONS, HEAVEN OR HELL."
—BUDDHA

The same priest that had conducted my father's funeral stepped out of the car with a nun beside him. I invited them into my home and sat them at the table. "Now what seems to be the issue?" the priest said, as if I was crazy. "Sister here tells me that you believe you have something in your house." I could tell by the tone of his voice that he was here as I had requested, but I was purely wasting his time. I explained a few things that had been happening, remembering what Suzannah had said to me. Sister listened intently, but he just sat there with his arms crossed like I was a complete idiot. I then thought I might as well show them the prints that have been coming through my walls.

I took them into the bedroom that had been attacked; the handprints were still very clear on the roof, and you could still see the lady on the wall. I explained that a very spiritual lady had come to do an extraction on my house and had gridded my land. I then showed them what was coming through the walls of my bedroom. The priest just sat there rubbing his chin with his hand, as if trying to take all this in. Above my main front door, I had stickers that read

"Bless this house and all who enter," which had been there for years. "Well, I don't really see anything religious in this house, to be honest, apart from this sticker. If you were really going through this, I'm sure you would have more things around the place." What an arrogant thing to say. I was just livid... I was SO angry with him. I told him that if he looked beside my bed, I had my father's Bible and rosary beads, and I showed him the cross I was wearing on my necklace that my mother had bought me.

I felt like screaming at him to GET OUT. He wasn't here to help me; he was just here to make me feel like I was going mad, and I could tell he was arrogant towards me, as I was obviously wasting HIS time. He went back, grabbed a palm leaf, and went to the room with the claw marks on the roof. He didn't even walk into it; he just stood on the outside in the hallway, threw the leaf with some holy water, and said a little prayer. They couldn't get out of my house quickly enough. For someone who was trained and ordained, I have never felt so terribly let down.

"OK, I think we are done here," he said.

"What, really?? What about the rest of the house? I have been waiting for you for nearly two and a half weeks, and that is all you're going to do? Can't you at LEAST do our bedroom and my daughter's room?" I asked, completely gobsmacked.

He looked at me, and his face flushed bright red. "NO, what I have done is fine. We really need to go. I think we have somewhere else to be now, Sister, don't we?"

I watched them both head for the door, and they were in such a hurry to get out that they slammed shoulders trying to get through at the same time. They got in the car and took off around the corner with such speed, spraying gravel all over my lawn, leaving me standing in the doorway in disbelief. I was just in shock. To this very day, I have never heard from either of them EVER again. Not once did they contact me to ask how I was or how my family was. I had never felt so betrayed in all my life. As I watched them drive off, I remember thinking that inviting them was the biggest regret of my life. They were both absolutely terrified—way more than I was. The more terror you feel, the more power IT gets. I remember Suzannah's words that I would feel ITS anger and ITS wrath. As I closed my front door, I began to hear my toilet growling. "OH my God, what the HELL have I JUST done?" I cried.

I lay in bed that night, absolutely terrified of what could happen. "Wear your black tourmaline to bed tonight and keep your shungite beside you," Suzannah had texted. My husband was away that night, and whenever there was no male energy in the house, things would really ramp up. After hours of exhaustion, I finally fell asleep. I remember feeling like I had sleep paralysis. I was trying to move, but I couldn't get away from IT. I woke up feeling like I was choking and found scratches all over my body. I knew I had been attacked or had started to be attacked, but thank God I had woken up in time. What happened to me that night I will NEVER forget, but I know I was being protected, which is why I woke when I did. I re-lived that night over and over in my mind for a long, long time and have finally been able to place it in a box and put it in the far corners of my mind that can never be reached or opened EVER again. I never want to re-live that memory for the rest of my life.

I ran into my bathroom and splashed water on my face. What the hell was happening to me? I think I'm honestly starting to go mad; my mind is sick. This is just not happening. My head and my thoughts were swirling as I looked at my reflection in the mirror. I saw a face staring back at me that looked so tired, exhausted, and completely terrified. I pulled my shirt back to find burn marks on my upper torso. There were also scratch marks on me too. As I was doing this, my toilet began to make those sounds again. "Get out of my house... just leave me alone... get out, get out... get out!" I screamed. I closed the door to my ensuite and ran out into my lounge. I grabbed my Dad's rosary beads, put them on, placed the Bible in my lap, and began to say the Lord's Prayer over and over. Eventually, out of sheer exhaustion, I must have fallen asleep. I awoke later that morning to the phone ringing. John had called to see how I was. I so wanted to tell him what had happened, but I knew that he would worry himself sick.

"Yeah, I'm fine," I lied through my teeth. "All good here; had a good night." When I walked back into my bedroom, I saw that all my curtains above my bed that I normally had tucked under the blind were all ripped out. No one could have done this, and the windows were shut—no breeze or wind. IT was letting me know that IT was definitely in there with me last night. I pulled my shirt back and once again saw scratches on my upper chest, legs, and abdomen. *Maybe I scratched myself in my sleep when I was having that horrific nightmare?* I thought. But how did the curtains get in that state? How did I get burns on me while I was sleeping? No matter how hard I tried to tell myself a logical explanation, deep down I knew the truth. I told my mother what had happened to me, and she told me that she went out to see Dad at his gravesite. She looked at his photo and told him that I needed him to ramp up his act. "I also asked him for a sign that he heard me, and I told him to blow a light—something, I didn't care. You got your feather; I came home that day to salt lamps blown in my house. This would have to mean that he was listening, so talk to him, Karen, and ask Dad for help," Mum told me.

When John came home, I could not hide the marks from him. How could I? It wasn't as if they were somewhere he wouldn't see them. I can still see the look of sheer shock on his face when he saw what IT had done to me. "Oh my God, what the hell happened to you? How on earth did you get all these scratches and burns all over you?" All I could do was just cry. I couldn't speak; I was too traumatised. That is when I knew deep down he truly understood what was finally happening to me. He hugged me gently, due to the pain I was in, and told me that we would get more help and that he would do everything he could to help me. I knew in my heart that there was nothing he could do. This was my journey, and this was a battle and path that I had to walk down alone.

PULLING BACK THE VEIL...

"REMEMBER TO LOOK UP AT THE STARS AND NOT DOWN AT YOUR FEET. TRY TO MAKE SENSE OF WHAT YOU SEE AND WONDER ABOUT WHAT MAKES THE UNIVERSE EXIST." —STEPHEN HAWKING

Joy asked if I had any of Cyndi's items still in my house. I explained that all the crystals had been collected, but she had left the wooden triangles and a few other things. "Ohhhh nooo, Steve said that those triangles are like portals and if they are open they can bring all sorts of terrible, evil malevolent beings into your home. Get rid of them, take everything back, and give it all back to her. You can do this by yourself, Karen. Do it as soon as you get home and after you have taken everything back, sage the absolute F**K out of your home, your yards, your cars, everything, including yourself and sprinkle holy water over all of you and call on Archangel Michael and your Dad."

Ohhh great what the hell could be in my home now after all this time, I thought to myself. Anne rang to see how I was. "It sounds like IT is trying to ramp up again, keep playing the Archangel Michael invocation, sage your house and make sure you put lots of holy water and salt all over your house, every door, every wall panel, absolutely everywhere. Keep asking for the angels to give you strength and courage to get through this. I know that you are on the right path and I know you are sick and tired of waiting but all will be revealed. You are coming out of the darkness and into the light. You are truly being so looked after and protected."

Anne told me that it was constantly coming up in her cards that she is going to love, guide, help, and heal an advanced soul. "Karen, I truly think that this is you. Every time that card comes up in my reading, you contact me, EVERY single time."

"What is an advanced soul?" I asked, completely confused.

"It means you have been here before many times and that you have a very spiritual journey ahead of you. You are going to help heal a lot of broken people. There is lots more information that you can read up on about it," Anne explained.

"Why was Campbell getting to see all these different things when he meditated and gets to experience lucid dreaming? He is seeing the most amazing things, and yet when I do it, I see absolutely nothing," I asked, confused.

"It's because it is finally his time to wake up, and I think he can see things more than you can because he didn't suffer the horrendous trauma that you did, Karen. When you start to heal from this trauma, the veil will be lifted for you too, and you will also experience amazing sights in these other realms. I honestly think that you two were very close in a past life together. I know he is Scottish; maybe you were in a past life, Karen. Maybe you were brother and sister? It is no accident or coincidence that you have found each other again in this lifetime," Anne explained.

Campbell began to get into spirituality way more than I was. He started to meditate for long periods, bought hundreds of dollars' worth of crystals, started visiting websites, and began wearing protective crystals on his necklace and specific oils. He let me borrow *The Crystal Bible* to help me with my development. He even told me that he suddenly had the urge to start making wands and had absolutely no idea why. He described in detail to me how he made them. I was just fascinated with how much he was embracing all of this; he was literally leaving me in the dust.

As I was looking at esoteric articles on my phone, I came across an advertisement for a lady overseas who dealt with spirit attachments. She had helped over 100,000 people all over the world since the sixties. It mentioned that common signs of spirit attachment include chronic fatigue, digestive disorders, frequent headaches, anxiety, powerful negative emotions, unexplained phobias, depression, mood swings, intrusive thoughts, suicidal thoughts, sleep problems, addiction, eating disorders, weight problems, hearing voices, alienation, always feeling cold, mental illnesses, feeling of a presence around you, concentration difficulties, not feeling yourself, hallucinations, relationship problems, severe allergies, unusual skin sensations, lack of clarity, panic attacks, abdominal pains, poor memory, insomnia, and more. I suffered from so many of these. Did I actually have a spirit attachment? I wondered to myself in angst.

Spirits are attracted by and feed off our negative emotions. Most people attract them when they experience intense, powerful negative emotions during really stressful events like losing their job, personal injury or illness, divorce, the death of a loved one or close friends, or marital separation. Other factors that can attract them include playing with Ouija boards, using alcohol or drugs, feelings of guilt, holding grudges, and playing violent video games. These can all make us extremely vulnerable to spirit attachments. Spirits can draw energy from us so powerfully that we no longer have the desire to do anything that we once enjoyed. Even just one is an extremely heavy burden on your energy system. Most people will not understand or even recognise what is actually happening to them.

When I was at work that afternoon, I had to go and do a wound dressing on a lady. I walked into her room and shut the door. "Hello," I said, and within seconds the door burst open, and all her wardrobe doors shook violently for around 30 seconds. We both just stared in amazement at what we witnessed. I looked down at her, and she said, "I must have a ghost in my room."

"As long as he is a friendly one," I told her. I went out and looked in the corridor in case some nurses had done this, but no one was there. Not that they would have done this; her windows were closed—it just baffled me. I spoke with Anne about it, and she told me that it must be getting near her time and that her family were coming for her. Exactly a week later, she died.

One of my residents was going to hospital a few days later to have a procedure done, and she was extremely apprehensive about it. When I spoke with her, she said something was telling her not to go through with it, but her family were all pressuring her to do it. She was still very much capable of making her own decisions and was worried out of her mind. That night, I dreamt that she went to hospital and died in the middle of the procedure. It really upset me, and the next day, I told one of my nursing colleagues about the dream. Patricia assured me it was just a silly dream and that our resident would be fine. Margaret was in good health, and it was just a routine procedure. Of course, I never told her about the dream, but it left me feeling unsettled. I was on shift when the ambulance came to get her, and she was visibly distressed as she got onto the trolley. I held Margaret's hand and reassured her that she would be fine and that I'd see her when she got back. I felt extremely uneasy saying this to her.

The next day when I arrived at work, Patricia was sitting at the desk and turned white after getting off the phone. It was the hospital; our resident had suffered a terrible heart attack in the middle of the procedure and didn't survive. I was heartbroken for her and her family. More and more breadcrumbs…

Another incident involved a resident who was on a syringe driver. I had to check on Joyce before night shift arrived. I went into her room and held her hand. I told her she didn't have to hold on anymore and that her family wanted her to be at peace. She seemed to acknowledge me very slowly. "You can go now," I whispered softly to her. "It's really beautiful where you're going; my Dad told me so." I went home, and in the early hours of the morning, I dreamt about her. She was showing me a book with photos of her as a child and growing up. She thanked me for all my help and asked me to thank the nurses for everything they had done. She was upset with herself for being cranky towards everyone in the end and never leaving her room. She hadn't intended for this, but the pain was horrendous, and nobody truly understood its severity. She hugged me and said she was going, asking once again to thank everyone.

Joyce got up, laid back in her body on the bed, and within seconds, the whole room filled with the most brilliant golden light, like fireflies dancing all over her room and around her. She went up sideways, not straight towards the ceiling, showing no signs of anxiety or fear. Joyce knew she was going home to see her loved ones, filled with incredible joy. I just stood there watching, knowing I didn't have to do anything. Her face was radiant, and she had a beautiful smile. This was her time, and she was going in her own peaceful way. I said a little prayer for her and wished Joyce a safe journey home. I could hear John saying, "Karen, wake up." I awoke to him looking over me. "You must have been having another nightmare," he said. I was sweating, bright red, and had torn the sheets apart, waking him up in the process. "WHAT THE HECK WERE YOU DREAMING OF? Did you have lions chasing you? My God, it must have been good!" he asked in exasperation. I replied, "I think one of my residents just died and came to say goodbye to me. Wow, that was intense." From my home computer, I logged onto work to check the report. "Go and see if any of your residents have passed away, and I'll make you some coffee," said John. As I logged on, I knew in my heart Joyce was gone. I read the report; the RN on night shift had just finished writing it—she had died just over 20 minutes ago. I knew she was finally at peace.

POWER OF DIVINE PROTECTION...

"A GOD WISE ENOUGH TO CREATE ME AND THE WORLD I LIVE IN IS WISE ENOUGH TO WATCH OUT FOR ME" —PHILIP YANCEY

"How are things at the haunted mansion?" texted Joy.

I replied, "Gosh, I have a traumatic near-death experience, and all this happens to me like in a movie script. It's all beyond comprehension. Anne said the more I heal, the more my gifts will come through. Still, I honestly have no idea what I'm supposed to do or what they even are. When I find my power... ha-ha. I'll definitely put a big protective light around you so nothing can ever happen to you. I'm still putting holy salt and holy water inside my toilet bowl, cistern, my house, around my land, and our cars."

While I was doing this, I said out loud, "I cast whatever darkness is in this house out FOREVER, you are not welcome here, and I send you to the light." I'm pretty sure the noise I heard next was my neighbour Paula falling off her chair in her pergola, which is right next to my bathroom ensuite... ha-ha. She must think I'm in some sort of cult or something; she's very wary of me. Hopefully, I've finally gotten rid of IT. I'm just so tired and exhausted from going through this every day of my life—I just wish IT would leave me alone. What does IT want, my soul? Well, IT tried that... lol. It felt like if I didn't laugh, I would cry, and I just wouldn't be able to ever stop.

My friend Maddie rang me. "Karen, I contacted a really good friend of mine, and she's got some holy salt and holy water for you. It's been blessed by the actual bishop. No names were mentioned, but he would like to meet you and hear more about your story." Maddie wanted to meet at a club because her family were very concerned about her coming over to our house due to what was happening. My mother also joined us there. "When you go home, I was told to tell you to put this holy salt in all four corners of your house, outside your window sills, and outside your doors." Maddie then pulled out a jar. "This is full of holy water. Go around to all your doors and handles and walls, make a sign of the cross, and say out loud, 'I bless this home in the name of the almighty Jesus Christ.'"

We talked at length about things that had happened over the years to my family since we arrived there, and I could start to connect the dots from a different perspective. We finally got up to leave, and we were all walking out to the car park together. Suddenly, I saw scratch marks all over the back of my bumper bar, glistening in the sunlight. "That son of a bitch," I said angrily. "Look what IT did to my car!"

I waited until John and Jenna were not at home and went around with the holy water. My heart was pounding in my chest. I called on Archangel Michael to be with me and slowly went to all my doors and handles, making the sign of the cross and saying aloud what I had been instructed to say. I felt like I was watching myself inside some set of a horror movie, and my mind just couldn't process that what I was doing was actually real—I felt terrified. At least I did it during the day and not at night. I told Jenna that I had put some salt out to keep the ants away because we were due for some rain and I'd heard it was an old wives' tale. I didn't want to tell her the real reason—she was already petrified enough.

The next morning, I awoke to the sounds of banging coming from all over the top of my roof. "What on earth is that sound?"

I thought. I went to the front door and opened it. All over my lawn in front of my house, across the road, and on my roof were about 30 ibis birds, and there was bird droppings everywhere. "Oh, come on, you've GOT to be kidding me... like, what the!!!" I got my two pet dogs, Bella and Beau, to chase them away at least ten times a day. Every day, they would be there, and every day would be the same routine of letting the dogs out to chase them away. I was so thankful that I wasn't at work and was on days off—I could only imagine the absolute mess that would have been created from so many birds if they'd been allowed to keep defecating all over my house.

John got a gurney from work, and we cleaned the entire outer exterior of our home, including the front road and the gutter. We felt like we were giving our house a thorough cleansing. We worked relentlessly for hours, and our home came out sparkling. To this day, touch wood, those birds have never returned. "Now you know it's not going to leave that easily—it may be quiet, but it's still lurking around, I'm sure," texted Joy. Suddenly, I felt a sting across my lower leg, and I texted back, "OMG, I just went to get up, and look what it just did to my leg." I felt a stinging sensation and looked down to see a big scratch mark across my lower leg. "Just sick to death of it scratching me—JUST OVER IT."

"It must know I'm talking to you... it's not gone, just lying in wait to make its next move. But you and hubby are so solid, and that makes a helluva difference. That's a rare and beautiful thing."

Joy took me to a German restaurant that had not long opened in our town. I knew it was her birthday, so I went down to the esoteric shop and saw in the display window a crystal bracelet that I was sure she would love. I bought it for her after everything she had done for me. It didn't feel like enough to say thank you—this friend of mine had literally saved my life. If it wasn't for her, I often wonder what might have happened to me or to my beautiful family. I feel forever indebted to this incredible woman who literally changed every facet of my life. Just SO, SO, SO incredibly blessed.

Joy told me she often wondered why she had come here to live and said that in her heart, she knew it was to meet me and help me on my journey. She was definitely my miracle. When I gave her the bracelet, she cried and told me how much it meant to her. That night she texted, "Thank you for a lovely day; it was fantastic. And I LOVE LOVE LOVE my bracelet—I will treasure it forever. Bless you, my beautiful friend."

I texted back, "So glad you loved your bracelet. I saw those beautiful colours and thought of my gorgeous friend. Wear it often, and may it give you the strength you need to follow your dreams. I SO hope this bracelet brings you everything you desire. Thank you, too, for a lovely day. I always know that when I see you, you'll make me laugh until my sides hurt. Love ya, sweet."

EMBRACED BY THE DIVINE...

> "I THINK IN EVERY LESSON THERE'S A BLESSING AND THERE'S SO MANY BLESSINGS FROM ALL THE LESSONS I'VE HAD TO GO THROUGH IN MY LIFE." —ALONZO MOURNING

"Have you ever tried to meditate, Karen?" Anne asked me.

"No, not really. I know Campbell does it all the time now sometimes for hours on end," I replied.

Anne told me, "It will help you to quieten your mind and allow you to find answers you are seeking. Some people need to listen to guided meditation when they are talking but others can just listen to music to achieve the same thing. Try and do it every day even if just at the start its only for 10 or 20 minutes. As you get the hang of it, you can increase the time limit. When you meditate, you can make contact with your spirit guides, spirit animals, and lots of other amazing things.

"Meditation can allow you to heal your spirit, mind, and body. Always make sure you put protection around you and intend to only allow benevolent energies to make contact with you. It will help you get rid of all that monkey mind chatter and negative thoughts that so incessantly plague us every day with the stress of what we call life. It helps to clear our mind from all of our frustrations, worries, resentments, anxieties, stresses, fears etc and helps us get closer to our own higher self. We start to understand about ourselves and our life and start to uncover and discover the precious gift inside us of who we really are."

Since I started meditating, it has certainly helped me on my journey of spiritual development and growth. It has helped my mind and body heal from the trauma I endured and has helped me deal with my inner conflicts. We can fill ourselves with love, joy, and happiness and, in a sense, become enlightened. It does require tenacity, persistence, patience, and practice, but the more you do it, the easier it becomes. I go into my meditation room, filled with my angels and crystals, and light a candle. I darken the room, turn on the air-conditioning to limit any outside noise and distractions, lie down, and let all my scattered thoughts float away. I surrender and let go.

We need to remember that our human mind can either take us to euphoric levels of joy or drown us in trenches of misery. We control our mind, but most people let the mind control them. My past was gone; it was over and finished with. I needed to learn from it and let it go. My future was still yet to arrive, so I stopped worrying about what was in it. Worrying is so worthless and unnecessary; I knew it could bring stress and heartache, and if that happened, I wouldn't achieve anything from it. I had to live in the present, be mindful, and let myself experience the joy and happiness that life wanted to bestow on me. I had to remember that everything is interconnected. I had to see God, my inner light, my true self. I had to let the light within me turn on and shower me with love.

I went home, put my phone on "Do Not Disturb," and found a heap of meditations on YouTube. I discovered that guided meditations worked best for me, though I often fell asleep. "That's okay; your subconscious mind can still hear the messages, and your mind will be relaxing," Anne told me. I started doing this every day, and most times, I would see a purple light swirling around me before drifting off and waking up with no memory of anything. Sometimes, I would feel a tingling sensation all over me, and it felt like I was being pulled forward. It frightened me, and I would pull myself out of it.

"That's your higher beings making contact with you when you feel that sensation," Anne explained. "It's nothing bad or sinister. Next time it happens, go with it and see what happens—don't be afraid. Your angels and spirit guides want to contact you."

When you pray, you talk to God; meditation is when He answers you. You don't have to sit in meditation for hours; some people find peace walking in nature, doing yoga, journaling daily, or watching sunrises over the ocean. What makes meditation successful isn't how quiet you can make your mind, but that you show up for it every single day. Some have said it has moved them so deeply that it has changed their whole perception of the world. Meditation helped me slowly develop the ability to focus and concentrate, allowing me to delve into my subconscious mind. Some people experience memories of past lives, while others gain insights so profound that they help solve issues in their current life. It brought me immense peace and helped me heal from wounds I had buried and wanted to keep hidden forever.

Anne explained, "Health-wise, it has helped many people overcome addictions like smoking, insomnia, and weight control. I really want you to consider meditating so you can also discover how amazing this is and develop your spiritual freedom. Always remember there is a reason and meaning for everything that happens in our life, whether we understand it or not. When you meditate, you can also raise your vibration. There are several ways to do this, including praying, Reiki, relaxing baths, positive affirmations, being in nature, showing gratitude, sound healing, eating fruits and vegetables, staying well-hydrated, moving your body, journalling, and spreading kindness, to name but a few.

"There is always a higher plan at work and an opportunity for you to grow at a soul level. Just remember to be patient with yourself and trust in the process; the results will be absolutely magnificent. When I meditate, I can reach higher levels of consciousness and self-awareness. I focus my mind, go within, and begin my own unique journey. Trust me, a truly breathtaking and incredible universe will be waiting for you, too."

WIDE AWAKE... FINALLY!

"IN THE MIDST OF CHANGE, WE OFTEN DISCOVER WINGS WE NEVER KNEW WE HAD." —EKATERINA WALTER

John and I were shopping when we saw a stall with lots of wooden frames with the most beautiful images on them. There were over a hundred to choose from. I stopped at one of a young Indian woman near a beautiful lake; it caught my eye. I was intrigued and thought of Anne. "She would just love this one," I told John as I pointed to it. The lady who sold it to me said it was an image from a movie made in 1953.

When I gave it to Anne the next time I had a healing session, she opened it and just loved it. "Oh Karen, that is absolutely beautiful."

"When I saw it, I thought of you for some reason. It's from the year 1953," I told her.

"Oh really? That's amazing; that's the year I was born," she said, giving me a big hug.

The white feathers I was finding were amazing. They were on the floor of my home, on the security grill of my front door, on my pillowcase, inside my car on my front seat. One day I was talking to Mum on the phone in the computer room when I felt something falling down on me and looked up and saw a white feather drift down right in front of me. It was just mind-boggling. A few nights later, I dreamt of being in some sort of bushland, but from where I was, I could see the ocean in the background. I knew I was near the water but didn't know exactly where. A man was pointing at the ground, telling me, "This is where I am. You need to let them know that this is where I am!" I was very confused as he was in front of me but was saying this was where he was. He was pointing at the ground, and when I looked down, I could see a pile of bones that looked human.

What the??? Who are you? I awoke in a cold sweat.

John asked, "Why did you say that name?"

"What? Did I?" I asked, confused, as I recalled my strange dream.

"Yes, you just said this name so distinctly. That name you mentioned is actually the name of a drug informant in this area who has been missing for many years. They've never found his body," John explained.

This was all becoming too much for me. I noticed that whenever Suzannah came into my house, she would start burping repeatedly.

"Are you okay?" I asked, really concerned.

"Sorry, I'm just having some downloads. When I burp like this, it can't attach to me or attack me. Remember, Karen, you have so much power. You can live with this thing around you—they're all over the planet. IT doesn't even have a body. You do! By Cyndi making you shut all your toilets and everything, it was giving IT power as it was filling you and your family with so much fear. No wonder it was having a field day with you all. The more fear you feel, the more power you give IT. They are parasites; they feed off your energy. The more negative energy around you, the more fighting between family members, the more they feed off that too. Have you noticed that your family members, like you and your kids, started fighting more than usual?"

"Well yes, as they've gotten older, the fighting has definitely intensified and ramped up. I just thought it was them being typical hormonal teenagers."

"Cameron asked what you were like, Karen, and I told him that you were VERY gentle, that you had a very sweet nature."

I laughed, "Don't know if my kids would agree with that one," I replied. Suzannah had told me previously that when we go through really bad trauma, like grief, accidents, or operations, we are more prone to being attacked.

"Well, no wonder it targeted her and had no trouble slamming her over and over again—she was so vulnerable," said Cameron. He believed that the lady who came through my wall was evil as she had no eyes.

"Do you sprinkle holy water and salt, use incense and sage?" she asked.

"Yes, I do now. I never knew about any of this until I started my new journey," I replied. At each door and window, I make the figure-eight sign, which represents infinity, as well as the sign of the cross, and say out loud, "May all that is pure, benevolent, good, holy, and true come into my home and into the hearts of all who live here, and may we always be protected forever in the name and power of the Almighty Jesus Christ." I do this while holding a candle; sometimes, I ring a bell to purify the energy in a room," I told her.

Suzannah then explained to me, "The problem with attempting to summon or communicate with spirits is the very real danger of summoning demonic, inhumane, or evil entities, and this should be avoided at all costs. Objects can be extremely dangerous and used as vessels to inflict suffering and pain upon unsuspecting victims, as their sole purpose is to wreak havoc upon innocent human beings. This thing is playing with you—get rid of it all.

IT is drawing all over your walls, and the more people that come to look at it, the more it is spoken about, the more power IT is getting. You need to get rid of everything off your walls, clean up your house, and show IT that this is YOUR house. An entity can't live in a place where the affected person takes the reins—not some guru who puts herbs or oils in there or those who consider themselves ordained in the eyes of the church. YOU have the power in this situation. Nobody else. This is YOUR home. YOU have all the power!"

THE VEIL WAS BEING LIFTED...

"EXPERIENCE, THAT MOST BRUTAL OF TEACHERS. BUT YOU LEARN, MY GOD, DO YOU LEARN." —C.S. LEWIS

"Remember, you have the physical body here; IT doesn't even have a body. You have got to remind IT and let IT know you have the power here. Don't provoke IT. Just make a firm statement; you need to be respectful but be very firm when you ask IT to leave and do not show any fear," said Suzannah. My heart was racing as I said goodbye to Suzannah. I walked into my ensuite to use the toilet, and every time, my exhaust fan would go ballistic like IT was angry. I could hear lots of sounds in the roof cavity and I never turned my fan on. It was starting to become very unsettling. I would look outside but there was never any wind, suddenly as it started it would abruptly stop.

"Remember, you know what to do. As you get stronger, IT will try and fight. Stay strong; you have a body IT would love to take over."

"Why won't IT just leave me alone and go find someone else?"

"IT is testing you in a way. DO NOT GIVE IN. Did you get all that tourmaline and put it out in the moonlight? It's holding negative energy. Put large pieces under your bed. I paid $150 for mine—it's HUGE. Remember, that's when I said entities kept leaving my house, opening doors and windows from the inside to escape. This is your big challenge, Karen."

"Yes, I did. I even put pieces in the cisterns of both my toilets. Gosh, being off work for these past few weeks because I'm so sick, the bills have piled up."

"Slow and steady, Karen. I know you're in a hurry to get rid of this thing, but there are many lessons for you on the way. A ladder has many rungs—one by one, you climb. Start to detox your body first, from the inside out. Herbs and fruit are the most healing things we have, especially fresh pineapple, melons, apples, lemons, berries, and oranges. Eat lots of green mixed salad, wholegrain rice, raw nuts, and drink plenty of water. Maintaining a vegetarian diet is the quickest route to developing your clairvoyance. Even faster is becoming vegan. Things like alcohol, dairy, chocolate, sugar, and red meat are the greatest blockers of your abilities. Remember to keep yourself grounded."

"Ohhhhhhh, it's just been such a long, hard, exhausting, and challenging 15 years. I'm just soooooooo tired—I haven't even gotten over my near-death experience yet. I was supposed to be recovering, and then this all happened. I was told IT was just enveloping me in my chair and bed… this is all just way toooooo much," I said in sheer frustration.

"I understand, but now you are about to make a difference. Don't give up now. I know it's tiring. I have fought through life for years as well. Now you have MET the problem. Now you can make a difference. Maybe you need a psychiatrist to talk to, and maybe you can get some sort of financial help to relieve the horrific financial pressure you are under. I truly believe you have the power to get through this and totally change your life for the better. You have been dealing with this so much for so long—you have ALREADY proved your strength, Karen."

"And you were sent back here to deal with it… please trust your Dad. That elite noble shungite is more feminine than black tourmaline and also super powerful for protection. It would be great for you to find a piece you can wear around your neck over your heart chakra," explained Suzannah.

"I'm just terrified that this thing is going to come after my daughter."

"I don't believe your daughter is of any interest to IT. Don't go back into your fear. YOU ARE POWERFUL, and your daughter has no fear of it. Just sit with it; maybe something will come to you."

"I remember seeing my friend's suicide, car accidents… even dreamt years ago of a plane crash and saw all the victims' photos in the newspapers. Most things for me don't happen until years after I dream them."

"Gosh, these are terrible things to dream. YOU have great power, Karen—it's a gift. When we have these kinds of gifts, we are more likely to be messed with by such entities. I've also had similar experiences with my dreams and even visions when I'm fully awake… it's like I could see ahead since I was very young. I can also leave my body."

"Wow, no, I have never seen anything when awake, always asleep," I replied.

"It's been a long journey for you, Karen, but you need to protect yourself. Sometimes our pineal is open, but our other chakras are not in line. I think this was my issue. Our chakras are like wheels; sometimes some of them are spinning nicely while others are very wobbly."

"Gosh, I think mine have wobbled so much they've all fallen off," I laughed.

"I can astral travel too. I used to be more out of my body than in. I'm much more grounded now. I see things like you have dreams, but I'm awake. You need to ground yourself; this entity has picked on you because you are so open and gentle. I believe it's a great lesson, not a curse."

"When I was saging my house, I would also play on both televisions, my home computer, and my phone a prayer called 'Removal of Entities, Dark Energy and Demonic Powers.' It was an exorcism prayer in Latin. While it played on YouTube, it showed a cross blazing with light, slowly rotating in circles. Gosh, there's SO much to learn… feeling like a deer in the headlights right now."

"There are lots of things to do, but you need to go at your own pace. As slow or as fast as you feel comfortable with. You will find your way. You will keep finding people to guide you, and you will know what is right for you. We are all so different. My best suggestion to start with is to detox your life—start with your body, and your environment will follow, and IT will leave. You don't need anyone else to help you. This is YOUR home… it's YOUR mind… it's YOUR body. No one else can deal with this but you. Stop letting other people play with IT and deal with IT yourself. You and John—his support will confirm to IT that you are serious, where two meet. There is such greater power."

"My husband is not in a good headspace right now. I'm not allowed to talk about IT, like EVER. He thinks people are putting all these strange ideas into my head, and that there has to be a logical explanation for all of this… blah blah."

"Stop talking to too many people. Listen to your inner voice—if you can't hear it, lay down, breathe, and wait. If you still can't hear it, carry on, and slowly you will get your answer the more relaxed you become. I also do colonics and my own enemas. I was going to suggest you do colonics… we are all full of parasites," said Suzannah.

"Yes, as well as being an RN, I am also a certified colonic therapist. You should see the parasites that we get out of clients—it is absolutely mind-boggling, the things I have seen coming out of people, and they have no idea what is going on inside them."

"OMG! I never realised that you held both those titles. You have great contacts, Karen. You really need to detox, as above so below, inside and out."

THE SHIFT...

"TRUE FORGIVENESS IS WHEN YOU CAN SAY THANK YOU FOR THAT EXPERIENCE." —OPRAH WINFREY

"You know how powerful you are, Karen. I'm just here to remind you."

"I know I have been told I have this supposed power, but I keep going over and over in my mind what happened to me that night, and that awful smell just won't stop looping in my mind."

"Let IT go; it served you to the next step. Now let it go. Go and buy some Frankincense oil. Use this to sniff whenever you need to. I wish you sweet dreams and a truly restful sleep. I have sent you a parasite frequency that kills parasites in case you need to play it to your unwelcome visitor. You will find so many more on YouTube. I follow Dr Robert Morse. Check him out... I've been detoxing for six years so I don't end up in my mother's position. It's so important to detox those buggers out, Karen."

"Gosh, I just finished my four-year Bachelor's degree in Nutritional Medicine, then nearly died, and now have this wealth of knowledge but just can't seem to get back into it. Ahhhhh, now I think I definitely know why. They told me this thing has oppressed me for many years, like a moth oppresses a flame."

"Like I said, I'm just here to remind you, yes… but you are now the butterfly about to leave the cocoon. And now you have all the knowledge ready to use. It's perfect timing, Karen… that is why your Dad sent you back. You have work to do. First you, then other desperate humans lost in this maze called life."

"My husband always said that unfortunately, I hadn't finished my studies in time to help my Dad, but his legacy through my studies trying to save his life is now how I can save thousands of others."

"Yes, I just need to save mine first."

"You have been through the worst of it. Remember, the most intimate relationship is the one you have with yourself. Take a break from the hectic world and reconnect with yourself. During your transformation, you might feel like everything is falling apart, but in reality, everything is coming together for your highest good. You're being pushed to evolve and get out of your comfort zone so you can live and experience your true greatness… welcome change.

"I truly believe that parasites are at play with all the images that they keep putting all around your house. I think moving out of there is a good response. Remember to put tourmaline around your bed and try to get some rest. I have sent you a podcast to listen to, Karen—it's awesome. It's called Occult Forces and Psychic Attacks, part one of the Cosmic Matrix Podcast. Thought you might like it."

"I was told that there were a lot of Aboriginal massacres on this land, and that when they were building houses here, they brought in landfill for months before to build it up, as this estate is prone to massive flooding. A friend of mine who had a friend living here for a few years did some research. She said that she and her husband had a terrible time after they moved here and within four years just couldn't deal with it anymore and moved down south.

Sophie was told that the landfill came from next to a cemetery that hadn't been expanded, so the council decided to use it. She also found on another website related to this suburb that many years ago, the council had used a section of land as the local cemetery. They realised that the bodies kept rising up after it rained because of the flooding, so eventually, the bodies were all dug up and reinterred in the main cemetery."

"Get off that land for sure, please get out as soon as you can."

"I was also told that when that lady came back and buried that necklace in the backyard, it stirred up this energy and made it very angry."

"Did she ask you for your permission to bury it in your backyard, or did she just tell you?"

"She said she needed to bury something and needed something hard like an old metal spoon that we could throw away afterwards."

"So, no actual permission from you? Karen, please stop letting these people do what they want. They are taking your power away. You need to stop giving your money away to all these people. You can live with this energy. Tell them thank you for all of your help and for making you realise who you truly are. You don't need anybody's help; you can do this all by yourself, Karen. You are POWERFUL! You don't think this energy is just here in this estate, do you? These entities are all over this planet," Suzannah replied.

After the necklace was buried, that same teaspoon was thrown down the drain at the front of our house. The very next day, when I went to collect the mail, I stopped in my tracks and my heart began to beat madly. I just froze on the spot. It took me a couple of minutes to process what I was seeing. There was that exact same teaspoon on the road in front of our driveway. I took a few steps forward slowly, as it felt hard to walk. I picked the spoon up and threw it in my garbage bin. How the hell did that spoon get out of the drain? It was impossible. But deep down, I already knew the answer.

"I was just so broken and had to try to put myself back together again. I think a lot of my friends think that I have abandoned them, but I just don't want them to know right now. I tried to talk with a few close friends of mine, but they just cut me off like I was having some sort of hallucination, and that I must be tired and need some sleep. I went out with friends we hadn't seen in such a long time. Leigh is actually Jenna's godmother. She and her husband came to have tea with us at one of our favourite restaurants. Near the end of the night, we told them a few things about how we had a smoking ceremony and that there was something in our house. I showed them both a photo. I have known Leigh for over 20 years; if anyone would believe me, it would be her. To my shock, she just stared at the photo and us like we had five heads coming out of our necks.

"'That is really creepy,' said Leigh, looking really unsettled. I suddenly understood that she didn't really believe us; she just had no concept of what I had been through. That was a major life lesson for me that night. I kept silent, fearing the repercussions from friends and other family members."

"Remember, Karen, not everyone will understand your journey. That's okay; it's all good. It's not their journey to make sense of—it's yours," Suzannah reassured me.

FINDING MY TRIBE...

"THE MIRACLE OF YOUR MIND ISN'T THAT YOU CAN SEE THE WORLD AS IT IS. IT'S THAT YOU CAN SEE THE WORLD AS IT ISN'T."
—KATHRYN SCHULZ

I felt like the few nonspiritual friends that I had trusted to tell this experience to thought it was a joke—laughing, rolling their eyes, discounting me, making me feel like I must have some sort of mental disorder to be saying such things. I had to find my own tribe, the people who did understand me, who knew exactly what I was going through. "It's really traumatising trying to tell my story, and I'm honestly not sure how my friends are going to react to me," I was explaining.

"Don't feel you have to," said Suzannah. "They are living in a completely different energy and frequency vibration to you. They cannot understand what you are saying or truly hear what you're telling them. They can only meet you as deeply as they have honestly met themselves. Please stop draining your energy by continually trying to explain yourself. They all have their own journey." From then on, I never spoke with any of my other friends about it again, and to this day, most of them have no idea what we went through and probably never will.

"I feel like now, though, I can finally start to reconnect with the world again, so to speak."

"Most people who have some sort of psychic gift are more likely to be slammed. You need to remove everything from this house and stop playing with IT," Suzannah told me. I had heard about a clairvoyant who lived in the same town and came highly recommended. I decided to ring her to see what her take was on my story and if anything came through for her. I called to speak with her, and once again, my phone kept cutting out. I rang back a couple of times, and Kath told me that I had an entity. WOW, she was good. I hadn't said a word to her about any of my story, and she was right on it. "That is why it keeps cutting your phone. Hang up now, and I will text you the details of my address so you can come to me," she replied.

Kath texted me her address, and the next day I drove over to see her. It was absolutely torrential rain that day; I hadn't seen rain like it for many years. Lightning and thunder were all around me. SO typical, I thought, of all the days. I normally would never be driving around in this sort of weather. I pulled up, and the gutters were overflowing with so much water. I ran in, absolutely drenched. "Thank you for seeing me." She told me that she too had an entity that had been giving her a very hard time for many months and had actually pushed her over and broken her ankle.

Kath told me that she had spent many months on crutches... OMG!!! I think I just stared at her, completely dumbfounded. This world was all so new to me, and it just kept getting bigger and bigger. "We have to understand, though; we can't blame them for everything bad that happens in our life, Karen. Sometimes our own choices and decisions will do that too." She explained that she would go under, connect, and see what messages she got.

Kath seemed to be squinting and having trouble looking at me. "Are you ok?" I asked, really concerned. She told me that I was so bright, like a white burning fire; my light was actually blinding her, and there were lots of beautiful pink orbs around me. As she connected, the lightning and thunder intensified, and I nearly fell off my seat when it cracked. She finally opened her eyes and said to me, "IT was an Aboriginal… he was very powerful in his human form when he was on earth—maybe a shaman, witchdoctor, or elder of the tribe. He had a daughter whom he loved dearly." She began to get overwhelmed and said she could feel terrible pain, and started to cry. "Oh, white man did terrible things to his daughter and made him watch, and then they did it to him too. He probably doesn't even realise that he is dead."

I told her about my youngest and that she had had so many accidents before she even reached the age of five. "He was protecting her. Children who are very young are very in tune with this world, as we all are, but as we get older, our ego mind takes over, and it becomes less and less. Please try and understand this, but he was most probably looking at your daughter like she was his own and wanted her to be with him." OMG!!! This was just too much to take in. I get chills now when I think about things and how much he must have always been around her.

She then went on to tell me that I have ramped his anger from one million to about twenty million now and that she feels it is best for me to leave that area. I explained that I had got another lady in to grid the land and do an extraction, but she told me that she felt it would not stop. I explained that we were not in a financial position to leave at present, so she gave me a Diamond Light protection. "Close your eyes, ask your guides to cleanse your chakras (all 360 of them). Ask your guides to cleanse your aura. Visualise a Herkimer diamond and step into it. KNOW that you are fully protected. Keep cleansing yourself for as long as you need, and remember to send him so much love and light." I thanked her for her help and left.

John had decided to take me away for the weekend after everything we had been through. As we were leaving that afternoon, the bin had to be put out as it was full. Leaving a garbage bin out where I lived was like putting up a great big neon sign letting the entire town know you were not at home. As there had been a lot of crime in our area and so many car thefts lately, I decided to go and knock on my neighbour's door two doors up. I just wanted to ask if they could put the bin away for us. I went down and knocked on the door. Scott only opened it up a few centimetres, and I could see the whole house was in complete darkness. "Oh, I'm so sorry, I was just wondering if you would be able to put the bin back for us tomorrow as we are leaving this arvo when John gets home from work."

His eyes were darting back and forth as I was speaking to him, and it scared the HELL out of me. "Yeah, no worries," he said, and with that, he promptly shut the door. OMG, what is wrong with Scott? I thought. Then I remembered Cyndi saying, "Say sorry to your neighbours." OMG, is this where IT had gone? Their house did have all those birds on it not long ago, after we finally removed them all from ours. There is always fighting coming from this house, I wonder?

I ran into his wife, Julia, a few days later at the grocery store. She looked terrible. I thanked her for putting the bin away for me and mentioned how wonderful the place was where we stayed, in case they might like to go away for the weekend too. Julia then told me, "Scott has lost his phenomenal-paying job, he's on some very heavy medication, and he never sleeps. His mood swings are so erratic... living with him is like being in a nightmare that I can't wake up from... my life is hell from the moment I wake up to the moment I shut my eyes at night, when I do actually get to sleep."

He had recently been to court for the first time in his life, and it had been splashed all over the papers about him. His behaviour and the things he was doing were so completely out of character. "I just don't know what to do. I feel like I have lost my husband, my kids never stop fighting, everything in our house keeps breaking down. I can't keep up with all the repair bills that keep coming in. I just feel like my whole family has been cursed or something in the last few months. It's just indescribable, the things that keep happening to us," Julia told me.

I SO knew exactly what she was going through; my family had endured it not for days, or weeks, or months, but for YEARS and YEARS and YEARS. I wanted to tell her, but would she actually believe me? But I have photos, I thought. My mind was racing. With that, she began to break down and cry. I went to give her a hug when her phone rang. "It's Scott. I have to go, thank you for listening to me, Karen," said Julia as she quickly wiped away her tears.

That night, I dreamt I was in a big white room, like on holidays. I was unpacking a suitcase, and when I turned around, an Aboriginal man was standing there. He wasn't really old, more middle-aged. He had the most piercing sky-blue eyes, and his white beard was curled under his chin. I gasped in fright and screamed at him to get out. He just stared intensely and then said to me, "I am coming for what I have been wanting." I yelled for John to come to me, even though I knew I was by myself. "You can call on him all you want, but he will NEVER be able to help you."

"Get out!" I screamed. "GET OUT!!!" With that, he gave me one last stare, turned, and left the room. I ran up and pushed all the bolts shut across the door, and then woke up in a cold sweat.

SO MANY SIGNS...

"WHAT'S MEANT FOR YOU WILL HAPPEN FOR YOU IN A WAY WHICH YOU COULD NEVER UNDERSTAND. BELIEVE IN IT. IT'S ALL HAPPENING FOR YOU." —IDIL AHMED

My Aunty, who lived down south, rang to tell me that she had been to her psychic and had told her what was happening to me. Her psychic friend told me that I needed to go through the house and play the song "Hallelujah" by KD Lang all the time. As often as I clean my teeth, and just make it a habit every single day, IT will absolutely hate it and IT will leave. So, for the next few weeks, I played that song religiously all through my house holding my phone in one hand and saging with the other.

I could only imagine what the neighbours must have been thinking, hearing that song all the time. When I think about the suburb where I live, lots of neighbours had been through so much bad luck too: Marriage break-ups, financial hardships and losses, houses being repossessed by banks, thefts, cars being stolen and burnt out. One of my cousins, who also lives in this same estate, had a terrible workplace accident and was off work for many months. There is even someone in this estate who is killing dogs. People have set up security cameras around their houses and have footage of a large-built man covered in a balaclava at night, putting letters into people's mailboxes warning them to shut up their dogs. After two warnings, the dogs are always found dead. He has never been caught. Over the years, a lot of dogs have been baited and died in this estate.

Years ago, I went to a hairdresser who had come to live in the same court as my family. The first time that I went to see her, she apologised for being a "bit out of sorts." When I questioned her further, she told me how, over the weekend, they had been picked to take the preschool pet guinea pig home, as one family did every weekend. Their daughter had been so excited and had played with it just about nonstop for the entire weekend. Yesterday, in the late afternoon, she had put him back in the cage and had started organising baths and tea for the family.

When she got up this morning to feed him and get her girls ready for school, she noticed that he was missing. Frantically, she searched before the girls realised, and then, to her horror, she found his body at the back of the yard, but his head had been cut off. She explained that it wasn't chewed off; it looked like a clean cut, as if done with a sword. She called her husband, who was also horrified at what he saw. Had someone broken in and decapitated it? But their house was locked up with triple bolts. It was just unexplainable.

They took the children to school and told the teacher that he had escaped, which devastated the kids. She came home and looked all around the entire front and back yards, but his head was nowhere to be found. When I went back to see her a couple of months later, she told me they never did find his head. Their daughter was bullied so badly at preschool for letting him get out of his cage that they ended up having to remove her and put her into another school. Within twelve months of them moving just a few doors down from me, they left. She told me that ever since moving here, they had suffered such terrible bad luck and just wanted to get the hell out. Oh, if only that was an option for us.

My Aunty May, who also lives in the same suburb, had her car stolen in the early hours of the morning and was nearly a victim of identity theft. She went on the local news to talk about what happened to her, but they kept her identity a secret. She also told me about a friend of hers who had endured negative entities, and he sleeps every night with over $8000 worth of crystals, but they still gave him a terrible time. He is determined not to let them win. My sister Jane and her husband, who also lived in the same area for only a few years, both lost their contracting jobs and had to leave town. There were no other jobs for them, so they ended up going interstate just to find work. Her husband also got very sick. Lots of fighting going on all around me—behind me, beside me—it just seemed to be everywhere I turned. Even the lady next door barely left her house anymore due to severe depression, and she was such an outgoing person when I met her.

I ran into an old friend who lived a couple of streets back from me. They moved here at a similar time, and our daughters attended preschool together, which is how we met. I remember when the girls were very little, her husband was constructing a large pool in their backyard. The hole had been dug and cemented, but there were still lots of steel pieces protruding out in all directions. One afternoon, she was washing up when she heard the most blood-curdling scream and found that her daughter had fallen in and dropped nearly 5 metres onto the cement below. It was a miracle that she wasn't killed or seriously injured. Must have been an angel looking after her, was all of our responses when she told us. I saw her recently, just a few weeks ago, and she looked really tired.

"How are you?" I asked.

"Ahhhhh, where do I start? My husband actually said to me, 'You know, ever since we moved into this estate, I feel like we have been cursed.'"

Gosh, if she only knew.

Suzannah texted me in the morning:

"How was your sleep?"

"Yeah, not good. Kept waking up and couldn't breathe. Felt like I was being choked again. I have lots of red marks around my throat this morning, but they have gradually faded as the day has gone on. Every time someone rings me on my mobile, it keeps cutting out continually... Another image appeared on the wall behind my toilet, on my kitchen pantry door. More scratch marks are all over every single one of my purple feature walls in my home. When I woke this morning, my entire mirror had what looks like scratch marks all over it... aarrgghhh..."

"Remember, Karen, try to let it all go. Relax, breathe, spend quiet time with yourself, focus on you, NOT IT," texted Suzannah.

I awoke the next morning and was just so grateful to be alive and that my body and my vestibular system were both finally starting to heal. I would go and spend time in church by myself and reflect on what had happened to me and why I had gone through so much. John and I had just spent a lovely weekend away together for the first time in so long. We also took all of my black tourmaline down to the ocean and washed it all in the salt water. We both walked along the water's edge, watching the sun come up. It was just so relaxing and refreshing.

I finally convinced John to go and have a healing with Anne after everything she had done for me. He was very reluctant at first but finally agreed. "He has also had his power taken away from him," Anne told me. Within a few weeks, John was given an interview for a brand-new job, and amazingly, he got it. He was just so VERY happy. I hadn't seen him so elated in a long time. I felt like I finally had my husband back—it was just a fantastic feeling.

I decided to take the black tourmaline off John and noticed that he didn't seem as stressed or angry as he was before. I was told that some people cannot wear it because it's so strong it can make them very aggressive. I replaced it with black obsidian, which is also very protective. We had actually been sleeping soundly for the past couple of nights, and we were planning to go for a drive to a valley with an esoteric shop that sold lots of beautiful crystals to see if we could get one to put under our bed. Suzannah contacted me again that morning to see how I was, and I told her that we were sleeping really well for the first time in such a long time.

"That is so wonderful. I will keep you and your family in my thoughts and keep grounding for you for a while longer—not for you, WITH you. And thank you for taking care of my mum; you really are all such special people. I am so happy to hear that you have found peace, which I know will increase by the day. Sweet dreams to you both; you are doing awesome work, you really are amazing. Thank you for walking into my mother's room."

"Oh gosh, no thank you sooooooo much for being in there. You have NO idea how much you have changed my life and the new perspective I now have on all of this because of you," I texted back, smiling.

I dreamt last night that I was walking through a white room and was looking at photos all over the walls. It was like a memorial dedicated to my niece. I saw my sister Jade and asked her what she was doing there, as she looked so sad. Unfortunately, my alarm went off and woke me up. I looked up the meaning of memorial dreams, and it said that it could signify an occasion for me to show kindness, as sickness and trouble threaten your relatives. "Oh no, is something going to happen to my sister or her daughter?" I thought. That same morning, my mother rang me to tell me that my niece was going for an MRI tomorrow as they had found a growth in her oesophagus.

Cancer of the stomach (gastro-adenocarcinoma) is what had killed her father when he was only 42. She was only in her early twenties and was just terrified. My sister was beside herself with worry. I told Anne that morning what had happened and how I had asked the angels and our Dad to intervene and give her the strength and courage she needed to get through this health battle.

"Oh, Karen, you are certainly starting to tune in now that you are meditating so much more. I will also ask the angels for courage and blessings and ask them to watch over your sister and your niece, so they can guide them both and give them strength as well. You and your family are beautiful; I am so honoured to send blessings to you all to help you through this time of need. It's in the hands of the angels, and they will do what is needed. In them I trust," said Anne. Thankfully, my niece was given the all clear.

GIVING MY POWER AWAY...

"SOME PEOPLE COME INTO OUR LIFE AS BLESSINGS. SOME COME INTO YOUR LIFE AS LESSONS." —MOTHER TERESA

The next day, John and I went for a lovely Sunday drive to a shop in the Valley about 45 minutes from where we live. I walked into the shop and saw so many sparkling crystals and geodes; it was truly beautiful. The colours were just bedazzling, and I didn't know where to look; it honestly took my breath away. I saw a lady at the counter and approached her to ask about black tourmaline crystals. She suddenly began to make dry retching movements and looked at the ground.

"Hi, um, I'm Karen," I stammered. She proceeded to look down at the ground and screwed her face up. … "Is everything ok?" I asked, worried.

"I'm really finding it hard not to vomit on you right now as you are standing in front of me," the woman replied. I was just speechless. This woman feels like she wants to vomit when she looks at me; well, that made me feel just wonderful about myself. She then went on to say that I had a dark energy around me and it was from a husband from a past life that has been looking for me for a VERY long time and that he had finally found me. My head honestly began to swirl exactly like you see on the movies. It was hard to describe; I just went SO dizzy and just saw colours spinning all around me.

Suddenly, I was thinking of the film clip to Meatloaf's song, "I'd Do Anything for Love (But I Won't Do That)." The very first words you see are: "I have travelled across the universe through the years to find her. Sometimes going all the way is just a start." I could hear the words being sung: "Will you get me right out of this God-forsaken town, and will you hose me down with holy water if I get too hot." I felt like I was the one who was going to vomit. This was JUST becoming too damn terrifying, and I just couldn't deal with it anymore. I wanted to burst into tears. Suddenly, my husband walked in and stood beside me at the counter. I remember grabbing his arm to steady myself as I felt like I was going to fall. He could see that I was as white as a sheet.

"What is wrong?" he asked, very concerned.

"She needs lots of protection around her. That shungite is not going to do anything for you."

"Did you need to see my photos of what I can see?" I asked, pulling out my phone.

"NO NO!!!! Put your phone away. I don't want to see any of it. This energy is so dark, evil, malevolent, and powerful. It probably doesn't even realise that IT is dead. IT has been looking for your energy blueprint."

Like my what??? Like WHAT THE!!! This is just too much, I was thinking to myself. She handed me a piece of foolscap paper completely full of writing. It talked about returning my blueprint, cleansing it, and clearing it of all negativity. It explained how to heal myself and what I had to do. I was too confused to even understand what I was reading.

"Well, what does she need?" my husband asked, absolutely gobsmacked.

"Well," she said as she walked around her shop, "you're going to need lots of sage and sage spray and smoky quartz with a point on it, as it will be a cutting tool. You need to put this all over your chakras. You need to say, 'I cut away and remove from myself all negative cords, ties, energies, and entities from my physical body, my spirit, and my soul.' Use this like a cutting tool and make a cutting motion as you say this. Do this all over your body—arms, legs, your whole front, the back of your neck, and your lower back. Do this as many times as you feel you need to." She told me to stand still and ran something over me. I folded my arms in front of myself.

"Get your arms away from your body," she hissed at me. "You're so used to having to protect yourself... your solar plexus is completely blocked. You need yellow jasper. Put this in your navel and cover it with a band-aid. You need to do this every night. Don't go near any hospitals or nursing homes as these places are crawling with entities. Spray yourself constantly with sage."

"What??... wait... I have to go to aged care, I work there, I'm an RN."

"Oh, well that makes a lot of sense then. You will need to sage spray as soon as you get out of your car. Keep it in your handbag and keep protection on you at all times while you are working. When leaving, spray yourself again with sage before you get back in your car. You need to do this EVERY TIME. As you are SO traumatised right now, you have the ability to pick up every piece of SHIT out there as you are so open and broken. I need to find you some black tourmaline you can keep in your bra."

This lady was handing my husband these items, and I was just walking around beside her like I was in a daze. This is a nightmare. PLEASE LET ME WAKE UP! Please someone just WAKE ME THE HELL UP! As I went up to the counter, she began drawing a grid that I had to keep under my bed: four black tourmalines in the four corners and a piece of clear quartz in the middle. I had to imagine invisible walls going up around me every night like steel doors so that they could not be penetrated... black tourmaline in four corners of my house, above every doorway. "If you have anything religious in your home, like Bibles, crucifixes, rosary beads, GET rid of them at once; that will just provoke this sort of energy."

I was aware that other people were walking into the shop as I could hear the buzzer going. Oh no, these people are going to hear what she's saying. I was very self-conscious and was trying to get her attention when suddenly, out of the corner of my eye, I saw Kyle walk in with his little boy. He could hear everything that was being said. He wandered around the front counter, and I knew he was listening to what I was being told. Of ALL the days... Of ALL the people... and of ALL the times.

We had to cross paths right at the moment she was telling me all this information. I stared at her intently, trying to get her attention when suddenly she looked up and saw my face. She instantly knew I was trying to tell her something. She stopped and then began to total up our purchase. I nearly fell over at the price, as we were both still out of work and had barely two cents to rub together. We lived on toast and spaghetti for the next week, as that was all we could afford to eat. I bought the items and went to leave. I passed Kyle, who said, "You know old mate is gone now, he's not there, he's moved on... you don't need to be buying all this stuff and doing all this." I just wanted to scream at him. NO, IT'S NOT GONE, IT IS STILL THERE, and things are WORSE than ever! but I politely nodded and agreed with him.

"Just some back-up supplies, just in case. We're picking up our daughter from a friend's place, so we just thought we'd pop in here and have a look—that's all, as we've never been in here before." He introduced me to his son, who looked about five. Kyle looked down at his son and said, "Remember me talking about Karen? We went to her house and did some ghost busting."

I suddenly had the soundtrack of the original theme song of the 1984 Ghostbusters movie playing over and over in my mind. I couldn't believe he said this, and his son looked at me with eyes as big as saucers… I could only imagine what must have been going through his little mind. Like, WOW, what a thing to say. She called Kyle up to serve him and then yelled out, "Can you please stay there for a minute longer, Karen? I just remembered something I wanted to show you."

Kyle was served and left, and she came up to me and said she was not surprised that this had happened, as IT was trying to keep causing dramas for me to keep the story and ITS power going for as long as possible. "Here is a piece of paper with a list of things for you to do. Don't talk to anybody about IT; it just gives IT power and could potentially bring IT into their lives. Be strong… Everyone who has photos of IT that you've shared, get them to delete IT. Get this energy out of their phones… This thing came to try and take you once, and trust me, IT will come back and try to take you again… IT is evil and will not stop until IT gets what IT wants. Do everything I've written down and good luck. And you need to keep your protection up. You've been getting a double whammy for years.

"You've been hit continually for many years in your home, especially in these past few when you've spent so much time in your house trying to finish your degree. IT has had unlimited access to you. IT has been slamming you like there's no tomorrow. Then you go to work in a place that's also filled with these entities. There has been no relief for you. I'm surprised, to be honest, that you're still alive and that you haven't ended up in a mental asylum with what you've endured. You truly are incredible; there is obviously great protection around you. You just haven't had a break from this for SO long. I am honestly in awe of you, Karen. Most people would not still be standing with what you have immensely suffered.

"I take my hat off to you. When you talk about IT, call it something sunny and bright that reminds you of something benevolent. IT will not like that. Do not refer to IT as dark and malevolent, and most importantly, PLEASE PROTECT YOURSELF!"

As I was about to leave, she suddenly spat at me, "You know you wanted this, you asked for this, and you deserve what is happening to you."

"Excuse me," I stammered back at her in complete and utter shock.

"You must have asked or wanted this to come into your life; that's why this is happening to you."

"I NEVER asked for any of this!" I felt like throwing everything I just bought from her shop back in her face. How dare she accuse me of such a thing? I spun around so fast that I nearly knocked over one of her shelves, and I walked out of there as fast as I could and never looked back. I walked over to the car, John started driving down the highway, and I began going over in my mind what she had said to me.

"Quick, pull over, I'm going to be sick." I got out of the car and began vomiting profusely on the side of the highway… I just couldn't stop. I was crying and vomiting at the same time out of absolute fear and terror. How on earth is this happening to me? I was thinking to myself as I vomited over and over again.

MY ILLUSION, MY REALITY...

> "SOMEONE ONCE ASKED ME HOW I HOLD MY HEAD UP SO HIGH AFTER ALL I'VE BEEN THROUGH. I SAID IT'S BECAUSE NO MATTER WHAT, I AM A SURVIVOR, NOT A VICTIM." —PATRICIA BUCKLEY

I opened up the paper the next morning that I had been given titled BLUE PRINT. I began to read the following words: "It is a theory that energy left behind by a living person can actually leave an imprint on the universe. It is like the same way that a paintbrush stroke can leave a mark on a canvas. Everything is made up of energy."

I was struggling to get my head around the words and what I was trying to actually understand. I contacted Suzannah the next morning and told her what had happened.

"Karen, this is YOUR story, YOUR body, YOUR family… YOUR life! No one knows you like you do. You're told it's Aboriginal, then it's other negative entities, then it's something else. Please stop putting so much faith in other people's stories and then giving them your hard-earned money. Be still with yourself.

"Black tourmaline stones are good for protection, but only if you cleanse them often, as they hold lots of negative energy. Shungite is softer and gentler. It also needs cleansing, but it's not as harsh as tourmaline. I feel like it's time for you to eliminate, stop adding, especially other people's opinions. Everyone has their own experience here based on many external influences and past, future life stories. GO inside, connect with YOU. Maybe your biggest lesson here and now is to trust yourself. You have great intuition!!!!!... remember all the dreams and experiences you have had. YOU have great intuition, Karen. Believe it... please...

"Stop talking to those people; I suggest you have all the answers inside. I can give you Cameron's number. He has seen all the pictures inside your house, the scratch marks, etc. He is used to all this! Now start to eliminate... when you clear your colon, you will clear your headspace. You know this. Small steps... slowly."

"It does feel more settled here... every now and then my toilet makes a funny sound, and my heart skips a beat and then it stops. Maybe IT is still here and is making me think IT is gone to lull me into a false sense of security, which will then make me not want to protect myself or become complacent, and then it will strike," I replied.

"NOOOOOOOOOO, you can feel for yourself... clean out your colon. You will feel clearer and more able to see. You have all the tools, start using them."

"I know you're right... I just feel so weak and tired. I've barely slept in a week since that attack. I'm so scared to sleep... I feel like I need to have a complete nervous breakdown and then I can start putting myself back together again. I can't seem to get those experiences out of my mind; it was just terrifying. I know I need to heal and believe in myself so much more."

"If you need to have a breakdown, do it. It's your body, do whatever it needs to do. Remember, the deeper you go down, the higher you rise. And please stop putting crystals on your solar plexus."

"She said this was to unblock it and help with my anger as this has been slamming me for so many years."

"Try putting your quartz point on your heart chakra, facing your head. Lay down and be still, do it as much as you feel. Smoky quartz is beautiful, and it will amplify your heart space. The solar plexus is the emotional chakra; leave it alone for now. Everything you are experiencing is for a good reason. It's time to stop and let it all pass. Stop trying to figure things out like each thing has meaning. It doesn't always have a meaning."

"She told me that I asked for this. That I deserved this. That I wanted all this to happen to me."

"WHAT…. NOOOOOOOO… SHE IS FULL OF CRAP, KAREN! Ask her how her colon is. Messed up for sure."

That woman really traumatised me to the point that I could never step foot back in her shop again. I found out from another friend a few months later that she has done the same thing to so many other people. It's like she can see how traumatised and broken you are and goes for your jugular. Knowing you are completely new to this world, she fuels your terror even more and then tells you that you need all these different products and crystals, making a small fortune out of you. I have never seen her or gone to that shop again, and I know I never will. Since this happened to me, she has now sold her shop and her crystals to other shops around the district and has left this entire area. She traumatised me beyond words, and it took me a very long time to get over what she said and did to me. I can only pray and hope that other people won't become victims of this terrible woman like I did.

"You are way more capable than any of these people. It's because these days, so many people are lost. Looking outside of themselves for answers. It's all inside, but humanity is full of shit. First clean out, then you can see the truth. It's your story. Keep others away from you for a while so you stop spinning around in THEIR story," Suzannah said to me.

"My manager wants to see me today... obviously, there are stories starting to get around my workplace. Should I tell her? I was told that every time I talk about IT, I give IT more power as IT is always listening."

"Don't go into detail, tell them as little as possible. Don't talk about IT. You've already been through so much physically and mentally. Just go with the flow, you are being supported. First, things might seem to crash around you, hit rock bottom... it's ok, even if it's scary, it's ok. Let go. Always remember to have gratitude in your heart. You will start to become aware of just how much has been given to you in your lifetime. When you do, be humble. Be humble for the people that have crossed your path, the love that you have been given, the deaths, the births, the beautiful experiences that you have had, the holidays, the journey you are on. Be humble for all the family and friends that have been on this journey with you and how desolate an existence it would have been without them in your life. Breathe in this amazing gratitude and breathe it out too."

I went and lay down and did what Suzannah suggested with the smoky quartz crystal. I dreamt of John, and he had his arms around me. He was kissing my forehead, and I could feel his love and support around me... I definitely felt so much better.

HEALING FROM THE INSIDE OUT...

"YOU WERE PUT ON THIS EARTH TO ACHIEVE YOUR GREATEST SELF, TO LIVE OUT YOUR PURPOSE AND TO DO IT FEARLESSLY."
—STEVE MARABOLI

Healing, I know, means a lot of different things to a lot of different people. Maybe for some, it is writing the years of trauma from your mind like I was doing right now. Maybe for others, it is hiding from the world, resting your soul, or laughing until you feel like you could cry. Sometimes it might feel like nothing at all. Do not fight it. Whatever your healing looks like or consists of, allow it to be. I had to do whatever made me feel happy. I had to remain calm, remember how loved I was and let the fear fall away. I decided to call my very unwelcome visitor that had been stalking and haunting myself, my family, and my home… Starlight.

I was getting ready for a walk when I began to hear lots of noises in my roof cavity. I turned and saw lots of birds at my bedroom window. As I walked into my ensuite, my exhaust fan went berserk like it was on high, but I didn't turn it on, and there was no wind outside. Oh no, could this energy now be out of my septic system and transferred into my roof cavity? I didn't acknowledge it. I just ignored it, but it made me feel so uneasy. Like I'm being watched. Suzannah told me that I was raining energy so that I could be spot on with thoughts with that. Remember, she told me this is YOUR story.

Everything is energy. "Whatever you are doing is working. Let the shit go. Remember, the only way out...IS IN.!!! You are being led to a new chapter. Everything will change for you now and your family. The more peaceful you become the more years will be added to your life. Get drama out of your life and balance your immune system."

My sister Jane has been told about my story, and I had spoken to her at length about some of the things that had happened to me. She sent me information about Solfeggio frequencies, something to raise my vibration. Cell DNA repair... it has been very relaxing... and I decided to take that yellow jasper out of my navel.

"Jenna has been doing my head in with all of this; it has really taken a toll on her too. I've had to refer her to a psychologist for her mental health. Things are starting to get more intense... more handprints on the walls in the house and on the roller doors in the carport attached to the house, the toilet growling on and off. Pictures intermittently appearing in my mirrors, trying so hard to ignore it, but this thing just won't seem to leave me alone. I just feel so exhausted and tired of the whole thing. I started eating better, started meditating, started detoxing. I knew it would clear my mind and my whole energy field.

"We have decided to sell and move out of this house; I just can't deal with it anymore. I feel like I am going to end up in a mental unit; I feel like I'm truly starting to go mad. Also having massive issues with my youngest," I texted Suzannah.

The text replied: "She is taking all of her frustrations out on you. You are her closest human. It's kind of a good thing that she is taking it out on you in a way. She trusts you and knows that you can take it. But she is also begging for direction, so stay calm when she does it and then give her a positive reaction instead of a negative one like frustration or anger. Focus more on yourself, get yourself grounded and focus on clearing out your body. That crap needs to go; it is more about what you can eliminate. Let it go, don't give it too much energy, it will totally exhaust you.

"Jenna is at an age where she is capable of doing her own thing in life, so focus on you. Tell her you love her and that you are always here for her, but you have your own shit to deal with, just as she does. And remove things from your diet like dairy, gluten, and sugar. This will be a good lesson for your daughter and will make you stronger too. Don't let her control you and your day; you have enough to deal with. You have come this far, you can keep going; this is the peak right now. Soon she will do her own thing in life and this too shall pass. Start on YOU, it will make you feel better. Remember, you must clean yourself up first. Go inside as deep as possible, let all the environmental shit go. IT will follow what you do to your body, flush that crap."

As I was getting out of the shower that night, I went into my bedroom and saw another image above my bedroom door. OMG, like seriously. What now? This was starting to become purely exhausting. Whenever I saw something new appear in my house and on my walls, I would not give it any time, thought, or energy, but this energy just would not leave me alone. It was like I had X-ray vision and was so hypersensitive to every part of my house. Images were appearing everywhere. I began packing my house up like a mad woman; I just wanted to get the hell out of there. There was just way too much trauma within these walls.

It was like they were starting to control my every thought.

"Yes, you are hypersensitive, I understand that… your house is an extension of you. Remember that you have choices about how you respond and react to what is happening in your life. When you react to your lessons with strength, you learn the lesson and move forward in your life. We are FULL of parasites, but for those of us who are sensitive, we become way more affected. Parasites are known to control your eating habits, thoughts, and many choices we make in our everyday life. They are POWERFUL! They absolutely love acids, so be careful. Always try to alkalise your body as much as you can. Eat lots and lots of greens and go easy on the sugars," Suzannah replied.

"Eventually, more and more of humanity will begin to acknowledge their presence and start to believe that they are real, which they are. Some people even take lots of Niacin (Vitamin B3) specifically to detoxify their body." I did recall in one of my lectures that *Mimosa pudica* seeds were deadly for parasites, as are pepitas, black walnut hulls, and Pau d'Arco also. "More than anything, Karen, do NOT give up the fight. This will not last forever, even though you feel like they have so much strength. Take great care of yourself and treat yourself with lots of dignity and respect. Trust me, it will not last forever. They are more concerned about exploiting you so that they can take and suck your energies like a parasite and completely disempower you collectively and personally. They feed on life force, and these vile and evil dark forces will not care how they manipulate, exploit, and use you for everything that they can get out of you. Just always remember: PROTECT, PROTECT!"

Even when I am in the shower, I have images and claw marks appearing on my shower screen.

"So take your favourite crystal in the shower with you, you have POWER. Please keep remembering how strong YOU truly are."

That night, I dreamt I was in a bathroom ensuite at work. My work colleague was trying to help with the door as it had come off the hinges. I could hear water running in the background. She was puffing and panting, and I said, "Stop, you are going to give yourself a heart attack." It made no sense to me. A few days later at work, I was in a room where a resident had fallen out of bed, and I could hear water running in the bathroom. The same work colleague was running, trying to get observation equipment and was frantic with worry. I grabbed her and said, "Stop, you're going to give yourself a heart attack." Unbeknownst to me, she had just been diagnosed with heart issues a few days before.

THE HARDEST BATTLE WAS IN MY MIND...

"JUST WHEN YOU THINK YOU'VE HIT ROCK BOTTOM, YOU REALISE YOU'RE STANDING ON ANOTHER TRAPDOOR." —MARISHA PESSL

I started to detox and was doing colonics, but this thing just kept overwhelming me. It started to put up faces everywhere I turned—on my windscreen, my mirrors, my lounge chairs… even on my shower screen. One morning, I walked into my bedroom, and every drawer had been pulled out from my duchess. I gasped in fright and quickly pushed them all back in again. Sometimes I would walk out into my dining room, and the chairs would all be pulled out from the table. Doors from the kitchen cupboards would be open, and photos on the wall would be hanging crooked. One morning, I turned on the TV and went into the kitchen to make my coffee. I had my toast in one hand and my coffee in the other, and as I walked around the corner, there in the middle of the lounge room floor were the two remotes for the TV. I always put them on the table beside my chair.

My heart nearly jumped out of my skin; I literally froze in terror. All I could hear in my mind was, *Don't show fear! This is your house!* I slowly picked up the remotes and tried to have my breakfast, but I couldn't stop shaking. I got dressed, got in my car, and got the hell out of there. I went down to my local church, sat on a pew, and just cried. I suddenly realised that throughout this journey, God had just fallen off my radar. I had completely forgotten about Him. All the years prior, I had always prayed to Him when I needed help, and I had not done that for so long. I had stopped going to church for years as I always worked weekends.

I prayed to God for help, I prayed for peace again in our life, and I prayed for whatever was haunting my house and my family to be gone. I prayed for God and for Dad to help me and my family. I just felt SOOOOOO completely and utterly exhausted. I couldn't remember the last time I actually slept properly, as it had been so long. I was starting to feel like this thing was SO angry, and I was getting no peace EVER. I was trying to work my shifts at aged care while trying to pack up this house. I was just so mentally exhausted beyond words. Some nights, my body was craving sleep so badly, but I just couldn't sleep due to the never-ending nightmares. Finally, I would fall into a restless sleep out of pure exhaustion. I would wake up with my whole body feeling like it had been hit by a freight train from being so tensed up all night, even in my subconscious. I must have always been bracing myself. I constantly felt so tired and so drained, no matter how much I slept.

"Keep that tourmaline around your bed and try and get some rest. Your third eye is so open, and you are now being exposed to visions, forces, and experiences that it wants to keep slamming you with," Suzannah told me. By this stage, Jenna was just causing her father and I so much grief. We were still trying to pack up our house, the bills just never seemed to stop piling up, and now our computer had broken down and had cost us nearly $1000 to fix—more money that we just didn't have to spare. Now I had the image of something coming through my wall, looking straight down at me when I was lying in my bed.

Above my head, looking straight down on me, another face appeared, and it looked like it had been made out of the dust on my curtains. I was just SICK and tired of waking up with scratches all over me. What was happening to me, I can honestly say, was one of the MOST terrifying and MOST traumatising experiences I have ever been through. It just NEVER stopped. I was dealing with some sort of malevolent force or forces that were just hammering me OVER and OVER and OVER again, and I couldn't see it. I needed to get out of this house… but it was like we were stuck here. I could not count how many dreams I had about spider webs and being cocooned and stuck inside them. It makes sense to me now, but at the time, I just couldn't understand what was happening to me. The sheer and absolute terror I felt was just indescribable.

We had a quote done to get our house painted inside and replace all the carpets so that we could put it on the market to sell, hoping to at least break even. The total cost was going to be around $15,000… I think I cried for days. Where on earth were we going to get that sort of money from? How were we ever going to leave this house when we had a massive mortgage from all the financial hardships we had endured? Apparently, Starlight had targeted John and I as we were the parents, the authority figures—the ones that had to have their power taken from them, which is exactly what IT had been doing to John for many years.

We went to the bank to enquire about a loan, but we were told that due to our financial hardship, they wouldn't even consider speaking with us until we could show that we could pay at least 6 months of repayments with no issues. We tried to explain that we wanted to sell the house so it wouldn't be repossessed, but the loans officer just cut us off and said, "I have nothing more to say to you," and within literally 60 seconds, we were walking back out the door. We felt so humiliated. Why was this still happening to us? Why couldn't we just get a break? What on earth had we done to deserve all this in our life? John was just so angry and frustrated. We both knew this thing was still there and so desperately wanted to get out, but how on earth were we ever going to achieve it? And we hadn't even begun to get quotes on getting the air conditioners fixed. We both got in the car and drove in silence, crying quietly to ourselves, back to a house that wasn't our home but more like a living nightmare.

I woke up the next day and wondered how Anne was going on her incredible journey to India to do her Shamanic healing. I was thinking of her and sending lots of love, light, and beautiful thoughts. Within seconds, she sent me a photo of herself in the early hours of the morning, watching the sun come up over the Himalayan mountains. Wow, wow, wow, so happy for you that you are living your dream. What an incredible and amazing experience for you.

We had some workmen coming over today to try and fix our main air conditioner in the roof and give us a quote. They told me that in all the years they've been doing this job, they had never seen a fault like mine before and had never seen a particular code displayed on the LED screen on the remote. Every time they come over, they finally manage to get it working again, and within half an hour of them leaving, it turns off. Then you have to wait hours to get them back again as they have so many other jobs to do. My exhaust fan in my ensuite keeps going ballistic every time I walk in there. I know it is STILL here in my roof cavity, and today the air conditioner started playing up in my car. Arrggghh... it is just never-ending. The boys just told me that they found another major fault in my whole power board and that the entire board will need replacing, costing hundreds and hundreds of dollars. I am down on shifts and money, and they also just found massive wasps next to my exhaust fan, and they are very active. Oh Dad, why didn't you just let me get on that plane?

"Do you think you will stay on in that house? There's just so much disruption to all of your lives," asked Joy.

"Jenna has become very withdrawn and is showing lots of depression. John, to be honest, is just holding it together; his work is very demanding and is definitely taking a toll on his health. I am having issues as they need to strengthen up my left side. I'm still getting lots of pain down my right side when I try to walk. Maybe IT is attacking all of us? Cyndi told me that while IT is still here in this house, my home will never sell. Sometimes I think in my heart it is time to get out. I'm just way too exhausted to keep all this up. And then another part of me feels like I am letting IT win, which is what I know it wants. Then I feel like such a failure. It is truly mentally exhausting beyond words. Last night, I had a terrible nightmare that a massive saltwater crocodile was attacking John and me… Ahhhhh on the bright side, at least we both survived."

MY GIFTS WERE AWAKENING...

"THE MOST POWERFUL WEAPON ON EARTH IS THE HUMAN SOUL ON FIRE." —FERDINAND FOCH

"Happy birthday for your beautiful Dad today. Be happy, have a happy day for him, and celebrate the good things in your life. There are many. Stop and think and take your time. Ask for your Dad's blessing; you have a lot to look forward to. You're moving forward into a more peaceful life. It's not your fault that this has happened. The poor person who is stuck in purgatory and has been stuck there through no fault of his own, just as you are. The sooner you are out of there, the better. Please have a celebration of your Dad's life… be happy, not sad. Take care. Thinking of you xx," texted Joy.

We went down south for a few days to visit our children. That night, I had a dream about a young boy named Travis. I could see his clothing and a cap but couldn't make out his face. He kept saying, "Please talk to me, why won't you listen? I need to speak with you." I was a bit perplexed as I had no idea who Travis was. I asked both my daughters, and they didn't know any Travis. It must have just been some silly random dream.

The next night, I dreamt that I was driving in a car, following another one in front. We turned down a road and eventually ended up on a property with an old run-down farmhouse on it. I remember walking inside and looking around; everything looked like a typical bachelor pad, with lots of dust covering everything. Then I was aware that a man was getting out of the car and coming towards me. He was an elderly gentleman, and he was very friendly. He had the kindest eyes and looked so tired. I could see his face distinctly, and I didn't feel threatened by him at all. He came up to me and introduced himself as Charlie. He shook my hand and told me that it was his time to go now and to please tell all of his family that he loved them very much and was so proud of them all. He hoped they wouldn't fight too much over what he had left for his kids in the will. I suddenly woke up.

I was having breakfast the next day, reading the local newspaper. As I turned to the Classifieds, there was a funeral notice for a gentleman named Charlie. I just sat there in complete disbelief. Was this the same man? Did he come to say goodbye? Why can't I keep dreaming? Why do I keep waking up like I do? I had so many questions that kept going around and around in my mind.

Later in the day, I could distinctly hear the name of something being repeated in my ear. I wasn't sure what it was… I looked it up and, to my surprise, found it was the name of an esoteric shop in one of the suburbs. I told John about it, and he said, "Well, let's go right now." We drove for nearly an hour on the highway before we finally arrived at the shop. I walked in, and it was really beautiful. I honestly had no idea why I was there. I spoke with the owner of the shop, who went and got their local psychic to come and talk with me.

I spoke at length with Davina and showed her some of my pictures.

"Wow, I have heard of people who can actually see things in the esoteric world, but I've never met anyone who can see things like you can and who has photos."

"What does that mean?" I asked, completely confused.

"It means you have great power, Karen, and you need to learn how to develop it. I think I know why you are here. We only just got these in a few hours ago. They are hard to get in the country; we could only access four of them. I bought one, and so did the owner of this shop. We only have two left." She took me to a tray and took out two beautiful crystals encased in a silver locket.

"These are from the Satyaloka mountains in Southern India. These powerful and rare stones are from the area of Southern India and have been gathered for you by the monks at the Satyaloka monastery for the purpose of spreading the energy of crystal enlightenment. The monks believed that this energy is a quality of the mountains where they live and that the stones are capable of carrying and dispersing this energy throughout the world."

Satyaloka quartz vibrates with the frequency of pure white spiritual light and carries one of the most rarefied energies of all the stones in the mineral kingdom. This is a very holy stone imbued with the energies of one of the Earth's most relatively unknown sacred sites, the mountains surrounding their Satyaloka monastery. It has been suggested that this area is the crown chakra of the Earth. Certainly, these stones resonate powerfully with the human crown chakra, and they can be of great assistance in building the emerging planetary consciousness. (Copied from the *BOOK of STONES*).

I was mesmerised by her story. They were just beautiful.

"I think you have been sent here for this, as they are also very protective. They are one of the holiest stones on this planet." She took me into a room and spoke to me about soul contracts and what we have all signed up for, and that this was all a part of my journey. She explained that herbal flower essences would help as I needed to meditate to connect more with my higher self and that all my answers lay within. She made up two: one called Meditation, the other Abundance, as I told her about all the years of financial hardship that we had endured. I was to put a few drops under my tongue every day before I meditated. When she told me the price of the crystal, I knew in my heart that we couldn't afford it. I thanked her immensely for her insight and for giving me the essences, and said that maybe one day I could afford to get the crystal. As we were leaving to go to the car, John asked about what had happened. I explained about the crystal.

"Jenna, take your mother to the car. You were told to come here. We have driven for over an hour to get here… you were directed here for a reason… I'm going to get that crystal… don't argue with me… wait for me in the car… I'm not taking no for an answer." He went back inside and spoke with Davina, who showed him the one I really liked. He came back out to the car within 20 minutes and said, "That was out there. Davina had put my crystal inside some sort of bowl to cleanse it, and the sound that came out of it was so loud and powerful. Everyone in the shop turned to see what it was, and even the owner came out, as no one had ever heard such a sound before.

"Davina said to me, 'This is a VERY powerful crystal. You need to pick it up—I'm not going to touch it—and you need to get this around your wife's neck and tell her to never take it off, except when it needs to be charged. It is VERY powerful. Go and buy a chain now and put it on her ASAP.'"

We drove straight to a jewellery store, and John purchased a chain and put it on me. I sleep, eat, and shower with it every day… the only time I take it off is when it is a full moon, and I charge it in the moonlight; otherwise, it is always on me constantly.

That night, I dreamt of Dad coming to me in a dream and telling me that he had sent angels around me to protect me and to take a photo of the crystal that John had bought me. I awoke in the morning and thought I must have been hallucinating. I grabbed my phone, switched to camera mode, and took a photo. When I looked at it, I was absolutely amazed. There, in the outline of my crystal, was the image of an angel. I could see his head and shoulders, his arms were outstretched, and I could also see the image of an older man near the bottom.

I was just in awe. Like WOW WOW WOW! What am I honestly looking at? My guardian angel? Archangel Michael? Someone was in my crystal. My grandmother used to tell me stories that her grandfather was very psychic and that people used to go to him for readings. We used to think she was just telling stories, but now I had to think that maybe this was him. I stared at it for ages in absolute disbelief. I sent a message to Joy, who was down south with her daughter, who had just delivered a gorgeous baby boy.

"Wow, that's amazing and so cool. You can live a fairly normal life, but if you have a gift unbeknownst to you, then you have to learn how to handle and live with it—which you will."

The crystal my husband bought from an esoteric shop for protection.

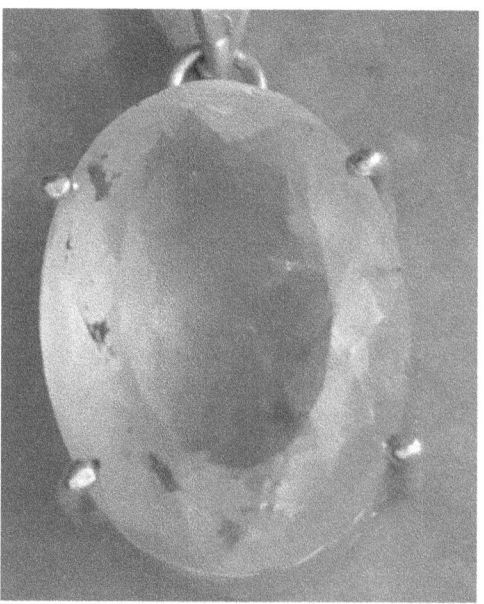

Is when an angel appeared in my crystal after Dad came to me in a dream and told me to take a photo of the crystal.

TRANSFORMING MY THOUGHTS AND MY LIFE...

"ONE DAY THE PEOPLE WHO DIDN'T BELIEVE IN YOU WILL TELL EVERYONE HOW THEY MET YOU." —JOHNNY DEPP

I received a letter in the mail marked urgent, as well as a follow-up phone call, as I had not long had my mammogram done. I was to attend the breast screen clinic within the next few days and was advised to bring a support person with me. If I needed the day off work, they would provide documentation for sick leave coverage. Specialists from another city would be here to consult with us only on that day. I didn't tell anybody but John and Anne. John wanted to come with me, but I wouldn't let him; he was only casual, and if he didn't work, we didn't get paid. I reassured him that I would be fine. I arrived in the morning with lots of other women who all had their support person but me.

We were taken in like cattle and put through a barrage of observations, paperwork, and the usual routine of having to speak with an RN, the doctor, having ultrasounds done, speaking to a counsellor, and lots and lots of waiting in between. We were shown where we could make tea and coffee and watch television, and were advised to bring some snacks as we could be there for hours until our final test results could be evaluated. When my name was called to speak with the doctor, she told me that she was very taken aback with my upbeat attitude and that I was being so positive. I just instinctively knew that after everything I had been through, the universe was not going to suddenly now strike me down with this horrendous disease or that I had cancer.

I couldn't explain it; I JUST knew I had gone through all of that journey for a reason, and this was just a bump in the road. She then explained, as she was putting up the images, that I had a number of cysts all in my right breast but none showing on my left. They were very concerned that I had breast cancer and would need immediate treatment. She wrote out the paperwork for the ultrasound and said that there was a very high probability that she would see me again later that day to discuss treatment options. I smiled at her and told her that I knew I wouldn't be back and wished her all the best. I can still see the look on her face as I walked out the door. Yes, I have no signs of any breast cancer, just like I knew in my heart that I wouldn't. Fingers crossed while I write this passage that I never do.

I was pondering to myself, with everything that I had been through, what was my concept of God. To me, God was a higher being that formed the great galaxies, the universe, and the most incredible beauty of nature on our Mother Earth. With her magnificent rainforests, deserts, waterfalls, great oceans, our plants, our insects, our animals, our marine life, and of course, the creation that is all of us. I cannot explain what God is, but I just know that God IS, and there is something very real about this presence. I had to walk my path and understand that the greatest thing I could do was what I could transcend in my mind.

I asked my spiritual tour guides, as I affectionately began to call them, to show me a sign today that would come completely out of the blue and to bring it to me in a way that I would never have expected, with such a surprise that I would know unequivocally that it was from them. I wanted to understand that I have the great power to transform my life. I had to start truly understanding how incredible my mind was—to let it take me to a higher level of consciousness, to the reality that was outside of me, to understand the world in a deeper way, and to connect to my spiritual self. I also had to give myself more self-love. This included resting, moving my body more, spending time in nature, investing in myself, drinking more water, meditating, eating healthier food, and telling myself that I am worthy.

I was consciously creating my destiny. My thoughts were creating my reality, my life, my environment, and my future. I had to let my ego go. I was here to create a phenomenal life for myself beyond my wildest dreams—I had been enlightened. I was here to step into my birthright, to surrender to the universe, to show amazing appreciation and gratitude, and to live my dream life. I had to raise my vibrational energy. I had to feel it in order to heal it, take action, release, and understand that the how was not up to me; it was up to the universe. I began to understand that I had to ask for help; once I was free, alignment would come quickly, and the manifestation I was desiring would not be far behind. I started to free-write until all the negativity was out of me. I had to be honest, brutally honest. My mind was my most powerful resource; there was guidance and magic available to me, just as there is to everyone. I had to accept my past, let myself heal, and make peace with my thoughts.

I began to say mantras like "I am okay, all is well, I am worthy of happiness, success, fulfilment, abundance, love." I was going to create miracles in my life. So many of us sit in our own self-created prisons of illusion. What is happening within us is what we are creating outside of us. Our brain processes 400 billion pieces of information a second, but we are only aware of 200,000. Who are we? Where did we actually come from? Why are we here? What are our thoughts made up of? So many questions. I believe that every time we speak and every thought we have, the universe listens and responds to us—that is how powerful we really are. I had to release all my fear, anger, powerlessness, victim mentality, and blame. I invoked angels into my life and knew that my life had unlimited possibilities. I had to start to value my own life, my own power, and know with every essence of my being that I was being divinely protected.

Suzannah sent me a text:

"I now release what no longer serves me... you won't know yourself soon. Things will change for the better as you take back your power. Maybe you went through it and survived it just so you could help someone else make it through too. Focus on YOU. Your daughter will follow. She has been surrounded by dark energy. It's not of her; it surrounds her. Love her—our girls are the future of our humanity. They carry the next generation. My mother is dying to teach me who I am. She is a beautiful human, Karen. Trapped but is motivating me to discover and fully be myself. There is always a balance of dark and light in absolutely every situation. What matters is what WE CHOOSE TO FOCUS ON. Focus on you; that darkness in your house will go. ITS time is OVER... Protect your space and your energy at all times. Remember, parasites will be attracted to your beautiful warmth, and moths will be attracted to your beautiful light... ALWAYS PROTECT... PROTECT... PROTECT!"

"My mum has been with me by my side through all of her disease. I think she spends more time with me at my home than here in her body. Trust your intuition; you have SO much power! It's what we can't see that is important and more real than ever. Our bodies are just a suit. Remember where you work—these places are packed full of entities... Protect yourself forever and always."

"Oh wow, really? In my workplace?" I texted back.

"Yes, everywhere. No light without the darkness. Laugh a lot, give IT little of your time, just enough to clean ITS crap up and remind IT whose house this really is. It's fine, Karen. You know what you are doing now. Just stay in your power. It might take a while, and it might get more intense before it gets better, like a Herxheimer reaction when one is detoxing their body, but just keep going and stay focused on you. Give IT NO power!"

BORN KNOWING WHO I AM...

"YOU CAN ONLY LOSE SOMETHING THAT YOU HAVE, BUT YOU CANNOT LOSE SOMETHING THAT YOU ARE." —ECKHART TOLLE

The next morning, I awoke to the sounds of what sounded like squawking. I opened up the front door and there all over my roof, my driveway, my garden beds, my lawn were magpies and crows and they were shitting all over everything AGAIN … "F**K YOU!" I screamed out… "Sorry, Dad, if you're here as I don't normally swear but I am JUST OVER THIS F**KING THING!"

I let my two Border Collie dogs out, and they chased the birds away over and over until they FINALLY never came back. The real estate agent, who lived in the same street as us, had come down that same morning to give us a quote.

"Good grief, look at all these birds everywhere! Never seen anything like it. You might have to get some rubber snakes and put them out to scare them away," she told me.

Mmmmmm…. if only she really knew.

Our daughter and I decided to go to the second-hand store to look for some clothes she needed. We were walking around the shop when I got to a certain corner and started to feel very uneasy. I walked to the front of the shop when I heard an almighty bang. The shelves where I was literally standing a few minutes before had crashed down with everything on it, causing an absolute mess. The ladies in the shop began to yell out, "Just go! Get out; you're not welcome here," not realising that my daughter and I were at the front of the shop. Suddenly, they saw us and told me that only a few days ago, a family had brought in a lot of items from a man who had passed away.

They had put them in the corner and had nothing but issues since the day his personal items arrived—shelves crashing down, the air con breaking down. I do remember reading that a lot of antique shops and second-hand stores that have certain objects can also carry energies and attachments, especially mirrors, as they can be a portal for energy to come through. If you buy anything from these places, you should always sage the items thoroughly before bringing them into your home space. *Mmmmmm... might have to get some sage*, I said and give it a good clearing out.

"Yes," they said, "he is a bit cranky, this one. Don't think he likes anybody buying his things, and he is definitely letting us know about it."

"Good luck," I said.

My shower and toilet were both leaking again, the hot water system was having issues and not working, and all our main air conditioners in the dining room, kitchen, and all bedrooms were still blown. Once again, we couldn't do anything for Jenna's 16th birthday, and Christmas was around the corner. John was out of work again... no money, no job, no nothing AGAIN!

"IT just won't leave you alone, will it?" said Joy. She could see how absolutely drained I was, and I honestly didn't know how much longer I could truly keep going. On my way to the grocery store the very next day, the air con in my car suddenly wasn't working anymore.

"Oh, great! WHAT NOW!" I screamed out loud. Of course, it had to break down in the oppressive heat. I took my car for a quote, and it ended up costing me over $2,400 to fix, as my entire condenser needed to be repaired. We were just devastated. How much more was this going to cost? We were quoted over $6,000 for the house air-conditioning, which we just didn't have.

OH GOD, WHY? I screamed, but deep down, I already knew the answer.

We ended up getting another man over with his apprentices, who spent a long time trying to find the leak. I ended up telling him all about our financial hardships and what we had been through. I prayed and prayed for Dad to help us, as we were just exhausted beyond words, and the heat was becoming intolerable. Amazingly, after nearly 10 days, they found the most minute hole and were able to get the whole system fixed for just under $1,500. It was truly a gift from Dad and from God too.

Thank you… thank you… thank you! I cried.

Mum came to visit to drop off my birthday present. It was a beautiful wall plaque that said, "He shall cover you with his feathers." It was really beautiful. My Aunty Alice had not long had a total hip replacement, and Mum asked if I wanted to go over to visit her to say hello. We went to the hospital and stayed for a while, and when I was sitting in the chair, I began to get stabbing pains all over me and started to feel really dizzy.

I wasn't sure if I was having a vestibular attack. I do remember being driven home and starting to feel lots of pain everywhere. Mum asked what was wrong, and I couldn't really explain. I got out of the car, and my vision was very distorted. I went and sat straight down and became extremely nauseous. What was this terrible stabbing pain I was experiencing? I thought to myself. John asked me what was wrong, and I told him that we had been at the hospital for the past couple of hours.

"Did you have your black tourmaline on you? You know you have to have protection on you when you go into those places."

"Of course I do." I went to pull it out of my bra when I realised I didn't have any on me at all.

"Ahhhhh nooo, I forgot to put it on."

"Where is your sage spray?" asked John.

"In the wardrobe." He went and got it, and I sprayed it all over me and visualised myself wrapped up in a brilliant white light. Eventually, in the course of the next half hour, the pain and nausea disappeared. To this day, I make sure that I am ALWAYS protected before I ever step foot into aged care facilities or hospitals.

After tea, I went for a shower, and when I stepped out to dry myself, the most hideous figure of a face covered in a black hood appeared in my mirror. Up in the top corner, another ghastly face began to appear right in front of me. I took a photo to make sure that I wasn't just seeing things, and as the third one started to appear, I yelled, "Leave me alone!" I used my hand to rub the images off and walked out. The next day, when getting dressed for work, there on my duchess mirror was another face, but this one looked Aboriginal—very distinct, and he looked VERY angry. I remembered Kath telling me that I had ramped up his anger, but I just ignored it and cleaned it off, asking again for protection from Archangel Michael and also from my Dad.

When I went out to the kitchen, there on the door grill was a white feather. The door was shut, so there was no way anything could have blown inside.

WOW WOW WOW! I felt just incredible. I knew in my heart that Dad had really come to me and that I indeed had so much protection around me. I began meditating again, and for the first time ever, I saw a lady with white flowing hair coming towards me. As she came up to me, all her hair turned purple, and she handed me three cards.

"Here are your cards of life, Karen," she said to me. I saw the Ace of Spades, King of Spades, and the Three of Spades, and then I woke up.

WOW! What a dream!

What was that all about, I thought, completely perplexed. I googled "Cards of Life" on the internet and was surprised to see that there was actually a site with this on there. I looked up the cards and was blown away by their meanings. The Ace of Spades was the most spiritual card in the deck. It is the card of transformation, representing rebirth and death, and has the ability to reach spiritual truths more than any other card. The King of Spades was the most powerful card in the deck. It has the ability to achieve great things in any chosen profession and achieve great success, with intuitive powers. The Three of Spades is highly creative if channelled in a productive way. The greatest success comes from focusing on a career that fulfils all their needs for creative expression and imbuing it with all their energy. With so many talents, they have the ability to achieve the success they desire when they apply themselves and work hard for it. They also need to watch their health and stress levels, as their health can ultimately pay the price.

When I typed in my birth date, it showed the Two of Diamonds. I looked up the meaning and read the following: can have innovative ideas that reach the public in a profound way; very powerful psychic ability; need to learn to trust their intuition; feels a certain calling in life, a special mission of sorts; this is a card of a missionary or a messenger, and they want you to share the truth with the world.

WOW! More and more breadcrumbs…

The Aboriginal face that appeared in my mirror.

FINDING MY TRUE SELF AND POWER...

"THE TWO MOST IMPORTANT DAYS IN YOUR LIFE ARE THE DAY YOU ARE BORN AND THE DAY YOU FIND OUT WHY." —MARK TWAIN

I had just finished doing eight afternoon shifts in a fortnight and to say that I was absolutely mentally and physically exhausted was an understatement. I was getting to sleep around 2 to 3 am and then having to get up again shortly after as I had to have our daughter at work by 5 am as it was too far for her to ride to work. This morning, I was exceptionally tired and irritable and could see that she had spilt a heap of muesli flakes all over the counter.

"Oh, for goodness' sake can't you just ever do anything right and clean up after yourself" I said to her angrily. "Why have I always got to clean up after you? Watch what you are doing."

"OMG! Calm down," she said, a bit taken aback. "I know you're tired, but don't take it out on me."

"Well, if you were more careful, you wouldn't always make such a mess. I'm just SO over cleaning up after you ALL the time."

With that, we got in the car and drove in silence all the way to her work. I dropped her off and headed home. It was still pitch black when I arrived back. I knew I had REALLY overreacted that morning and hadn't needed to yell at her so much. I will say sorry to her when she gets home, I thought to myself. I arrived back and sat down on the lounge near the kitchen for a few minutes to compose myself, as I was just so dizzy. I turned the light on as I couldn't see. Within minutes of me sitting there, I could hear a distinct crackling noise coming along my walls from the hallway towards my kitchen.

What the hell is that? I thought. I had never heard it before. I got up to walk towards the sink to start cleaning up the mess and doing the dishes and to investigate where this sound was coming from. Suddenly, as quickly as it started, it stopped. Gosh, I must be imagining things; I'm just so tired.

As I began to put the dishes in the sink, the air around me suddenly went cold and heavy, and it felt really hard to breathe. I felt the presence of something directly in front of my face. I then looked down to see a flake move across in front of me, then another, and then another. They had been arranged into an upside-down U shape.

What the??? I was SO angry—I instantly knew what was happening. I put my hands over the flakes and scattered them all over the floor.

"GET OUT OF MY HOUSE... DO YOU HEAR ME... GET OUT! YOU ARE NOT WELCOME HERE. I AM A CHILD OF GOD. THIS IS HIS HOUSE... MY FAMILY AND I BELONG TO HIM. YOU WILL NEVER HAVE ANY OF US, DO YOU HEAR ME? GET THE F**K OUT OF MY HOUSE!" I screamed at the top of my lungs.

Suddenly, I saw a vision of myself falling backwards, spiralling into a never-ending black abyss. I could actually feel my body spinning out of control; my mind was numb, my terror was palpable, and no one could hear me screaming.

I know the word FEAR could mean two different things for me... Forget Everything And Run... or I could use it for Face Everything And Rise. Deep down I knew the choice was mine and I knew which one I wanted. As I was falling slowly down into blackness, it felt like something caught me. I could not understand what was happening. I then heard whispers from the abyss... 'Hold on Karen... we've got you... your miracle is coming.'

www.ingramcontent.com/pod-product-compliance
Lightning Source LLC
Chambersburg PA
CBHW040240130526
44590CB00049B/4029